Trial and Tribulation in the Qur'an
A Mystical Theodicy

Other Books by Gerlach Press:

Colin Turner
The Qur'an Revealed: A Critical Analysis of Said Nursi's Epistles of Light
ISBN 9783940924285, 2013

Aziz Al-Azmeh
The Arabs and Islam in Late Antiquity: A Critique of Approaches to Arabic Sources
ISBN 9783940924421, 2014

Sadik J. Al-Azm
On Fundamentalisms
ISBN 9783940924223, 2014

Sadik J. Al-Azm
Islam – Submission and Disobedience
ISBN 9783940924247, 2014

Sadik J. Al-Azm
Is Islam Secularizable? Challenging Political and Religious Taboos
ISBN 9783940924261, 2014

Sadik J. Al-Azm
Critique of Religious Thought: English Translation of *naqd al-fikr ad-dini*
ISBN 9783940924445, 2015

Wahhabism – Doctrine and Development
Edited by Esther Peskes
ISBN: 978-3-940924-50-6, 2015

www.gerlach-press.de

Nasrin Rouzati

Trial and Tribulation in the Qur'an
A Mystical Theodicy

With a Foreword by Colin Turner

 Gerlach Press

First published 2015
by Gerlach Press
Berlin, Germany
www.gerlach-press.de

Cover Design: www.brandnewdesign.de, Hamburg
Printed and bound in Germany by
Hubert & Co, Göttingen
www.hubertundco.de

British Library Cataloguing in Publication Data.
A catalogue record for this book is available from the British Library.

Bibliographic data available from Deutsche Nationalbibliothek
http://d-nb.info/1059934140

ISBN: 978-3-940924-54-4 (hardcover)
ISBN: 978-3-940924-55-1 (ebook)

Contents

Foreword

It may be argued that among the grassroots believers of all religions, and perhaps particularly among believers who are Muslim, there has for all too long been the perception that Divine trial and tribulation appear in the form of events, situations and scenarios which are inherently disruptive of the status quo ante and are thus shot through with negativity: hunger, poverty, illness, "natural" disasters such as fires, floods and earthquakes are but a few of the "acts of God" which are, as the word tribulation suggests, sent to try us.

Almost as deeply entrenched as this perception is the idea that when tribulation does strike, it is sent primarily to punish, and it has to be said that at first glance, Islamic revelation presents some of the calamities which have befallen certain communities over the millennia squarely in the framework of retributive justice. One thinks of Noah and the flood, of the destruction of the idolatrous people of "Ad by ferocious winds", and, of course, one thinks of the community of Lot, whose cities were visited by fire and brimstone on account of their persistent disobedience.

Yet there is another side to the issue of tribulation – as yet virtually unexplored – which would suggest that the notion of Divine trial is not only more multifaceted than popular perception would allow, but also that the concept of the test is fundamental to the very act of creation itself. To uncover this other face of Divine trial and tribulation is to uncover a world in which the default setting, as it were, is one of continuous examination – one in which all of the things which mankind finds taxing or abhorrent, as well as all of the things that mankind finds pleasurable or welcome, are posited as instruments by which man is subjected to the Divine test. More significant still, it would seem, is the fact that the very creation of the cosmos in general, and of mankind in particular, is presented by revelation as an act that is mediated by the Divine will to "try" human beings, as it were, in the vast courtroom of existence, and in so doing to determine whether man is worthy of the title of "vicegerent of God" (*khalifat Allah*) on earth.

It is this hitherto uncovered face of tribulation which is one of the central concerns of Nasrin Rouzati in this ground-breaking piece of scholarship. Drawing on, *inter alia*, the works of Toshihiko Izutsu, Jalal al-Din Rumi and Ghazali, Rouzati's *Trial and Tribulations in the Qur'an: A Mystical Theodicy* is a remarkable amalgam of semantic analysis, exegesis criticism and theological speculation. Through her critical analysis of the Qur'anic narratives in which the concept of test and examination is revealed, the author unpacks the notion of trial and lays it bare, revealing for the first time in a Western academic work its all-embracing inclusivity. Through her painstaking semantic study and inter-textual interpretation of the Qur'anic *balā* narratives, augmented by various works of gnostic theology, Rouzati argues for an understanding of Divine trial quite unlike any that has gone before. With elegance and eloquence, she emphasizes the wholly positive nature of Divine trial, rescuing it in a sense from the popular perception of tribulation as punishment. For Rouzati, while suffering may indeed be experienced as a result of subjection to Divine examination, the test itself is meant not to make man suffer, but to help him actualize his potential and realize his destiny as God's vicegerent on earth.

Apart from having intrinsic value as an example of contemporary exegesis, Nasrin Rouzati's work provides us with a new lens through which to view and explore how the challenges of life, be they fortunate or unfortunate, in prosperity or in adversity, can in reality be seen as opportunities – opportunities for the unfurling and development of latent human potentialities and spiritual growth. Even those for whom the central tenets, themes and motifs of the Islamic revelation are unfamiliar, and the Muslim understanding of theodicy unknown, will be able to gain access to these ideas through Rouzati's penetrating, darkness-dispelling analysis, thus opening up another window onto one of the most perplexing yet thought provoking areas of our shared human condition.

Colin Turner
Durham, June 2015

Acknowledgements

First and foremost, I am grateful to Professor Colin Turner, my mentor and academic advisor, for his continued guidance throughout the original research, as well as his support during the publication of the book. His wealth of knowledge in the field of Islamic Studies, as well as his commitment in engaging me in the intellectual discussions, particularly during the early stages of the study, produced invaluable fruits. His interest, and the value he placed on the study of the Qur'anic themes, as well as timely suggestions and encouragements throughout the study, were instrumental in the successful completion of the thesis and the book.

Without doubt, I am indebted to Dr. Mahmoud Ayoub, family friend and a paragon of scholarship in the field of Qur'anic Studies, for his genuine assistance in the selection of the theme of the study, and Dr. Ali Aliabadi for sharing his extraordinary knowledge with the literature, as well as his ongoing moral support. I would like to thank Michael Laterza and Janet Mathews, two English teachers and compassionate colleagues, for proof reading the manuscript, and providing excellent suggestions. My heartfelt gratitude also goes to my dear friend, Dr. Susan Guiney, for believing in me and the value of this research, as well as for her ongoing motivation.

I am extremely grateful to my husband and best friend, Muhammad, for his love, encouragement, and understanding during the years that I devoted to this work. And last but not least, my children, Ali and Leila, have been a tremendous moral support during the study; their love and words of reassurance made it possible to overcome the many challenges throughout this journey.

Every soul is certain to taste death:
We shall test you all through the
bad and the good, and to Us you
will all return.

(Qur'an, 21:35)

Introduction

This book aims to provide a critical examination of one of the central themes of the Islamic revelation: the notion of trial and tribulation, *balā / ibtilā*, and throw light on its all-inclusive, multi-dimensional, and wholly positive meaning. The significance of the notion of *balā*, within the context of the Qur'anic teachings, becomes evident through the following narrative whereby *balā* is introduced as the *raison d'être* of the creation itself: *"It is He who created the heavens and the earth in six days...so as to test you, which of you does best"*[1]. However, traditionally, *balā* is discussed in the context of evil and human suffering, and thus largely with negative connotations; hardly ever is it pondered as something which is positive, meaningful and ultimately benign. And even when it is discussed as a benign phenomenon, there is no nuanced exposition of *balā* which accords with its all-inclusive meaning as established in the Qur'an.

Furthermore, *balā* is seen almost exclusively as being an issue of Muslim theodicy[2], in which it appears fleetingly against the backdrop of discussion on the justice of God and the apparent inconsistency between Divine justice and the existence of trials and tribulations which mankind encounters as an inevitable corollary of being human.[3] What has thus far been overlooked is the all-encompassing nature of *balā* as portrayed by the Qur'an, which actually posits *balā* as being the reason for creation. If the very reason for creation is *balā*, this naturally brings into question the ontological status of *balā*. If the whole of the cosmos was brought into being in order for man to experience *balā*, then it raises the question of whether humankind was created only to suffer adversity, for adversity and hardship are the things which *balā* commonly connotes.[4] A closer reading of the Qur'anic verses on *balā*, however, reveals that while it is indeed all-encompassing, to see it as only the harbinger of negativity is to fail to understand the multi-dimensional nature of *balā*, and the fact that it deals not only with adversity but also with prosperity and well-being.[5] Moreover, in positing the all-reaching nature of *balā* the Quran confirms that as a phenomenon, Divine trial, whether in adversity or prosperity, is always positive and charged with good. Therefore there appears to be a serious mismatch between both the popular and, for the most part, the scholarly perceptions of *balā* and the notion of Divine trial that is portrayed in the Qur'an.[6] An understanding of the Qur'anic approach to *balā* is crucial if we are to understand exactly how the process of human spiritual development is envisioned by the Islamic revelation. It also adds dimensions to the Muslim understanding of theodicy.

The Qur'an also affirms that the creation of the universe in general, and mankind's creation in particular, is purposeful, decisive, and not in vain: *"It was not without purpose that We created the heavens and the earth and everything in between!"*[7] Furthermore, at the core of the Qur'anic discourse on the creation of the universe, also appear the divine attributes and the affirmation that this world is the creative work of an Omnipotent, Omniscient, Wise, and absolutely Compassionate and Merciful God. The facts of adversity, misfortune, illness, and suffering, all of which may be considered as negative forms of *balā*, however, seem to question the very foundation of the aforementioned belief. Is this world, with all of its apparent imperfections, the creative work of an all-loving and powerful God? Therefore, the fact that mankind's experience of *balā* is interrelated with the purpose of the creation of the universe further necessitates a critical analysis and an in-depth study of the notion of *balā*.

Moreover, the popular perception of *balā*, and to a large extent the scholarly work, often tends to imply that God is testing mankind in order to establish a basis for either reward or punishment.[8] However, a closer reading of the Qur'anic text reveals that while Divine trial may be a measure for reward or punishment in the world to come, its primary role seems to serve a more comprehensive purpose: to provide a context for the actualization of man's full potential in this world. Therefore, *balā* is one of the key concepts needed to understand better the purpose posited by the Qur'an for the existence of beings in general, and mankind in particular. It is also one of the main issues that need to be unpacked in order to facilitate a more rounded understanding of Divine justice and the notion of evil.

Background

As already stated, the notion of Divine trial, *balā* / *ibtilā*, and its various versions, appears as a central theme in the Qur'an.[9] Nonetheless, there is a noticeable paucity of scholarly literature on the concept of *balā*. Most of what exists is found in the classical works of Qur'anic exegesis, and in the theological debates. The exegetical material on *balā*, however, is scant, and there is a lack of serious intellectual engagement which renders a literature review difficult to say the least. Therefore, while *balā* is a Qur'anic concept, it is not dealt with, in its all-inclusive nature, in the literature which purports to have as its main aim the exposition and clarification of the meanings of the Islamic revelation.

The review of the exegetical material, presented in Chapter Two, illustrates that the primary literature on the Qur'anic teachings is largely silent on the in-depth meaning and significance of *balā*. An example of the exegete's lack of engagement with this concept can be observed from their elucidations on the following narrative: *"It is He who created the heavens and the earth in six Days – and His throne was on water- so as to test you, which of you does best…".*[10] One of the most comprehensive Qur'anic commentaries, *Jāmi' al-bayān 'an Ta'wīl ayy al-Qur'ān,* by Muhammad ibn Jarir al-Tabari (d. 310/923), fully elaborates on the first part of the narrative and offers detail discussion on how and why the universe was created in six days. Tabari, however, offers very little on the second part of the verse which posits *balā* as the reason for the creation, and simply points out that God created the heavens and the earth to test peoples' commitment to their religious duties.[11] A similar approach is taken by another major exegetical work, *al-Kashshaf 'an Haga'I al-Tanzil wa 'Uyun al-Agawil fi Wujuh al-Ta'wil* by Abu al-Qasim Jar Allah Mahmud ibn 'Umar al-Zamakhshari (d. 538/1144). In Zamakhshari's opinion God created the universe, granted man countless blessings, and commanded him to perform certain religious duties; He will then reward the one who obeys Him and punish whoever disobeys the commands. According to Zamakhshari, similar to the goals set by any test giver, the purpose for having mankind experience *balā* is for God to find out, or to know, whether or not people act according to His commandments, and to establish the criteria for rewards and punishments.[12]

Another source where material on *balā* is found seems to be those scholastic theological works which discuss theodicy in general. Nonetheless, due to the fact that the discussion of *balā* in the theological discourse is generally discussed under the category of natural or moral evils and its relation to the overall "problem of evil" and justice in the world, it only treats the concept in a limited scope and does not offer the all-inclusive meaning of *balā* as emphasized in the Qur'an.[13]

Finally, the works of the mystic scholars and the poets, though scattered, seem to offer more in-depth exposition of this concept.[14] The notion of Divine trial from the perspective of Muslim mystics and its significance in man's spiritual development will be discussed in Chapter Four.

The relative silence of the sources on this issue may have contributed to the popular misconception of *balā* as something unpalatable and undesirable. As such, an in-depth study of *balā* which figures only incidentally in the scholarly literature is long overdue.

The Objective

The premise of the present book is that *balā* is not equated with suffering; it is not intended to punish the sinful; and that its manifestation is both in adversity and prosperity. Furthermore, the sole purpose of *balā* is not to put human beings into difficulties in order for God to establish their status in the world to come, but is a means whereby man's inherent potentialities for spiritual growth are allowed to flourish and be made manifest. This study aims to show that the Qur'anic notion of *balā* is seriously at odds with both popular, and to a large extent, the scholarly perceptions of this concept. The leading research questions for the study include the following: do classical and modern works of exegesis, which are deemed to be the prime source of elucidation of the Qur'an, throw light on the all-encompassing and entirely positive nature of the notion of *balā*? Is *balā* represented as a negative or positive phenomenon in the Qur'an? Is *balā* God's way of punishing the sinful; how is that related to the *balā* of the prophets mentioned in the Qur'an? If *balā* is a "test", what is the purpose of this test? If God is Omniscient, He can clearly have no need of a test which throws light on man's abilities and deficiencies. Similarly, if the test is for man, to what end?

Defining Key Terms and Methodology

The concept of Divine trial is mostly connoted by two main terms in the Qur'an, *balā* and *fitna*, both of which are subsumed under the general term *ibtilā*. Translation of these terms into English is problematic, since any translation will inevitably fail to give a full picture of the term as it is used in the Qur'an.[15] Although translation may serve as a preliminary guide and the first step, more often than not, it misrepresents the original term under study. For this reason, although the term "Divine trial" is used, it is used only for the sake of the English–speaking reader, and then merely as a rough equivalent. Therefore, the use of the original words *balā* and *ibtilā* has been deemed more appropriate than the term "Divine trial".

As mentioned above, the notion of Divine trial becomes visible in the Qur'an through *balā* and *fitna* narratives. In an effort to provide a clear understanding of the meanings of the two terms, I have employed the methodology of semantic analysis and contextual interpretation discussed by Toshibiko Izutsu in his book *Ethico-Religious Concepts in the Qur'an*.[16] According to Izutsu, any Qur'anic term needs to be understood within the whole semantic framework of the verses in which it appears and which surround it. In Izutsu's opinion the best method for analyzing the Qur'anic terms is to bring together, compare and put in relation, all the narratives in which the terms under study appear, so that the semantic value and the context of the narratives are examined. Utilizing the Izutsuian methodology, all *balā* and *fitna* narratives were surveyed first, followed by a careful examination of the context of each narrative which involved the occasion of the revelation, the targeted audience, and the historical context (revealed in Mecca or Medina). The contexts of these narratives were then compared and studied against similar and opposing verses prior to grouping them in a specific category. Taking this contextual analysis approach, the study allowed the Qur'an to interpret itself and further guide the research to its full development. Therefore, the result of this analysis which is based on the Izutsuian methodology, serves as the backbone of the study; the result is the complete typology of *balā* and *fitna* narratives which is presented in Chapter One.

In addition to Izutsuian methodology employed in Chapter One, textual and historical analysis method has been utilized in Chapters Two and Three. These chapters also include an intra-textual hermeneutics method whereby the narratives under study are examined in light of their overall context, as well as their relationship, whether implicitly or explicitly, to other closely related themes of the Qur'an. The historical analysis method becomes especially noticeable in discussing *balā* in lives of the Prophets and other faith communities in light of their historical settings. It also needs to be noted here that "critical" analysis, used in various parts of this work, refers to a tool in the examination of the concept of *balā* through textual analysis in the form of deconstructionist approach. Therefore, the methodology of deconstructionism is utilized in Chapters Four and Five of the study. To this end, the term *balā* is first un-packed and decomposed so that its in-depth meaning can better be studied in light of the mystical and theological discussions. Accordingly, the utilization of the deconstructionist method in the final two chapters of the work enabled the study to shed light on the wholly positive nature of *balā* which the Qur'an seems to import.

Scope and Structure

As stated above, the Muslim exegetical literature is regarded as the primary source for the study of the Qur'anic concepts. Consequently, in order to pursue the aforementioned research questions, the works of the mainstream Muslim exegesis, as they pertain to the notion of *balā*, will be scrutinized and their level of engagement with the all-inclusive meaning of this concept will be highlighted. However, it needs to be noted that, while the task of the Muslim exegetes has traditionally been defined as the interpreters of Divine revelation, their elucidation is not solely based on the Qur'anic text itself – the semantics and linguistic aspects – but is also influenced by external factors which affect their comprehension of the Qur'anic themes. The exegetical literature, therefore, reflects the various school of thoughts and approaches in Muslim history (Ash'arite/Mu'tazilite; Sunnite/Shi'ite sectarian views; rationalistic, philosophic, or theological orientations), as well as the cultural, theological, and political climate, and the personal interests of their respective authors. This research, however, is not concerned with these external elements which inevitably influence the extent of the exegetes' understanding as it relates to the notion of *balā*. Consequently, the study limits itself to the context of the Qur'an, and examines the Qur'anic commentaries, without analyzing their particular social and anthropological setting, to find out if, in fact, the exegetical literature deals with the all-encompassing meaning and the wholly positive nature of *balā* emphasized in the Qur'an. Correspondingly, the examination of various factors underpinning the development of mystical tradition of Islam (various Sufi orders), and the establishment of different theological schools of thought (Ash'arite/Mu'tazilite) are beyond the scope of this work. Thus, the interpretations of *balā* from mystical and theological perspectives, presented in Chapters Four and Five, are not concerned with the socio-political and anthropological contexts of the sources used in the study; rather, the aim is to throw light on their overall exposition of the concept of *balā*.

This book is comprised of five chapters that are chronologically organized and also represent a logical order. The first chapter is dedicated to the typology of the Qur'anic narratives whereby the notion of Divine trial is revealed in its various contexts. The chapter is organized according to the statistical survey of the fifty *balā* and *fitna* narratives, as well as the narratives' historical context, the occasion of the revelation, the objective, and the audience to whom they were addressed. Therefore, by taking a textual hermeneutics approach, the narratives are grouped in four distinct categories with certain overlap between them. This part of the study produced a framework which demonstrates the overall Qur'anic approach to the notion of Divine trial and establishes the importance of the concept of *balā* within the Qur'anic teachings. The impact of this typology becomes visible in various parts of the book.

In Chapter Two, the concept of Divine trial will be examined in light of the two major Muslim scholarly sources: the prophetic traditions (*hadith*) and Qur'anic exegesis (*tafsir*). The chapter begins by highlighting the importance of *hadith* and *tafsir* and the instrumental role that they play in elucidation of the Islamic revelation, followed by discussing the rationale for selecting certain scholars and their respected work. Since the number of prophetic traditions that pertain to the concept of *balā* in its all-encompassing meaning are not significant, *hadith* literature is discussed first. The following section which occupies the major portion of this chapter discusses the Qur'anic exegetical materials and deals directly with one of the leading research questions of the study: does the exegetical material deal with the all-inclusive meaning of *balā* which accords with the Qur'an? To this end, a total of twelve *balā* and *fitna* narratives – three verses from each of the four categories indicated in the typology chapter – were selected and examined in light of six major *tafsir* works. The Qur'anic exegeses were selected to best represent the viewpoints of the Sunnite and Shiite schools of thought from classical and contemporary time. In its final analysis, this chapter establishes the fact that the mainstream Muslim exegetes generally do not engage in an in-depth discussion of the notion of Divine trial which the Qur'an seems to emphasize.

Chapter Three is tasked with the examination of Divine trial in the lives of the prophets, *nabi / rasūl*, and pertains to the *balā* and *fitna* narratives grouped in the fourth category indicated in the typology. The responsibility of the prophets, as well as the many challenges they encountered in leading their addressee communities, occupy a major portion of the Qur'an and require a careful examination. The chapter begins by a brief overview of the Qur'anic approach to the notion of prophethood (*nabuwwa*), and the vital role of the prophets as the exemplars and the best role model to be followed by their communities. Next, the stories of ten Qur'anic prophets whose particular trials are emphasized in the Qur'an are examined in the following subsequent sections of the chapter. To this end, each section begins by a brief synopsis of the tale of a prophet as it is reflected in the Qur'an, followed by a discussion of the unique *balā* of each prophet; the Qur'anic exegetical literature is reviewed to illustrate the commentator's understanding, or misunderstanding, of the significance of that particular *balā*. Further responding to the leading research question – the exegetical materials on the concept of *balā* – this chapter illustrates that the mainstream Qur'anic commentaries, for the most part, are generally concerned with the non-essential details of the stories of the prophets, and seem not to engage with the notion of *balā* to its full potential.

Chapter Four of the study is charged with the mystical dimensions of the notion of *balā* and investigates the perspectives of the Muslim mystics relating to this concept. Due to the fact that the typology chapter clearly demonstrates the significant position that the notion of *balā* occupies in the Qur'an, and since the exegetical literature seem to have opted not to engage with this concept in a comprehensive manner, the study will now turn to the mystical and Sufi literature to examine their understanding of *balā*. To this end, first, the chapter will provide the reader with the universal definition of the term "mysticism" and its roots in the teachings of perennial philosophy, as well as a general overview of the mystical tradition of Islam which historically has been represented by Sufism. The chapter will then demonstrate the comprehensive engagement of Muslim mystical literature with the notion of *balā*, as reflected in the teachings of a selected mystic and poet, and show that it is through this mystical approach that one engages in an in-depth understanding of the concept of *balā* which appears to accord with the all-encompassing approach that the Qur'an seems to emphasize. The material presented in this chapter supports the notion that *balā* – in adversity and prosperity – is a necessary component of the creation of the universe in general, and man's creation in particular; that *balā* is the means by which man's potential will be realised; and as such, it is a wholly positive phenomenon.

Chapter Five, which is the concluding chapter of the study, is devoted to the investigation of Divine trial as it relates to the notion of "the best of all possible worlds". Due to the fact that *balā* is seen traditionally as being synonymous with suffering and hardship, the objective of this chapter is to examine *balā* from the Muslim theological perspective and the attendant concepts of "good" and "evil". The chapter begins by an overview of the "problem of evil" and the various theological and philosophical debates surrounding it, followed by a summary of the theodicies which attempt to explain the existence of "evil" from a theistic perspective. The chapter will culminate in an in-depth scrutiny of al-Ghazālī's famous dictum of "the best of all possible worlds" and demonstrates that, from the Ghazālian perspective, this world, including all of its apparent imperfections, is indeed the best possible world that it can be.

*It is He who created the heavens
and the earth...to test you, which
of you does best.*

(Qur'an, 11:7)

1

Divine Trial Narratives in the Qur'an:
A Typology

The Qur'anic approach to the notion of Divine trial becomes visible mostly in the *balā* and *fitna* narratives. These narratives reveal that *balā* is a fundamental pillar of the creational structure of the Cosmos, functioning as an instrument to actualize the purposes of the Creator. The Qur'an clearly illustrates that humankind, regardless of religious belief, individually and collectively as a community, will be put to the test as part of their human experience: *"He created death and life to test you, and reveal which of you does best"* (Q. 67:2). The depth and comprehensiveness of the concept of *balā* in the Qur'an reveals that even the prophets are not exempted from this meaningful encounter: *"... And we tried you [Moses] with many tests"* (Q. 20:40).

In this introduction, the notion of *balā* will be discussed in various themes as it can be observed from the Qur'an. These include: the link between *balā* and the creational structure of the universe both as a whole, and in relation to man's creation, means by which *balā* is actualized in man's life, and *balā* as punishment.

Trial and Tribulation: Purpose in Divine Plan

The strength and universality of the concept of *balā* within the Qur'anic context posits *balā* as one of the components of the formation of the universe: *"It is He who created the heavens and the earth in six Days – and His throne was on water – so as to test you, which of you does best. Yet [Prophet] if you say to them, 'You will be resurrected after death', the disbelievers are sure to answer, this is clearly nothing but sorcery!"* (Q. 11:7). Furthermore, the notion of *balā* is intertwined with the Qur'anic concept of purposefulness of the Cosmic Creation. Repeatedly the Qur'an reminds us that the Creation of the universe is purposeful, decisive, and not in vain: *"It was not without purpose that we created the heavens and the earth and everything in between!"* (Q. 38:27). It can further be noticed from the Qur'an that the creation of man (*insān*)[1] is distinguished from the rest of the Creation, for the reason that his inner-nature (*fitra*) is composed of the Divine Spirit, hence, making him the highest creature in rank: *"...I have fashioned him, and breathed my spirit into him..."* (Q. 15:29).

As Rahman points out, "While the purpose of man is to serve God, i.e., to develop his higher potentialities in accordance with the 'command' *(amr)* of God, through choice, he must be provided with adequate means of sustenance and of finding the right way."[2] To this end, the very first Qur'anic revelations point out that the essential knowledge, which is imperative for man's survival, is ingrained in his nature by the Merciful God: *"Your Lord is the Most Bountiful one who taught by the pen, who taught man what he did not know"* (Q. 96:3-5). Additionally, the endowment of knowledge is illustrated in the Qur'anic narrative of Adam's creation, whereby the angels are commanded to bow down before him (Q. 2:30-34). According to Yusuf Ali, "Allah teaches us new knowledge at every given moment. Individuals learn more and more day by day; nations and humanity at large learn fresh knowledge at every stage. This is even more noticeable and important in the spiritual world"[3]. To this fact, in an early Meccan[4] *Sura*, the Qur'an exposes a colorful portrait of man's soul, illustrating the extent of man's capability in making his spiritual destiny. It is worth mentioning here that it is in accordance with the concept of man's spiritual development emphasized in the Qur'an that the present work will discuss the notion of *balā* from the Muslim mystical perspective in Chapter Four to shed light on the wholly positive nature of *balā* as it relates to man's creation and his spiritual journey.

By creation of the soul (*nafs*), and granting it the power to distinguish between right and wrong, God has positioned man in charge of his own life. His spiritual success is dependent on whether he makes the "choice" to purify his soul or corrupt it: *"...And by the soul and how He formed it and inspired it [to know] its own rebellion and piety! The one who purifies his soul succeeds, and the one who corrupts it fails"* (Q. 91:7-10). Hence, having the necessary cognition to create knowledge, and the ability to differentiate between wrong and right, man's crucial test, Rahman informs us, is "whether he can control history towards good ends or whether he will succumb to its vagaries."[5] Thus, it may be noted that the Qur'an approaches the notion of *balā*, as a means to constantly remind man of his mission on earth, and his final return. *"Did you think we had created you in vain, and that you would not be brought back to us?"* (Q. 23:115).

The instrumentality of *balā* as it relates to serving the purposes of God, whereby the Divine Plan is actualized, therefore, is the context in which the Qur'an approaches the concept of *balā*. It can also be observed that the underlying principle of *balā* seems to arise from the notion of "Divine Guidance" *(hedaya)* which is the ultimate goal of the Qur'an, guidance for humanity *(hudan li'l-nas)*. The notion of Divine guidance and its direct relationship to *balā* is discussed in more detail in other parts of this study. Furthermore, it is in conforming to the instrumentality aspect of *balā* and its entirely positive nature that this concept must further be discussed in light of the theological debates. Consequently, to shed light on the all-inclusive meaning of *balā*, Chapter Five of the book is tasked with the interpretation of *balā* as it relates to the overall "problem of evil" from the Muslim theodicean thought in general, and the Ghazālian perspective formulated in his famous dictum of "the best of all possible worlds" in particular.

Means of Divine Trial

While the vast majority of the Qur'anic narratives in which the concept of *balā* is elucidated point to manifestation of *balā through* adversity and hardship, nevertheless, the Qur'an noticeably reveals that *balā* will, without a doubt, present itself in prosperity and abundance as well: *"We will test you all through the bad and the good"* (Q. 21:35).

The manifestation and objects of *balā* are clearly represented in the Qur'an, signifying all that matters to man, wealth, power, health, offspring, etc., are means by which man will be put to the "test"; how man perceives the specific circumstances of his life is of tremendous importance in the Qur'an. As the commentator Tabarsi writes, "This world is the realm of tests and afflictions. People of faith will face trials in order that they may develop patience and know spiritual blessings."[6] To this fact, the Qur'an points out that, in reality, "everything" on this earth is meant for the purpose of the test: *"We have adorned the earth with attractive things so that We may test people to find out which of them do best, but we shall reduce all this to barren dust"* (Q. 18:7).

Divine Trial as Punishment

The popular understanding of *balā* and *fitna* carries a negative connotation and, for the most part, represents an undesirable and unconstructive image. This perception may be viewed from different perspectives. Whether an individual is experiencing a hardship, an illness or financial difficulty, or an entire community is affected by a natural tragedy, such as an earthquake, the popular tendency is to view the situation as a punishment from God. This accepted perception goes further to justify the hardship as a deserved punishment, which is a direct consequence of sinful conduct on the part of the recipient of the calamity. However, as it can be observed from the following verse, the Qur'an indisputably clarifies this misperception: *"No blame will be attached to the blind, the lame, and the sick"* (Q. 24:61). Therefore, as Bowker points out, "the Qur'an warns the faithful not to make the mistake of Job's friends and to assume that where they see suffering there also they see sin".[7] The overall Qur'anic view which noticeably identifies the purpose of adversities in human lives as tests and not punishment can be elucidated from the following narrative: *"We shall certainly test you with fear and hunger, and loss of property, lives, and crops; but [Prophet], give good news to those who steadfast"* (Q. 2:155).

Nevertheless, the Qur'an includes a small number of narratives which support that suffering may, in fact, be a punishment from God. Appealing to past history, these "punishment narratives" illustrate that as a result of continuous persistence in disbelief and rejection of the prophetic message, an entire community is eradicated. According to the Qur'an, God's sending of a prophet may be accompanied by calamities afflicting the community[8]. However, the purpose of the tragedies or misfortunes is to serve as supporting evidence for the warnings of the prophet, thereby providing the opportunity to embrace the prophetic message. However, as a result of peoples' choice of ignoring the prophet's warnings, and their endless tenacity on the disbelief path, God eradicates the hardship, bestows prosperity, and whilst people are ignorant of the Divine, wills the total destruction of the community through a natural disaster.

> *Whenever we sent a prophet to a town, we afflicted its [disbelieving] people with suffering and hardships, so that they might humble themselves [before God], and then we changed their hardship to prosperity, until they multiplied. But then they said, "hardship and affluence also befell our forefathers", and so we took them suddenly, unawares.* (Q. 7:94-95)

Although annihilation of a particular community is perceived to be a punishment from God, nevertheless, this paradigm serves a decisive role within a broader scope: a test and a learning opportunity for other addressee communities. The Qur'an repeatedly demonstrates that the underlying principle of the hardships was meant for the community to become humble in the way of God, transform their attitude, and willingly accept the monotheistic message. Time and again, the Qur'an reflects on human understanding with regard to signs (*ayāt*) from God; in this case, asking people to think about the adversity and the prosperity visited on them, and recognize the Divine purpose. Had they not ignored the signs which resulted in their insistence on the wrong path, they would have been guided to salvation. Instead, their heedlessness leads them to destruction.[9] It needs to be emphasized that the term *balā* is not utilized in the "punishment narratives"; nonetheless, the popular understanding equates these calamities with *balā*.

Man's Response to Divine Trial

In the case of the individual who is going through hardship, by and large, the circumstance is perceived as an undesirable condition, with no benefit or purpose. The person views himself as the victim of an objectionable occasion, someone unlucky who is being humiliated by God: *"And man, when his Lord tries him through the restriction of his provision, he says, 'my Lord has humiliated me'"* (Q. 89:16). Identifying a particular situation as misfortune, which has happened due to bad luck, the person refrains to reflect on the circumstance, and perhaps, fails to discover a meaningful purpose with an opportunity to grow. In the language of the Qur'an, whether the individual is experiencing a hardship, or enjoying life in prosperity (Q. 89: 15-16), he is going through a *balā*. What is expected of man is to act in accordance with the Will of God: patience during hardship, and humility and kindness in prosperity. However, man, more often than not, gets "puffed up in prosperity and depressed in adversity, putting false values on this world's goods".[10]

This analogy, of course, lends itself not only to the individual who, in any given situation, might be experiencing the *balā* (Divine test), but equally to those who are observing a particular circumstance. In other words, man is always going through some sort of test; either he himself is the direct subject of the trial, or his response towards the ordeal and / or prosperity of other fellow human beings indirectly becomes his own *balā*. To illustrate the latter, the Qur'an speaks of people who are not willing to spend part of their wealth in charity, thus not realizing that their *balā* is with their wealth. Therefore, their refusal of help to the needy is a testimony to their failure in the test: *"And when they are told, 'give to others out of what God has provided for you', the disbelievers say to the believers, why should we feed those that God could feed if He wanted? You must be deeply misguided"* (Q. 36:47).

Contrary to the popular perception of *balā* and *fitna*, the Qur'an paints a very different portrait of these terms, to the extent that it regards *balā* as part of the structure of Divine Creation, and a very purposeful encounter for human beings. The Qur'anic view on *balā* as a fundamental pillar of the creation of the Cosmos is exposed through many narratives whereby not only adversity is viewed as trial; prosperity is also a condition in which man is put to the test. This aspect of *balā*, as part of the "Divine Plan", and the fact that *all* human beings, including the prophets, encounter diverse purposeful trials in both adversity and prosperity, will be an essential part of this study.

Preceding the linguistic overview of the terms *balā* and *fitna*, it should be noted that the Qur'anic view on the general notion of trial is presented in more than one hundred narratives by utilizing four verbs and / or verbal nouns. However, by and large, the notion of Divine trial becomes known in *balā* and *fitna* narratives; therefore, this typology is concerned only with these two major terms. The two fewer used terms, each appearing only in two Qur'anic accounts, are: *mahhasa*, trial, (Q. 3:141; 3:154) and *imtahana*, test, (Q. 49:3; 60:10). Nonetheless, based on the context and the level of their relevancy, these two terms will be highlighted during the discussion of various categories and types of *balā*.

A Linguistic Overview of *balā* and *fitna*

Edward William Lane describes the term *balā* as: "God tried, proved, or tested him, [by, or with, good], or [by, or with, evil]; for God tries his servant by, or with, a benefit, to test his thankfulness; and by, or with, a calamity, to test his patience"[11]. According to Abdolnabi Ghayyem, *balā* simply means "to put to the test".[12] Although the term *balā or ibtilā* is not referenced in the *Encyclopedia of the Qur'an*, the notion of trial is cross-referenced to *balā* and the definition of "challenge to be endured"[13] is given.

Prior to providing the reader with the various meanings of *fitna*, it has to be noted that, historically, Muslim culture portrays a symbolic meaning of *fitna* to refer to "the great rift in the community shortly after the death of the prophet"[14]. Therefore, more often than not, the use of the word *fitna* carries a negative connotation. This study is not, however, concerned with the cultural aspects of *fitna* as it applies within the historical context, but rather will focus on the Qur'anic aspect of the term as it relates to Divine trials and tests.

An overall review of the meaning of the Arabic word *fitna* reveals multiple definitions. According to Lane, its most general meaning seems to be:

Melting of gold and of silver in order to separate, or distinguish, the bad from the good, it signifies a trial, or probation; and affliction, distress, or hardship; and [particularly] an affliction whereby one is tried, proved, or tested.[15]

The Arabic lexicon of Ibn-Manzūr defines a similar meaning for *fitna*:

It denotes a process of extracting and purging the impure from the pure in the metal. This basic idea of purification was then extended to the moral condition of humanity where a demanding situation acted as a watershed, a moral test or trial.[16]

According to Abdolnabi Ghayyem, the following definitions may be applied to *fitna*: "disparity between people, riot, trial, learning experience, affliction, and disbelief."[17] Similarly, the *Encyclopedia of Islam* gives the primary definition of the term *fitna* as "putting to the proof, discriminatory test."[18]

In an effort to inductively bring clarity on the meanings of terms *balā* and *fitna*, taking a hermeneutical approach, I have applied the methodology of Toshihiko Izutsu outlined in his book *Ethico-Religious Concepts in the Qur'an*.[19] In his book, Izutsu explains the importance of "contextual interpretation", whereby the terms are analyzed according to the framework of the Qur'an, hence allowing the Qur'an to interpret itself. According to Izutsu, "for any passage to acquire a peculiar semantic significance, it must work as a specific context revealing in a full light some aspect or aspects of the semantic category of a given word"[20]. Izutsu's methodology is constructed on seven distinct principles by which the Qur'anic terms must carefully be examined before the interpreter is able to provide the intended meaning.

Applying the Izutsuian methodology, namely the employment of "contextual interpretation", *balā* and *fitna* narratives in the Qur'an underwent a careful examination, both individually and collectively. I have located all the verses of the Qur'an in which the word *balā* and / or *fitna* have been utilized; examined each verse by studying its occasion of revelation, the historical context, and its thematic concept by employing the intra-textual hermeneutic approach. Furthermore, the purpose of the narratives and the addresses were also examined. With this method, my goal is to shed light on the notion of *balā*, as expressed in the Qur'anic context, by grouping the narratives in specific categories, keeping in mind potential overlaps between them. Through this process, the context and themes of each individual verse were cautiously studied and compared with other similar verses in which the words were utilized. Based on this analysis, the *fitna* and *balā* narratives reveal a deeply rooted principle indicating why and how people are put to the "test".

A General Overview of *balā* and *fitna* Narratives

The *balā* and *fitna* narratives appear in both Meccan and Medinan chapters of the Qur'an. Although much research has been done on the chronology of the Qur'anic scripture, there is still no consensus as to the exact sequence of the chapters (*sūras*). However, categorization of the Qur'an based on whether the *sūras* were revealed during the first phase of the prophetic message in Mecca, or after the prophet and his followers migrated to Medina, is generally accepted.[21]

The numerical analyses of the terms *balā* and *fitna* shows a total of eighty-nine accounts. However, this typology is concerned only with fifty of these narratives, whereby the contextual format directly alludes to Divine trial. Of the twenty nine occasions of *balā*, fifteen are revealed in Mecca and fourteen in Medina; where as from the twenty one *fitna* accounts, Mecca has a share of fourteen narratives, with Medina chapters containing only seven. The fact that the twenty nine *balā* verses are almost equally divided between the Meccan and Medinan chapters seems to suggest that the notion of Divine trials and tests was part of the Qur'anic teachings from the early stage of the prophetic message, and continued to be the case throughout the Medinan phase. Furthermore, the fact that the vast majority of *fitna* verses are revealed during the Meccan phase also points to the importance of the notion of Divine trial from early on.

Classifications of *balā* and *fitna* Narratives

The overall representation of the *balā* and *fitna* narratives in the Qur'an appears to suggest four distinct types or categories, with a certain amount of overlap between them. The individual narratives have been grouped in each category according to their theme and the overall context in which they are revealed. What follows is the explanation for each of the four categories and their corresponding narratives.

(a) Divine Trial as the Central Pillar of the Creational Structure of the Cosmos

Prior to providing the reader with an explanation of the narratives in this category, an important distinction between the terms *balā* and *fitna* needs to be made. While both terms are utilized to mean "trial" in the Qur'anic context, *balā* seems to be used in a broader spectrum presenting itself in all four categories. *Fitna*, on the other hand, is mostly used in the Qur'anic accounts in which specific subjects of trial are mentioned, offering more detailed elucidation of the means by which man will be tested. Consequently, since *fitna* does not seem to appear in any of the verses where "trial" is presented as part of the creational structure, this category will only include the *balā* narratives.

The verses classified in this category are mainly those in which the concept of *balā* is introduced as an integral part of the cosmic plan. Therefore, this category provides us with an overall umbrella of the Qur'anic view on *balā* as part of the structure of the Cosmos. The fact that out of the six narratives in this category, four are from the Meccan period (11:7, 18:7; 67:2; 86:9), and two appear in Medinan *sūras* (5:48; 76:2), points to the importance of the concept of *balā* from the early phase of the Qur'anic teachings.

Meccan *balā* Narratives

The first verse in this category appears in *sūra Hud*:

> *It is He who created the heavens and the earth in six Days – and His throne was on water - so as to test you, which of you does best. Yet [Prophet] if you say to them, "You will be resurrected after death", the disbelievers are sure to answer, this is clearly nothing but sorcery!* (Q. 11:7)

In this verse the concept of *balā* is not only directly linked to the story of the Creation, it is highlighted as its foundation: without *balā* the Creation would be aimless. It can be further observed that this narrative is the focal point which acts as the bridge for verses 6-11, whereby key Qur'anic concepts are linked through the concept of *balā*. We are told in verse six that there is no creature on this earth but its provision rests with God; He knows where it lives and its final resting place. Therefore, verse six emphasizes that everything in this universe happens with the knowledge of God and according to Divine Law. Subsequently, verse seven, which is the narrative in discussion, reveals that *"God created the heavens and the earth so as to 'test' you: which of you does best in conduct"*, hence emphasizing that *balā* is part of the structure of the universe. The narrative then goes further to introduce the concept of resurrection while pointing to the fact that disbelievers' response will be *"this is clearly nothing but sorcery"*. In summary, this narrative illustrates that the creation of the universe is purposeful, that man's conduct is tested through *balā*, that *balā* is the medium in which his spiritual life will be flourished, and that ultimately man's return is to God.

Following along the same path, verses nine through ten illustrate man's behavior at the time that he is experiencing *balā*, whether he is being tested in adversity or prosperity.

> *How desperate and ungrateful man becomes when We let him taste Our mercy and then withhold it. And if We let him taste mercy after some harm has touched him,*

he is sure to say, "misfortune has gone away from me", he becomes exultant and boastful. (Q. 11:9-10)

These narratives illustrate that human beings, for the most part, do not act in accordance with God's plan during *balā*; they get disappointed while experiencing hardship and proud during blessed times. However, the next verse in this sequence paints the picture of those who have developed the sense of steadiness in life, and who neither get depressed whenever a calamity befalls them nor overjoyed with pride during prosperity[22]: *"Not so those who are steadfast and do good deeds: they will have forgiveness and a great reward"* (Q. 11:11). The Qur'an, therefore, demonstrates what is expected of man by guiding him to the correct path and the right course of actions during the time of *balā*.

The second narrative in this category is revealed in *sūra al-kahf*: *"We have adorned the earth with attractive things so that We may test people to find out which of them do best"* (Q. 18:7). This narrative demonstrates the Qur'anic view on the materialist aspect of this life, such as power, fame, wealth, social status, and all that man strives for, to be nothing but a magnificent show and means of trial to test man. It can be observed from this verse that beautification of all things on this earth, "everything" that man desires, is part of the Divine plan in order to test man in his conduct, hence positioning *balā* at the center of God's Creation and an instrument by which His plan is actualized.

The next narrative in this group presents itself in *sūra al-Mulk*: *"He who created death and life to test you and reveal which of you does best – he is the Mighty, the Forgiving"* (Q. 67:2). The creation of death and life for the purpose of trial is once again a clear indication that *balā* is an essential part of the Divine plan. This narrative also confirms the point made previously that the Creation of the universe is not in vain or without a purpose. As Yusuf Ali points out: "The state before our present Life, or the state after, we can scarcely understand. But our present Life is clearly given to enable us to strive by good deeds to reach a nobler state."[23] It can be further observed that *balā* is the medium by which man's conducts and deeds will be evaluated, and therefore, based on his attitude towards Divine trial, he will be able to reach the higher state in life.

The final narrative revealed in Mecca appears in *sūra al-Tāriq*, *"On the Day when secrets are laid bare"* (Q. 86:9). This verse points to Judgment Day when the secrets of the hearts are put on trial, all that man attempted to hide will become apparent. The term used in this verse is *tubla* from the root *balā*, signifying the fact that the result of the trial will be bluntly clear on this day.

Medinan *balā* Narratives

From the Medinan period we have two narratives which can be classified in this category. The first of these appears in *sūra al-Mā'idah*:

> *We sent to you [Muhammad] the Scripture with the truth, confirming the Scriptures that came before it and with final authority over them: so judge between them according*

to what God has sent down. Do not follow their whims, which deviate from the truth that has come to you. We have assigned a law and a path to each of you. If God had so willed, He would have made you one community but He wanted to test you through that which He has given you, so race to do good: you will all return to God and he will make clear to you the matters you differed about. (Q. 5:48)

While this narrative discloses the relationship between the Qur'an and the previous scriptures, it provides clarification on the underlying principle which validates the variety of rules, *sharia*, and practical conduct. The verse also explains that a diverse code of law which, in fact, is the consequence of diversity of the people, is part of the Divine plan. It can further be observed from this narrative that, while God could have made people into one single community, He has constructed the universe to accommodate different people and a variety of rules in order to "test" people. While this verse sheds light on the fact that scriptures and laws are means by which each community will be put to the "test", it commands people to compete in virtue and strive on the right path. The concluding part of the narrative reminds us that everyone's return is to God, and the truth of disputed matters will be known to all communities on the Day of Judgment. It has to be noted that this verse may also be classified in Category Two of this typology (the manifestation of *bala*); however, it is included in this category due to the fact that the subject of *bala* is directly related to the creational structure of the universe.

The second narrative of the Medinan phase appears in *Sura Insān*: "*We created man from a drop of mingled fluid to put him to the test; We gave him hearing and sight*" (Q. 76:2). This narrative which is one of the key Qur'anic verses on the creation of man consists of three sections: first, it discloses the origins of man by showing the animalistic dimension of his creation; second, it points to the notion of Divine trial (*bala*) and the fact that man will go through tests and trials; finally, it concludes by shedding light on man's potential and abilities which will enable him to thrive in his life. Therefore, "man as an animal has this humble origin, but he has been given the gift of certain faculties of receiving instruction (typified by hearing) and of intellectual and spiritual insight (typified by sight)"[24].

(b) Manifestation of Divine Trial

The narratives identified in this category are mainly those in which the manifestation of *bala*, i.e., how *bala* is materialized in the lives of human beings, is the central theme and appears at the core of the discussion. By providing clear examples of tangible means through which *bala* is realized, these Qur'anic accounts shed light on the overall view of the Divine plan as it relates to man's trials. Furthermore, the narratives equally emphasize man's response in dealing with different situations, i.e., the variety of *bala*. This collection also illustrates what is expected of man during the time of *bala* and provides guidelines to reflect upon as man experiences *bala*. An overall observation on narratives presented in this group also reveals that, while *bala* is manifested mostly through adversity and hardship, prosperity and abundance, nevertheless, are also viewed as a type of *bala*. This observation further tends to suggest that the purification of man's personality to create a more authentic and truthful exposition is the focal point of the verses in this category. The following is a brief explanation on four *bala* verses (6:165, 21:35, 89:15-16), as well as four *fitna* narratives (6:53, 21:35, 21:111, 39:49), whereby the manifestation of *bala* is discussed.

The Meccan *bala* Narratives[25]

The first narrative of this category appears in *sura al-An'am*:

> *It is He who made you successors on the earth and raises some of you above others in rank, to test you through what He gives you. [Prophet], your Lord is swift in punishment, yet He is most forgiving and merciful* (Q. 6:165).

This verse is the concluding narrative of the *Sura;* therefore, it summarizes the previously discussed contents. While pointing to the Divine plan in creating generations after generations who are the inheritors of earth, the narrative emphasizes that God positions people in different ranks and provides them with diverse opportunities in order to test them. Hence, the goal is to test you in what He has bestowed upon you.

The second verse of this collection is a key narrative which appears in the late Meccan *sura al Anbiya'*: "*Every soul is certain to taste death: We test you all through the bad and the good, and to Us you will all return*" (Q. 21:35). The structure of this narrative is unique mainly for two reasons: firstly, both *bala* and *fitna* terms are used; secondly, the manifestation of *bala* both in adversity and prosperity is elucidated. While the narrative begins by confirming mortality, that everyone's time on this earth is limited and that death will visit us all, it quickly reminds man that his entire life is a test. The narrative further provides a detailed explanation of the means by which the Divine test will be conducted: through the bad (*sharr:* sickness, lack of wealth, etc.) and the good (*khayr:* abundance, health, etc.). The concluding section of the verse expounds upon the fact that everyone's return is to God; once again reminding man to be attentive of the diverse circumstances of his life and not lose sight of the fact that, at any given time, he might be experiencing a test.

The following two narratives present themselves in *Sura al Fajr*:

> *The nature of man is that, when his Lord tries him through honors and blessings, he says, "My Lord has honoured me", but when He tries him through the restriction of his provision, he says, "My Lord has humiliated me"* (Q. 89:15-16).

These narratives substantiate the point already made by the previous verse in this category, emphasizing that God will try man in both prosperity and adversity. Furthermore, the verses illustrate the likelihood of man's response at the time of *balā:* when he is the recipient of God's blessings, he gets puffed up and thinks he is special in the eyes of God; on the other hand, when his provision is restricted by God, man gets depressed and thinks that God has humiliated him. Had man recognized God's plan in both of these circumstances, he would have responded differently: show kindness to others during prosperity and patience during hardship.

The Meccan *fitna* Narratives[26]

The first narrative in which *fitna* is used to mean "trial" appears in *Sura Al – An`ām:* "*We have made some of them a 'test' for others, to make the disbelievers say, 'is it these men that God has favoured among us?' Does God not know best, who are the grateful ones?*" (Q. 6:53). In conjunction with the surrounding verses, this narrative demonstrates that the social and financial status of a group of people may in fact happen to be a test for others, i.e., the wealthy of a society are tested through the disadvantaged within the same society. The historical evidence indicates that the people of Mecca did not respond positively to the prophetic message, and a small number who did follow the prophet were the poor and the disadvantaged of that society[27]. The more wealthy people of Mecca who viewed themselves superior to others found it degrading to listen to Muhammad's preaching in the company of the poor. Therefore, by failing to realize that the financial status of the followers of the Prophet was how they were being tested, the materially well-off polytheists rejected the monotheistic message of the Prophet.

The third narrative[28] of this category is revealed in a late Meccan *Sūra al Anbiyā'* "*I do not know: this [time] may well be a test for you, and enjoyment for a while*" (Q. 21:111). Appearing at the end of the *Sura*, this verse represents the Prophet's final remarks in reminding his audience that what he has been asked to warn them about may be a test.

The final verse in this group appears in *Sūra Al Zumar:*

> *When man suffers some affliction, he cries out to Us, but when We favor him with Our blessings, he says, "All this has been given to me because of my knowledge" – it is only a test, though most of them do not know it* (Q. 39:49).

While this narrative clearly illustrates the manifestation of *balā* (test / trial) through prosperity, it also sheds light on man's response at the time of hardship or abundance. It can be understood from this verse that when man is faced with distress or adversity, he realizes his powerlessness and turns to God as the source of all good. However, when God bestows on him a favor, a gift, or mercy, man attributes it to his own doing, and fails to remember that God is the source of the received mercy. The narrative promptly reminds us that while man remains ignorant of the true source of the happiness or mercy he has just been blessed with, more importantly, he fails to realize that ultimately the goal was to test him. Time and again, the Qur'an reminds the reader that God is the sole source of all things; therefore, remembering God in times of distress and turning to Him during adversity, and yet being ignorant during abundance and happiness, will result in ungratefulness. It can further be observed from this narrative and other similar verses in the Qur'an that afflictions and hardships, as well as happiness and abundance, are both means in which man will be put to the test; in both circumstances man should be mindful of God and act according to what is expected of him.

(c) Objects of Divine Trial

The narratives included in this category are largely those in which various objects of *balā* are identified and presented as the focal point of the narratives. Additionally, the Qur'anic accounts which refer to the Muslim community's trials and tests at the time of battles or conflicts are grouped in this cluster as well. This collection includes eleven *balā* verses, two of which appear in Mecca (16:92 & 68:17) and nine of which belong to the Medinan phase (2:155, 3:152, 3:154, 3:186, 5:94, 8:17, 33:11, 47:4, 47:31). The nine *fitna* narratives are almost equally divided between Meccan (17:60, 29:2, 29:3, 72:17, 75:31) and Medinan periods (8:28, 9:126, 22:11, 64:15). That the frequency of the *balā* verses, with references to tangible objects, appears mostly in Medina seems to correlate with the historical context of Medina. Historians have written much about the cultural-social context of Medina, where this newly formed faith-community must thrive, as well as the challenges that the followers of the prophet had to face[29]. Therefore, this group of narratives symbolizes the Qur'anic view as it relates to unforeseen situations, whereby concrete objects of *balā* are entailed. Furthermore, man's perception of, and his emotional attachment to these precious and worldly goods, are questioned and warned about by these narratives.

The Meccan *balā* Narratives

The first narrative of this group appears in *sūra al Nahl*:

> *Do not use your oaths to deceive each other – like a woman who unravels the thread she has firmly spun – just because one party may be more numerous than another. God tests you with this and on the Day of the Resurrection He will make clear to you those things you differed about* (Q. 16:92).

It can be observed from the previous verse, which leads to the verse in discussion, that sometimes oaths and promises were used as a tool in deceiving other members of the community. By instructing people to keep their oaths and remain faithful to their promises, the narrative runs a comparative analysis between the actions of a female character that untwists the strands of the yarn after she has spun the yarn. The concluding section of the narrative reminds us that, while making an oath may bring security and strong sense of community to man, in actuality, the oath is one of the means by which God will test people.

The second Meccan narrative of this category presents itself in *Sura Al Qalam*: "*We have tried them as We tried the owners of a certain garden, who swore that they would harvest its fruits in the morning*" (Q. 68:17). In the preceding verses, mention is made of those people who have rejected the Prophetic message, basing their rejection on their false belief that the Qur'an is "nothing but ancient fables." The narrative in discussion, then, reminds the reader that the rejecters are, in actuality, being tested, i.e., experiencing a *balā*, the same way the owners of the Garden were put to the test[30].

The Medinan *balā* Narratives

The first verse of the Medinan period in which tangible items are referenced as *balā* appears in the longest *sūra* of the Qur'an, al- Baqarah: "*We shall certainly test you with fear and hunger, and loss of property, lives, and crops. But [Prophet], give good news to those who are steadfast.*" (Q. 2:155). In this narrative the most precious items within man's life are considered as objects of *balā* or Divine tests. While these objects may present themselves at various times and according to specific situations, lack of security and fear during conflicts, loss of property throughout harsh economic crisis, etc., they are, however, in the Qur'anic context, viewed as means by which man is tested. The concluding section of the narrative clearly demonstrates that what is expected of man during these difficult times is to have patience and act according to the will of God. Furthermore, by instructing the Prophet to give glad tidings to those who patiently persevere, it grants the believers the ultimate assurance to endure the situation and remain faithful to God.

Continuing with the discussion of concrete objects of *balā*, the following narrative appears in *sūra al –Imrān*:

> *You are sure to be tested through your possessions and persons; you are sure to hear much that is harmful from those who were given the Scripture before you and from those who associate others with God. If you are steadfast and mindful of God, that is the best course* (Q. 3:186).

This narrative emphasizes three distinct subjects of *balā* by means of which the believers are put to the test: their belongings (wealth, social status, and children); themselves (their own life); and the insults or harm imposed by the non-believers. The concluding section of the narrative briefly demonstrates the Qur'anic view on the expectations on the part of the believers, i.e., proper response while they are experiencing any of the mentioned *balā* – endurance with patience and mindfulness of God.

The concluding narrative of this section makes itself known in *sūra al-Mā'ida*:

> *You who believe, God is sure to test you with game within reach of your hands and spears, to find out who fears Him even though they cannot see Him: from now on, anyone who transgresses will have a painful punishment* (Q. 5:94).

By informing the believers that gaming is an object of *balā* in which they will be put to the test, this narrative sets the stage for the following verse: *"You who believe, do not kill game while you are in the state of consecration [for pilgrimage]..."* (Q. 5:95). Therefore, it can be understood from the two narratives that, since gaming is prohibited during the pilgrimage, they should refrain from killing any kind of animal during that time. Consequently, observing the rule as it relates to this object of *balā* is the sign of obedience to the command of God.

Balā on the Battle Field

As mentioned previously, a number of Qur'anic narratives signify *balā* during warfare. By and large, these verses pertain to some of the major battles that took place between the newly formed Muslim community in Medina and the Meccans. While they may deserve their own category, they have been included in this collection to show the relevancy of objects of *balā* to specific circumstances. This collection includes the following narratives in chronological order as they appear in the Qur'an: 3:152, 3:154, 8:17, 33:11, 47:4, and 47:31.

The first two narratives with an analogous theme appear in *sūra al Imrān*:

> *God fulfilled His promise to you: you were routing them, with His permission, but then you faltered, disputed the order, and disobeyed, once He had brought you within sight of your goal – some of you desire the gains of this world and others desire the world to come – and then He prevented you from [defeating] them as a punishment[31]. He has now forgiven you: God is most gracious to the believers* (Q. 3:152).

Continuing with more details of the same story, verse 154 reads:

> *After sorrow, He caused calm to descend upon you, a sleep that overtook some of you. Another group, caring only for themselves, entertained false thoughts about God, thoughts more appropriate to pagan ignorance and said, "Do we get a say in any of this?" [Prophet], tell them, "Everything to do with this affair is in God's hands". They conceal in their hearts things they will not reveal to you. They say. "If we had had our say in this, none of us would have been killed here." Tell them. "Even if you had resolved to stay at home, those who were destined to be killed would still have gone out to meet their deaths." God did this in order to test everything within you and in order to prove what is in your hearts. God knows your innermost thoughts very well* (Q. 3:154).

The above two narratives refer to one of the major battles in which the Muslims were engaged, namely the battle of *Uhud*, whereby the followers of the Prophet experienced an enormous *balā*[32]. The story has it that while the Meccans, who were the enemy of the

Muslims, outnumbered the supporters of the Prophet, the battle turned out in favor of the Muslims in victory. However, as the enemy was withdrawing from the battlefield, a group of Muslim soldiers who were instructed to remain on the top of the hill disobeyed the order and left their post to join the rest of the army in capturing valuables left by the Meccans. Taking advantage of the opening left by the archers, the Meccan army attacked again and killed many of the prophet's companions, including his uncle, Hamza. Although the Prophet was hurt, he was able to regroup the remaining members of the army, and return to the battlefield the next day to force the enemy out.[33] It can be observed from the context of 3:152 that going against the direct orders of the Prophet, which resulted in leaving the post and aiming after the booty, is referred to as the *balā*. Moreover, the entire story of the battle of *Uhud*, with its gains and losses, disappointments and excitements, is referred to as *balā* in 3:154.

The next narrative in discussion appears in *sūra al Anfal*:

> It was not you who killed them but God, and when you [Prophet] threw [sand at them] it was not your throw [that defeated them] but God's, to do the believers a favor[34]: God is all seeing and all knowing (Q. 8:17).

This narrative is related to another major battle, namely the battle of *Badr* which was a "turning point in the history of Islam as a political and military, as well as expanding religious movement".[35] The story has it that "before the battle, the Prophet prayed and threw a handful of sand at the enemy as symbol of their being defeated."[36]

The psychological hardship of war as a test for the Muslims also appears in a short narrative of *sūra al Ahzāb*: "*There the believers were sorely tested and deeply shaken*" (Q. 33:11). Drawing on the previous narrative whereby the enemy attack during the battle of *Ahzāb* is discussed, this verse reminds the believers that all of what they felt was in fact a *balā*.

The final two narratives of this category where *balā* is discussed in the context of the battlefield appear in *Sura Muhammad*: "*When you meet the disbelievers in battle, strike them.…, God could have defeated them Himself if He had willed, but His purpose is to test some of you by means of others…*" (Q. 47:4). In this narrative the followers of the Prophet are reminded that, while God is definitely able to wipe out the enemy and grant victory to the believers, the extent of their commitment to support the Prophet and defend their faith is, in fact, their *balā*, i.e., the means by which they are being tested. Furthermore, in another verse of the same *sūra*, the believers are, once again, made aware of the fact that *balā* does in fact serves a purpose within the larger part of the Divine plan: "*We shall test you to see which of you strive your hardest and are steadfast; We shall test the sincerity of your assertions*" (Q. 47:31).

The Meccan *fitna* Narratives

The fist *fitna* narrative of this category appears in *sūra al Isrā'*:

[Prophet], We have told you that your Lord knows all about human beings. The vision
We showed you was only a test for people, as was the cursed tree [mentioned] in the
Qur'an. We warn them, but this only increases their insolence (Q. 17:60).

At the beginning of this *Sura*, the Qur'an speaks of an extraordinary incident, namely
the Night Journey,[37] performed by the Prophet Muhammad. However, in the narrative in
discussion, this miraculous experience is referred to as prophet's vision[38], which was intended
as a *fitna* (test) for the people.

The next two narratives under discussion belong to another Meccan revelation, *sūra*
al 'Ankabūt:

Do people think they will be left alone after saying "We believe" without being put to
the test? We tested those who went before them; God will certainly mark out which ones
are truthful and which are lying (Q. 29:2 & 29:3).

While the notion of faith remains at the heart of the Qur'anic context[39], the first narrative
in discussion clarifies that a simple profession of faith is necessary but not sufficient.
The verse goes on to inform the believers that, without a doubt, the sincerity of their
assertion as it relates to their faith will be put to the test by God. Having established
the foundation for this understanding, the following narrative promptly reinforces the
idea by informing the Muslims that the genuineness of faith in other faith communities
prior to Islam was also tested, hence ruling out any exemption from this type of
Divine test.

The next narrative of this collection appears in *sūra al* Jinn: *"A test for them, but*
anyone who turns away from his Lord's Revelation will be sent by Him to spiraling torment"
(Q. 72:17). While the term *fitna* is used in this narrative, the preceding verse contains
the context of the test: *"if they had stayed on the right way, We would have given them*
abundant water to drink" (Q. 72:16). It can be observed from this Qur'anic account that,
while God in His Mercy grants "abundance" to people who are firm in their belief, the
bestowed blessing is, in fact, a *fitna*, i.e., means by which God will test the recipients of
His blessings.

The concluding narrative of the Meccan revelations in this group, present itself in
sūra al Muddaththir:

We have appointed only angels to guard Hellfire – and We have made their number
a test for the disbelievers and so that those who have been given the Scripture
will be certain and those who believe will have their faith increased and neither
those who have been given the Scripture nor the believers will have any doubts,
but the sick at heart and the disbelievers will say, "What could God mean by this
description?" In this way God leaves whoever He will to stray and guides whoever

He will – no one knows your Lord's forces except Him, It is only a reminder to mortals (Q. 74:31).

This narrative seems to act both as a clarification and an extension to the previous verse, whereby the number of the guardians of the fire is set to nineteen. The verse begins by providing the rationalization to point out that *fitna* or trial is, in fact, the reasoning for setting the number of the angels. The different groups of people and their response to this trial are elucidated in the concluding section of the narrative, while reminding the reader of God's ultimate power in providing guidance or leaving people to stray.

The Medinan *fitna* Narratives

We now turn to *fitna* narratives revealed in the Medinan phase of the prophetic message. The first of this group appears in *sūra al Anfal*: "*Be aware that your possessions and your children are only a test and that there is a tremendous reward with God*" (Q. 8:28). This narrative elucidates two of the dearest objects in man's life, namely possessions and offspring, and reminds the reader that both of these subjects are means by which people will be tested. Additionally, the verse affirms that trusting in God remains a wonderful compensation for the trial they face and the hardship they encounter in the way of God.

Next in the chronological order is the following verse which presents itself in *sūra al Tawbah*: "*Can they not see that they are afflicted once or twice a year? Yet, they neither repent nor take heed*" (Q. 9:126). The preceding narratives (9:123-125) expound upon the conflict between the believers and the unbelievers, while they shed light on the unbelievers' response to the Truth which lies before them. The verse in discussion, then, corresponds to the opportunity that is given to the unbelievers so they may repent and join the believing community. The concluding section of the narrative confirms the unbelievers' failure to recognize the *fitna* and take advantage of the once or twice a year opportunity granted to them, hence missing their chance to join the faith community. By denying themselves the chance to repent, the unbelievers remain on the wrong path.

The next narrative dealing with the objects of trial appears in *sūra al Hajj*:

> *There are also some who serve God with unsteady faith: if something good comes their way, they are satisfied, but if they are tested, they revert to their old ways, losing both this world and the next – that is the clearest loss* (Q. 22:11).

It may be observed from this narrative that the depth and firmness of people's faith, and their dedication and commitment towards God, become evident while they are experiencing a test. Some people's faith is only firm while all is well with their lives; once tried, however, their faith in God is weakened and their path deviates from Him, resulting in an ultimate loss in this life and the hereafter.

The final narrative of this category presents itself in *Sūra Al Taghābun*: *"Your wealth and your children are only a test for you. There is great reward with God"* (Q. 64:15). In this narrative, two of the most important attachments in man's life, mainly wealth and children, are specified to be among the objects of *balā*. This short narrative concludes by reminding man that the ultimate reward is with God.

(d) Divine Trial Visited on Prophets and Their Communities

The narratives classified in this category are primarily those in which the concept of *balā* in the life of Prophet Muhammad, as well as in the life of other prophets and messengers prior to the birth of Islam, is introduced[40]. Included in this group are eight *balā* narratives, from which four are revealed in Mecca (7:141, 7:136, 14:6, 37:106, 44:33), and three belong to the Medinan chapters (2:49, 2:124, 2:249). Additionally, from the six *fitna* narratives grouped in this cluster, five belong to the Meccan period (7:155, 20:40, 25:20, 44:17, 54:27), and one appears in a Medinan chapter (60:5).

By throwing light on the central role of the Prophets, in which they act as the exemplars for their communities, this group of verses provides us with a Qur'anic view of the manifestation of *balā* as it relates to the Prophets. While, by in large, these verses elucidate how a certain prophet or messenger deals with, or reflects on, the specific form of *balā*, there are, nevertheless, those narratives in which the life of a prophet becomes the object of *balā* for the addressee community. Furthermore, the Qur'anic accounts demonstrating the various forms of *balā* as it relates to other faith communities are also grouped in this category.

Life of the Prophets as Divine Trial

The first Meccan narrative in this section appears in *sūra al Furqān*:

> *No messenger have We sent before you [Muhammad] who did not eat food and walk about in the marketplaces. But We have made some of you a means of testing others – will you stand fast? Your Lord is all seeing* (Q. 25:20).

This narrative seems to expand upon another verse of the same *sūra* (Q. 25:7), whereby, the Meccans objected to the fact that Muhammad is an ordinary man with no extraordinary or magical ability, questioning why an angel is not accompanying him in bringing God's message. The narrative in discussion, therefore, sheds light on an important historical fact, namely that no other messenger was sent before Muhammad unless he, too, would eat food and walk through the street as any normal human being. In the context of this Qur'anic narrative, therefore, the fact that Muhammad is an ordinary member of society, who lives in much the same way as others, is in fact a *fitna* (test) from God. Moreover, this narrative concludes by confirming the previously made point that a group of people may become the means by which a different group within the same society is being tested by God.

Divine Trial in the Lives of the Prophets

The two narratives of this section signify _balā_ in the life of the Prophet Abraham. The first appears in the Meccan _sūra al Sāffāt_: "_It was a test to prove [their true characters]_" (Q. 37:106). This narrative sheds light on the story of Abraham and his son which is disclosed in previous verses (Q. 37:102-107), whereby Abraham's dream regarding the sacrifice of this son is discussed in full detail. The above Qur'anic accounts reveal an intimate dialog between Abraham and his son, in which God's command to Abraham to sacrifice his son emerged. Additionally, the narratives illuminate the act of submission to the will of God; father and son both realize God's command and submit to His will. Therefore, the narrative in discussion (37:106) reminds the reader that God's command to Abraham was, in fact, a _balā_, a Divine test for both Abraham and his son.

A wide-ranging _balā_ manifestation in relation to Abraham is also discussed in the Medinan _sūra al Baqarah_:

> _When Abraham's Lord tested him with certain commandments, which he fulfilled, He said, "I will make you a leader of people". Abraham asked, "And will You make leaders from my descendants too?" God answered, "My pledge does not hold for those who do evil"_ (Q. 2:124).

This narrative clearly illustrates Abraham's fulfillment of God's commands in everything that he was asked to do.

The next Qur'anic account in this group relates to the story of Prophet Moses and is revealed in the Meccan _sura, al A'rāf_,

> _Moses chose from his people seventy men for Our appointment, and when they were seized by trembling, he prayed, "My Lord, if You had chosen to do so, You could have destroyed them long before this, and me too, so will You now destroy us for what the foolish among us have done? This is only a trial from You – through it, you cause whoever You will to stray and guide whoever You will – and You are our Protector, so forgive us and have mercy on us. You are the best of those who forgive"_ (Q. 7:155).

It can be observed from this narrative that the Prophet Moses and a number of his companions faced a Divine _balā_; the companions failed the test while Moses prayed for their forgiveness.[41] Furthermore, the manifestation of _balā_ in the life of Moses is also discussed in the following narrative revealed in another Meccan _Sūra, Ta Ha_:

> _Your sister went out, saying, "Shall I show you someone who will nurse him?" then We returned you to your mother so that she could rejoice and not grieve. Later you killed a_

man, but We saved you from distress and tried your with other tests. You stayed among the people of Midian for years, then you came here as I ordained (Q. 20:40).

This narrative elucidates the story of Moses from his infancy to adulthood, recounting all the events in his life while referring to a variety of *balā* visited on him from God.

Divine Trial Relating to Other Faith Communities

The Qur'anic narratives grouped in this cluster are mainly those in which other faith communities and their respective *balā* are discussed. It needs to be noted that, thematically, five out of the eight narratives of this subsection (2:49, 7:141, 7:163, 14:6, and 44:33) demonstrate *balā* and *fitna* as they relate to the Children of Israel. Each of the remaining three narratives discusses *balā* as it pertains to various other communities: people of Talūt (Q. 2:249); people of Pharaoh (Q. 44:17), and people of *Thamūd* (Q. 54:27).

The first Meccan narrative disclosing the *balā* of the Children of Israel appears in *sūra al A'rāf*:

Remember how We saved you from Pharaoh's people, who were subjecting you to the worst of sufferings, killing your male children, sparing only your females – that was a mighty ordeal from your Lord (Q. 7:141).

The same message is conveyed through a similar passage which makes itself present in another Meccan *Sūra, Abraham*:

And so Moses said to his people, "Remember God's blessings on you when He saved you from Pharaoh's people, who were inflicting terrible suffering on you, slaughtering your sons and sparing only your women – that was a severe test from your Lord" (Q. 14:6).

Furthermore, this particular *balā* visited on the Children of Israel, i.e., the hardships imposed by Pharaoh, is also highlighted in the Medinan *sūra, al-Baqarah*: *"Remember when We saved you from Pharaoh's people, who subjected you to terrible torment, slaughtering your sons and sparing only your women – this was a great trial from your Lord"* (Q. 2:49). It can be observed from the above three narratives and their surrounding verses that, while all three accounts signify *balā* visited on the Children of Israel, they are, nevertheless, discussed within different historical contexts.[42]

Following the same path of demonstrating the *balā* of Children of Israel, another Qur'anic narrative in a Meccan *sūra, al Dukhān* reads: *"We gave them revelations in which there was a clear test"* (Q. 44:33). The story of the Children of Israel, their afflictions and *balā*, and their freedom is also discussed in this *sūra* (Q. 44:30 -33); hence, the narrative under discussion concludes the section by referring to an overall indication of their *balā*.[43]

The final narrative relating to the Children of Israel makes itself present in a Meccan *sūra, al Aʿrāf*:

> *[Prophet], ask them about the town by the sea; how its people broke the Sabbath when their fish surfaced for them only on that day, never on weekdays – We tested them in this way: because of their disobedience* (Q. 7:163).

As can be observed from this narrative, the Children of Israel were put to the test on the Sabbath day when fishing was prohibited. As it turned out, there were many fish that came up to the surface ready to be caught on the Sabbath day but not on the other days of the week. While some were obedient to the law, there were others who could not resist the temptation, disobeyed the law, and followed their desire to fish.

As mentioned above, there are three Qur'anic narratives in which *balā* on other faith communities are discussed. The first of these relates to the people of Pharaoh and is revealed in a Meccan *Sura, Al Dukhān*: *"We tested the people of Pharaoh before them: a noble messenger was sent to them"* (Q. 44:17). This narrative refers to the people of Pharaoh when Prophet Moses was sent to them; by refusing to accept his message, they failed the test.

The second narrative representing another faith community, namely the people of *Thamūd*, appears in *Sura Al Qamar*: *"For we shall send them a she-camel to test them: so watch them [Sālih] and be patient"* (Q. 54:27). While the story of the people of *Thamūd* and their messenger *Sālih* is presented in several Qur'anic narratives[44], the verse under discussion sheds light on their trial through a she-camel: they slaughtered the camel while they were instructed not to harm her.

The third narrative in this group corresponds to the people of *Talūt* and makes itself present in the Medinan *sūra al-Baqarah*:

> *When Talūt set out with his forces, he said to them, "God will test you with a river. Anyone who drinks from it will not belong with me, but anyone who refrains from tasting it will belong with me; if he scoops up just one handful [he will be excused]." But they all drank [deep] from it, except for a few. When he crossed it with those who had kept faith, they said, "We have no strength today against Goliath and his warriors." But those who knew that they were going to meet their Lord said, "How often a small force has defeated a large army with God's permission! God is with those who are steadfast"* (Q. 2:249).

This narrative discloses the story of the army of Talūt and sheds light on their *balā* to be a river; those who consume the water will fail the test, while abstaining from drinking the water will be a sign of obedience. Moreover, the narrative under discussion emphasizes the importance of believing in the day when all will meet God, hence remaining faithful and ready to fight on the path of God.[45]

Conclusion

The notion of Divine trial in the Qur'an is presented mostly through the Qur'anic accounts in which one of the two major terms of *balā* or *fitna* is utilized. These narratives illustrate that *balā* is a fundamental component of the structure of the universe and plays a purposeful function in the Divine plan. Consequently, all individuals and communities, including the prophets, will be put to the test according to God's Will. Although the manifestation of *balā* is mostly through hardships and adversity, the Qur'an, nevertheless, specifies prosperity and abundance as a type of *balā*.

The statistical survey of the Qur'anic narratives confirms that the notion of *balā* was revealed during the Meccan phase of the prophetic message, as well as the Medinan period during which the Muslim community was established. Therefore, the concept of *balā* remained at the heart of the Qur'anic teachings throughout the period when the Scripture was revealed.

Taking an intra-textual hermeneutics approach, whereby the themes and the context of the narratives are examined, the fifty narratives included in this typology were grouped in four major categories, with a certain amount of overlap between them. In discussing the categories, a logical order was followed whereby the most comprehensive category, namely "Divine trial as the central pillar of the creational structure of the Cosmos" was presented first, followed by "manifestation of Divine trial", "objects of Divine trial", and "Divine trial visited on prophets and their communities".

The next chapter of this study will examine *balā* in the *hadith* traditions as presented in both Sunni and Shi'ite collections. Also in this chapter, a number of key *balā* and *fitna* narratives will be examined in the light of major exegetical works from the classical period to the present day.

He who created death and life to
test you and reveal which of you
does best – he is the Mighty, the
Forgiving.

(Qur'an, 67:2)

2

Divine Trial in Prophetic Traditions
and Qur'anic Exegesis

The Qur'an is viewed by Muslims as the literal word of God sent down to the Prophet Muhammad over a period of twenty-three years. As the scripture of the religion of Islam, the Qur'an has not only served as the solid rock of the great Muslim venture of the past, but continues to be the source of guidance for more than one billion followers around the world today. The revelation stands at the center of Muslim life, influencing thought, shaping behavior, offering comfort at the time of hardship, and above all, providing the best guidance for the one who submits to the will of God. As Smith notes, "The Qur'an represents the eternal breaking through into time; the unknowable disclosed; the transcendent entering history and remaining here, available to mortals to handle and appropriate."[1]

As the alleged miracle of Islam, the Qur'an plays a dynamic role in the lives of Muslims regardless of their cultural, historical, political, or intellectual background. While the Qur'an was revealed in seventh century Arabia, its authority and influence continue to be as vibrant and significant today. As Ayoub notes:

Although the Qur'an has taken on the form of and character of human speech, it remains 'in its essence a celestial archetype free from the limitations of human sounds and letters.' Because the Qur'an intersects the human plane of existence and the transcendent word of God, it is imbued with this quasi-human personality, imbued with feelings and emotions, ready even to contend on the

Day of Resurrection with those who abandoned it in this life and to intercede for those who have lived by its teachings.[2]

While the Qur'an is viewed as the highest authority in Islam, the *hadīth* or Prophetic traditions, "constitute a kind of secondary scripture for Muslims, with an authority exceeded only by the Qur'an."[3] The root of a remarkable connection between the two sources of Islam, namely, the Qur'an and the *hadīth*, is articulated in the *shahāda*, which is the obligatory profession of faith: *there is no god but God, and Muhammad is the Messenger of God*. Moreover, the Qur'an, time and again, illustrates the exemplary role of the Prophet and reminds the community to follow in his footsteps: *"The Messenger of God is an excellent model for those of you who put your hope in God and the Last Day and remember Him often" (Q. 33:21);* and: *"Whoever obeys the Messenger obeys God"* (Q. 4:80). As Denny observes: "The two – prophet and book – are inextricably bound up in each other in a manner perhaps unduplicated by any other scripture."[4]

The Qur'anic emphasis on the exemplary role of the Prophet, along with the Prophet's extraordinary qualities: *"Truly you have a strong character"* (Q. 68:4), is the underlying principle for preservation of the Prophet's *Sunna* or mode of life. While the Prophet's *Sunna* - all that he left in the way of example and teachings - was remembered and handed down through personal teachings, the literary form of transmitting the *Sunna* emerged as a vital undertaking.

The companions of the Prophet made a conscious effort to record the actions and deeds of the Prophet, which led to the development of *hadīth* literature. Although many prophetic traditions were transmitted by diverse groups of people and in a variety of contexts, eventually the scholars adapted a methodology to distinguish between the authentic and forged traditions. After the completion of this process, which took over two centuries, the major collections of *hadīth* were introduced as authentic and solid sources of Prophetic tradition.[5]

While there are six major *hadīth* collections within the Sunni school of thought, the two that are widely used throughout the Muslim world are *Sahīh* Bukhārī (d. 256/870) and *Sahīh* Muslim (d. 261/875). As Brown observes, "al- Bukhārī and Muslim were thus the first to produce *hadīth* collections devoted only to *hadīths* whose *isnāds* [chain of transmission] they felt met the requirements of authenticity."[6]

In addition to exploring the major Sunni *hadīth* sources, I will draw on a well-known *hadīth* collection from the Shi'ite school of thought, namely, *Kāfi* of *al-Kulaini*, as well as, *Nahjol – Balāgha* of Imam Ali.

In this Chapter, by taking an intra-textual and historical interpretation approach, the notion of *balā* will be examined in the light of the two major textual sources, namely, the prophetic traditions (*hadīth*) and Qur'anic exegesis (*tafsīr*). Due to the fact that the number of *hadīth* traditions in which the subject of *balā* is discussed is not significant, the prophetic traditions will be discussed first. Furthermore, the characteristics of the selected exegetical sources, as well as justification for the particular Qur'anic narratives chosen to be examined in this part of the study, will be provided.

Divine Trial in the Prophetic Traditions (*hadīth*)

The statistical survey of prophetic traditions relating to the notion of Divine trial reveals a greater number of traditions than those covered in this section. This is mainly due to the fact that, while one report may appear in various *hadīth* collections, others convey the same message with minor alteration; therefore, a conscious attempt has been made to avoid repetitious traditions.

The *hadīth* collection of Sahīh Bukhārī has the following report which indicates the Prophet Muhammad's positive attitude towards afflictions: "If Allah wants to do good to somebody, He afflicts him with trials."[7] In another report, Bukhari references the following tradition which sheds light on the reward aspect of hardships: "No fatigue, nor disease, nor sorrow, nor sadness, nor hurt, nor distress befalls a Muslim, even if it were the prick he receives from a thorn, but that Allah expiates some of his sins for that."[8]

Sahih Muslim transmits an important tradition from the Prophet, which draws a comparison between a believer and a non-believer with regards to calamities of life:

> The example of a believer is that of a fresh tender plant; from whatever direction the wind comes, it bends it, but when the wind becomes quiet, it becomes straight again. Similarly, a believer is afflicted with calamities (but he remains patient till Allah removes his difficulties.) And an impious wicked person is like a pine tree which keeps hard and straight till Allah cuts (breaks) it down when He wishes.[9]

Additionally, the following *hadīth* sited in the *Sunan* of Abu-Dawūd highlights an important aspect of *balā*, namely, the positive rewards: "When man's deeds are inadequate Allah tests him by means of his health, wealth, or children; as he deals with these calamities with endurance, Allah grants him the high status that He had intended for him."[10] It is in accordance with this positive reward that various prophetic traditions point out man's response to *balā*. To this end, al-Tirmidhi's *Sunan* transmits the following *hadīth* which provides a guideline for a person who is experiencing *balā*: "A believer should not humiliate himself by declaring that he cannot tolerate a *balā* that has afflicted upon him".[11] Tirmidhi also reports a *hadīth* which stresses the importance of man's acceptance of the *balā*: "Certainly, the highest reward is granted for the hardest *balā*; a community which is favored by Allah will receive *balā*, whoever can tolerate it, Allah will be pleased with him."[12]

The final *hadīth* transmitted by Tirmidhi implies that a person who is experiencing a *balā* is not favored by Allah; therefore, the observer of such a circumstance must thank Allah for not engaging him in the same trial: "Whoever becomes aware of a *balā* that someone else is going through and offers gratitude to Allah for not being tested with the same condition, he will never, as long as he lives, be tested by Allah through the same means."[13] This *hadīth*, one may point out, inspires people to be sympathetic towards those who are tested through a major affliction or calamity.

Furthermore, the *hadith* works of the Shi'ite school of thought also make references to *balā* in its various aspects. The major work of *al-Kafi* cites the following tradition from the Prophet: "The greatest reward comes from the greatest trials and suffering. There have never been a people whom Allah loved but were not put to trial."[14] Another *hadith* which highlights the link between the greatness of trial and the level of belief is mentioned in *Kāfi* which reads: "The believers are like the two sides of a balance, as his belief increases in strength; his trial also increases in intensity."[15]

The book of *Nahjol-Balāgha*, which includes the sermons and letters of the first Shi'ite Imam, Ali bn Abi-Tālib, has several passages about the notion of *balā*. In sermon 191, considered to be one of his longest sermons, Imam Ali discusses various aspects of *balā* and sheds light on its impact on human lives.

What follows is the summary of his treatment of trials and tests as it appears in the context of sermon 191. After praising Allah through two of His divine attributes, Imam Ali discusses the creation of Adam, angels' obedience of Allah's command in prostrating before him, and Satan's lack of submission due to his feeling of supremacy, i.e., his creation from fire makes him superior to Adam who is created out of clay, hence refusing to prostrate before him. Imam Ali points to this event as the means by which the sincerity of the angels was put to the "test", therefore causing Satan to be expelled from his position which further provides the context for man's trials and tests.[16]

> If Allah had wanted to create Adam from a light whose glare would have dazzled the eyes, whose handsomeness would have amazed the wits and whose smell would have caught the breath, He could have done so; and if He had done so, people would have bowed to him in humility and the trial of the angels though him would have become easier. But Allah, the glorified, tries His creatures by means of those things whose real nature they do not know in order to distinguish (good and bad) for them through the trial, and to remove vanity from them and keep them aloof from pride and self-admiration.[17]

As can be seen from the above quote, according to Imam Ali, man's self-admiration, egotism, and lack of consideration for others, all of which are characterized as satanic qualities, can be altered through trials and tests. To further ground his point and to illustrate this concept in a more authentic and tangible format, Imam Ali reminds his audience of the Prophetic trials.

> Certainly, if Allah were to allow anyone to indulge in pride He would have allowed it to his selected prophets and vicegerents. But Allah, the Sublime, disliked vanity for them and liked humbleness for them. Therefore, they laid

their cheeks on the ground, smeared their faces with dust, bent themselves down for the believers and remained humble people. Allah tried them with hunger, afflicted them with difficulty, tested them with fear, and upset them with troubles.[18]

In another part of this sermon, Imam Ali makes an example of the Ka`ba to illustrate that the location of Allah's house of worship is one of the ways in which the believers' sincerity will be put to a test.

If Allah, the Glorified, had placed His sacred House and His great signs among plantations, streams, soft and level plains ..., the amount of recompense would have decreased because of the lightness of the trial. If the foundation on which the House is borne and the stones with which it has been raised had been of green emerald and red rubies...., then this would have lessened the action of doubts in the breasts, would have dismissed the effect of Satan's activity from the hearts. But Allah tries His creatures by means of different troubles, wants them to render worship through hardships and involves them in distresses, all in order to extract out vanity from their hearts, to settle down humbleness in their spirits and to make all this an open door for His favour and an easy means for His forgiveness (for their sins).[19]

On another occasion, while delivering a sermon to an audience about the creation of man, Imam Ali speaks of some of the means by which human beings will be tested.

Allah ordained livelihoods with plenty and with paucity. He distributed them narrowly as well as profusely. He did it with justice to test whoever He desired, with prosperity or with destitution, and to test through it the gratefulness or endurance of the rich and the poor. Then He coupled plenty with misfortunes of destitution, safely with the distress of calamities and pleasures of enjoyment with pangs of grief.[20]

The "Letters" section of *Nahjol-Balāgha* – Imam Ali's correspondence to various governmental authorities under his rule – includes a number of references to manifestation of *balā*. In the letter to the governor of Damascus, Mu'āwiyya ibn Abī Sufyān, Ali reminds his disobedient governor and opponent that while the material world will come to an end, our deeds and actions of this life will make up the essence of our life in the hereafter.

Allah, the Glorified, has made this world for what is to come hereafter, and put its inhabitants to trial as to which of you does good deeds. We have not been created for this world, nor ordered to strive for it, but we have been made to stay in it and stand trial therein. So, Allah has tried me with you and tried you with me. He has therefore made either of us a plea for the other.[21]

In his sermon of "Praying for Rain", Imam Ali speaks of the positive value of Divine trials, and points out that through despair lays the opportunity to return to the path of Allah, repent, and ask for forgiveness. Below is the summary of his speech on this occasion.

> Certainly, Allah tries his creatures in respect of their evil deeds by decreasing fruits, holding back blessings and closing the treasures of good, so that he who wishes to repent may repent, he who wishes to turn away (from evil) may turn away, he who wishes to recall (forgotten good) may recall, and he who wishes to abstain (from evil) may abstain.[22]

Our concluding reference from *Nahjol-Balāgha* is Imam Ali's speech on the deputation of Prophets, where he illustrates the link between the mission of the prophets and the community's trials.

> Allah deputed prophets and distinguished them with His revelations. He made them as pleas for Him among His creation, so that there should not remain any excuse for people. He invited people to the right path through a truthful tongue. You should know that Allah fully knows His creation. Not that He was not aware of what they concealed from among their hidden secrets and inner feelings, but in order to try them as to who from among them performs good acts, so that there is reward in respect of good acts and chastisement in respect of evil acts.[23]

An Overview of Qur'anic Exegesis (*tafsīr*)

For more than fourteen hundred years, the teaching of the Qur'an and its meanings has occupied the minds of the ordinary as well as the intellectuals within the Muslim community. This has led to the development of the science of *tafsīr*, or the systematic scholarship of Qur'anic commentary. As Ayoub notes, "The science of *tafsīr* is primarily concerned with the interpretation and elucidation of the text of the Qur'an as a given entity."[24]

A historical review of the Qur'anic commentaries reveals diverse types of exegesis which have been composed throughout the years. While the early *tafsīr* began mostly as *hadīth* transmissions, gradually commentators started to compile Qur'anic commentaries through the lens of their sectarian views, school of thought, their particular approach and personal interest. For the purpose of this study, six *tafsīr* works have been selected to best represent the chronological order, classical and modern periods, as well as sectarian views of both Sunn and Shi'ite commentators.

Sunnite Commentaries (tafsīr)

The first selected *tafsīr* amongst the Sunni commentaries is *Jāmi' al-bayān 'an Ta'wīl ayy al-Qur'ān,* by Muhammad ibn Jarir al-Tabari (d. 310/923). *Jami'al-Bayan* is the first major work in the development of Qur'anic exegesis, known for its comprehensiveness and clarity, and it is widely used by other commentators after him.[25] As Mcauliffe observes, while Tabari's commentary is heavily based on *hadīth,* it nevertheless contains his own analysis and critical view of the different *hadīth* incorporated in his work.[26] The following is Tabari's description of his own work:

> We shall relate in it arguments wherein agreement was achieved and where disagreement persisted. We shall present the reasons for every school of thought or opinion and elucidate what we consider to be the right view with utmost brevity.[27]

The second selected commentary of the Sunni exegetical work is *al-Kashshaf 'an Haga'I al-Tanzil wa 'Uyun al-Agawil fi Wujuh al-Ta'wil* by Abu al-Qasim Jar Allah Mahmud ibn 'Umar al-Zamakhshari (d. 538/1144). *Al-Kashshaf* is highly valued as an important tafsir work which offers indispensable linguistic explanations for the Qur'anic verses. As a great scholar both in religious and linguistic sciences, Zamakhshari is regarded as the great authority on the Arabic language who has contributed to the study of the Qur'an through his *tafsir.*

While Zamakhshari is known for his Mu'tazilite ideas, his theological thoughts are presented so delicately that "a number of commentaries have been written to determine where and how his theological bias has influenced his work."[28] Zamakhshari completed this major work only in two years while he was living in Mecca, for which he was given the nickname of *Jar Allah* (God's neighbor).

> In his introduction to the tafsir he notes that he had expected to spend more than thirty years on the task. The swiftness of its consummation he credits to the miraculous power of the Ka'bah [shrine/house of God] and the blessed influence (*barakah*) that emanates from it.[29]

In a poem ascribed to Zamakhshari, he reveals how proud he was of his work: "Truly *tafsirs* in the world are uncounted, but surely none among them is like my *Kashshāf;* if you would seek guidance then constantly read it; for, ignorance is like disease and the *Kashshāf* like the cure."[30]

The third selected Sunnite Qur'anic exegesis is *Tafhim al-Qur'an* by Sayyid Abul A'la Mawdūdi (d. 1979), which is representative of the *tafsir* literature in the modern period.

As the founder of the Islamic movement of the *Jamā'at-i-Islāmi* in India, Mawdūdi's commentary is heavily grounded on his revivalist and revolutionary ideas.[31] Although his *tafsīr* is primarily written for an educated audience, Mawdūdi "skillfully provides simple and clear explanations on the complex topics which are also of assistance to the general reader."[32] While the literary aspects of the Qur'an are illustrated in *Tafhim*, the main goal of Mawdūdi, however, is to emphasise the ideological message of the Qur'an. In his own words: "The key that can open every locked door is called a master-key. So to me, the Qur'an constitutes the master-key which resolves every problem of human life."[33]

Shi'ite Commentaries (tafsīr)

This group of Qur'anic exegeses includes the commentaries composed by Shi'ite interpreters, whereby the views of the Imams, i.e., descendants of the Prophet Muhammad are highlighted.[34] According to Ayoub, "The sacred text of the Qur'an, or what is contained between the two covers, is what Muhammad taught the generality of the faithful. Its exegesis, however, he reserved for the Imams, the elect of his household (*ahl al-bayt*)."[35]

The first selected *tafsīr* of this genre is *Rawḥ al-Jinān wa-rūḥ al-Janān* by Abū al-Futūḥ Rāzi (d. 525/1131). I have selected this commentary as it is one of "the earliest Shi'ite commentaries composed in Persian, and is ranked as one of the most comprehensive and useful *tafsīr* work."[36] Although not much is known about Rāzi, he is positioned among the leading literary figures of his era and holds a special position in Shi'ite intellectual history.[37] "He brings out particularities of morphology, syntax, and stylistic matters; issues concerning the occasion of revelation and differences about the reading of words, and also *hadīth* applicable to the subject."[38]

The second Shi'ite commentary is *Minhāj al-sādigin fi ilzām al-mukhālifīn* composed by Mullā Fath Allāh Kāshānī (d. 988/1580). While Kāshānī composed three exegetical works on the Qur'an, two in Persian and one in Arabic, the most significant is *Minhaj al-sādigin*. As McAuliffe notes, "This is among the most comprehensive and renowned of Persian *tafsīrs*, dealing at length with points of Qur'anic lexicography and grammar."[39] Kāshānī comments on the literary aspects of the verses, as well as occasions of revelation which, for the most part, are in the form of *hadīth*. Although theological discussions are included in *Minhaj al-sādigin*, however, Kāshānī's writing style offers coherent and understandable explanations for the general audience as well.[40]

The third of the Shi'ite commentaries selected for this study is *al-Mīzān fi tafsīr al-Qur'an* by Allāmeh Sayyid Muhammad Husayn Tabātabā'i (d. 1982). This commentary represents the modern period of Qur'anic exegetical works, and "reflects the wide and profound learning of one of the most respected recent religious scholars of the Shi'ite community."[41] Composing for the intellectuals of the Shi'ite community, Tabātabā'i approaches the Qur'an from a rational and philosophical viewpoint, while dedicating a section to the prophetic traditions from Sunni and Shiite sources. As Nasr observes:

This monumental commentary is written based on the principle of having one part of the Qur'an interpret other parts (*al-Qur'an yufassiru ba'dahu ba'dan*), is a *summa* of Islamic religious thought, in which the sciences of the Qur'an, theology, philosophy, gnosis, sacred history and the social teachings of Islam are all brought together.[42]

Trial from an Exegetical Perspective

As discussed in the previous chapter, the Qur'anic view of the notion of *balā* is illustrated through fifty narratives, which, depending on their theme and the contextual framework, may be grouped in four distinct categories, namely: *balā* as the central pillar of the creational structure of the cosmos; manifestation of *balā*; objects of *balā*; and *balā* visited on prophets and their communities. While each narrative plays an important role in painting this overall portrait, clearly, given their number, an examination of all of the narratives is beyond the scope of this chapter. Therefore, the exegetical section of the study will concentrate on twelve selected verses, three narratives from each of the four categories. The decisive criterion was to select verses which best represent their group in a broader scope, and offer a more in-depth understanding of the concept of *balā* in the Qur'an.

In this section selected Qur'anic exegetical works will be examined and their perspectives on the notion of *balā* will be discussed. A total of twelve Qur'anic narratives, three narratives from each of the four categories of *balā* classified in Chapter One, will be the focus of this part of the study.

From the first category in which the concept of *balā* is introduced as the central pillar of the creational structure of the cosmos, the following narratives will be studied: 11:7, 67:2, and 18:7. The second category, in which the manifestation of *balā* is revealed, the discussion will focus on 89:15, 89:16, and 39:49 (*fitna*). The third category on the objects of *balā* will include 2:155, 8:17, and 64:15 (*fitna*). Finally, from the fourth category, representing *balā* visited on prophets and their communities, the study will include 37:106, 2:49, and 25:20 (*fitna*).

In an effort to shed light on the sectarian viewpoints of the Qur'anic commentaries, if any, as well as drawing attention to their individual contributions, the opinions of our Sunni scholars appear first, followed by the commentaries of the Shi'ite exegesis.

Verses on Divine Trial as a Fundamental Pillar of the Creational Structure of the Cosmos

The significance of notion of *balā* and its central function within the creation of the cosmos will be studied through the following three narratives:

> *It is He who created the heavens and the earth in six days – and His throne was on water – so as to test you, which of you does best...*" (Q. 11:7); "*We have adorned the earth with attractive things so that We may test people to find out which of them do*

best" (Q. 18:7); and, *He who created death and life to test you and reveal which of you does best...* (Q. 67:2).

Tabari's discussion on 11:7 is centered on the first section of the verse — the creation of the universe in six days — therefore, he writes very little on the part of the verse in which *balā* is referred to as the ultimate reason for the creation of the cosmos. To this end, Tabari writes: "God created the heavens and the earth to test people on the level of their obedience towards God's commands, i.e., to assess who performs the religious duties in the best way."[43] Tabari goes further to quote a tradition from the Prophet Muhammad: "To test you is to see which one of you performs the best deeds, stays away from the prohibited acts, and is the one who constantly remains in the path of God."[44]

With reference to 18:7, Tabari follows the same pattern in that he provides a brief description of the narrative first, and further supports his points with *hadith* reports. His commentary of this narrative is summarized below.[45]

According to Tabari, God is telling us that He has made all that is on this earth attractive so that He may test the people to find out which one of them attaches less to these adornments, and concentrates more on obeying His commands. It can be observed from Tabari's comment that his interpretation of *balā* points to the level of attachment and dependency on the material aspects of life. He further goes on to quote a tradition from Prophet Muhammad: "Life is full of sweet and green things, and God has left you in full control of all its beauty; He observes how each of you acts". He continues with citing another *hadīth*: "To test you means to see if you avoid committing sins". Tabari's concluding remarks reference the third tradition: "This is a test for the people to see which ones are more obedient and strive to stay in God's path".

Tabari's interpretation of 67:2 emphasizes the meaning of the creation of death rather than the concept of *balā*. However, he does provide us with a brief explanation of *balā*: "To test you means to find out which one of you is more obedient to Allah and strives to act in accordance with what pleases Allah."[46]

Zamakhshari's commentary on 11:7 begins by an explanation of the part of the verse which refers to the creation of water and God's throne. According to Zamakhshari, before the creation of the heavens and the earth, the only created entity was water; hence, water and God's throne were created prior to anything else. He goes on to say:

> To test you is in conjunction with the act of "creation". This means that His creation is based on His wisdom, He brought all sorts of blessings to the human beings, and He commanded them to perform certain duties and stay away from sins. He will then reward whoever expresses his gratitude and obeys Him, and punish whoever ignores the blessings and disobeys Him. Therefore, since this is similar to what a test giver does, the purpose is to find out, or to know how you act.[47]

He continues his discussion by asking a hypothetical question:

> And if you ask me how come it says "which one of you does best", when we
> know that deeds of the believers are classified into good and great, but when
> compared to the deeds of the un-believers, the deeds are divided into good and
> bad; in which case it is not possible to say which one is better. I will tell you that
> the best deeds belong to the believers; hence, the verse only refers to the acts of
> the believers and does not include the others.[48]

Zamakhshari ends his explanation by pointing out a _hadīth_ from the Prophet: "To test you
means to find out which one of you has the best wisdom, does not go near prohibited acts,
and is eager in obeying God."[49]

Commenting on 18:7, Zamakhshari offers a short explanation: "all that is on this earth
can potentially be of interest and a means of attraction for the human race."[50] He further
observes that "to excel in conduct means detaching oneself from the attractions of this life
and not being misled by it; then refraining from getting close to it."[51]

Zamakhshari reflects on 67:2 by first providing a brief note on the concept of _balā_,
and quickly focusing his attention on the meaning of "good deed". To this end he writes:
"Allah puts people to the test to examine them in their deeds. A good deed is a deed that is
appropriate and if it is done purely for the sake of Allah."[52]

Our third Sunni commentator, Mawdūdi, offers a more in-depth interpretation on
the _balā_ aspect of 11:7, and sheds light on man's responsibilities. He argues that the purpose
of the Creation is to set the stage for man to exercise his vicegerency potential on earth.
He further observes that while man is free to utilize such a power in any direction, he will,
however, face the consequences of his actions.

> This enunciates the purpose of the Creation: Allah created the heavens and the
> earth for the sake of the creation of mankind and He created mankind to rest
> human beings by delegating to them the powers of vicegerency and making them
> morally responsible for using or abusing them, just as they liked. Thus it has been
> emphasized that the sole purpose of the Creation is the moral trial of man and
> his consequent accountability to the Creator for the use or abuse of the delegated
> powers, and the award of rewards and punishments. For without this basic purpose,
> the whole work of Creation would have become meaningless and useless.[53]

Mawdūdi's reflection on 18:7 emphasizes the fact that man's entire life is a trial, which
further grounds the previously made point from the above commentary.

> Things that you see in the world and which allure you, are a transitory adornment
> which has been arranged merely to test you, but it is a pity that you have been

involved in the misunderstanding that all these things have been created to cater for your pleasure and enjoyment. You must understand it well that these things have not been provided for pleasure but are actually a means of testing you. You have been placed among them to see which of you is allured by these from the real aim of life and which of you keeps steadfast in the worship of Allah, for which you have been sent to the world. All these things and means of pleasure shall come to an end on the Day your examination is over and nothing will remain on the earth because it will be turned into a bare plain.[54]

With reference to the final narrative of this category, 67:2, Mawdūdi makes an effort to define the characteristics of good deeds.

That man has been given the power to do both good and evil, is not purposeless; the Creator has created him in the world for the test: life is for him the period of the test and death means that the time allotted for the test has come to an end; that for the sake of this very test the Creator has given every man an opportunity for action, so that he may do good or evil in the world and practically show what kind of a man he is; that the Creator alone will decide who has done good or evil; it is not for us to propose a criterion for the good and the evil deeds but for Almighty Allah; therefore, whoever desires to get through the test, will have to find out what is the criterion of a good deed in His sight; the fifth point is contained in the meaning of the test itself, that is, every person will be recompensed according to his deeds, for if there was no reward or punishment the test would be meaningless.[55]

We will now turn to the Shi'ite exegeses and shed light on their opinion regarding the above-mentioned three narratives.

Rāzi's explication on 11:7 is heavily centered on the creation of the cosmos in six days, and his rationalization for why water was created before anything else. His brief note on the *balā* aspect of the narrative is as follows: "To put you to the test means to test you with your deeds and know who from you has the best conduct."[56] He goes further to say: "the means of this test is whether or not people will perform what has been mandatory for them, i.e., the duties (*taklif*)."[57] Furthermore, Razi quotes a tradition from Prophet Muhammad in this matter: "the person with the best deed is whoever is more cautious to obey Allah and refrain from committing sins; or more steadfast, or with stronger will to detach from worldly matters."[58]

Rāzi provides a similar clarification on 18:7 and the aspect of *balā*. To this end he writes: "the test is on performing the mandatory obligations."[59]

Reviewing Rāzi's explanatory notes on 67:2 reveals no more than what he has written on the previous two narratives. On this verse, he notes: "the best deed is to perform the obligatory duties."[60] Furthermore, he quotes another tradition from Prophet Muhammad who said: "The wisest from you is the one who is afraid of Allah, performs the mandated prayers, and does his best not to engage in the prohibited acts."[61]

Kāshāni's commentary on 11:7 begins by a discussion regarding the significance of the creation of the universe in six days. The following is a summary of his viewpoints.[62] According to Kāshāni, Allah was certainly able to bring the cosmos into existence in a moment of time; however, He made the universe in six days, to illustrate gradual process in completing a task. This process educates man to take great care in planning his actions and refrain from rushing through a task, which may result in compromising quality. He continues by expounding upon the *balā* aspect of the narrative and points out that the creation of the cosmos was completed so that man can be put to the test in an environment which allows him to grow and actualize his full potential. Kāshāni concludes by illustrating that people with the best conduct are the ones who, through knowledge and wisdom, increase their faith in Allah, worship Him only, and strive to do good deeds.

With reference to 67:2, Kāshāni provides his readers with an in-depth discussion about the creation of death and life as it is revealed in this narrative. He then continues with an elucidation on the notion of *balā* which is summarized below.[63] As Kāshāni observes, while man must make every effort to do good deeds during his life on this earth, nevertheless, the level of his sincerity (*ikhlās*) in performing the deeds is of high importance. Moreover, he quotes a tradition from the Prophet who said: "The best of you in conduct is the one who acts according to his intellect and ponders upon the effect of his deeds in this world and the hereafter."

Kāshāni's brief commentary on 18:7 is as follows. He starts off by reminding the reader that the Meccans' persistence in opposing the prophetic message had caused Prophet Muhammad much distress and concern. Through this narrative, Allah eradicates the Prophet's concerns and points out that We have created and beautified everything on this earth, i.e., all that man strives for, to provide an appropriate environment so that man may be put to the test. He then elucidates "to find out which of them do best", to mean "which one is most grateful who utilizes Allah's blessings in His path"? Kāshāni further observes that one of the adornments on this earth is the existence of prophets and imams; to have respect for them and follow in their footsteps will position man amongst those who have performed good deeds.[64]

Tabātabā'i, our contemporary commentator from the Shi'ite school of thought, offers an in-depth explanation of 11:7 and sheds light on aspects of the narrative not discussed by the other scholars. What follows is a summary of his discussion. According to Tabātabā'i, the universe is created in the most systematic and organized fashion for the purpose of *balā* or Divine Trial. The Creator, therefore, with His outmost creativity and wisdom, has provided the best environment whereby human beings are put to the test through their conduct. Starting with a linguistic explanation for the word *leyablowakum* (to put you to the test), Tabātabā'i builds his discussion by emphasizing the first letter (L/ *lām*), which conveys the meaning of "consequence or outcome". He goes on to explain that *balā* becomes the means by which pious people are distinguished from the non-pious, providing the context for reward or punishment. Tabātabā'i's commentary adds a whole new dimension to the meaning of this verse by illuminating the fact that not only is *balā* part of the creation, but more importantly, it is considered as the objective of creation. Being the highest ranked creature of the cosmos, man's guidance and salvation must, therefore, be of high importance within the creational structure of the universe. To further ground his argument, Tabātabā'i refers to 18:7, which is the second narrative in this cluster and will be discussed next. He references this verse as supplementary material by pointing out that all things on this earth act as agents for Divine trial and ways by which people's level of devotion to virtuous life can be measured.[65]

Tabātabā'i's elucidation of the link between *balā* and the creational structure of the cosmos is extended in his commentary on 18:7. The summarized version of his interpretation is as follows. According to Tabātabā'i, this narrative reveals a profound truth about the nature of human life on this earth. The essence of man's true nature (*fitra*) is created at such an elevated level that he is not interested in attaching his heart to worldly matters, i.e., his *fitra* guides him to search for more meaningful and spiritual levels of being. However, God in his wisdom has willed for man to reach his full potential by exercising his free will, and through conscious choice, find belief and perform good deeds during his lifetime. Therefore, the beautification of all that is on this earth is for the sole purpose of putting man to the test. In this fashion, the self-centered ego of man continually feels attracted to worldly manners, and as he goes through the journey of life he will find himself interested in pleasures of life and seek comfort in them. However, the test is for man to perform good deeds, and not lose sight of the fact that realization of his potential can only take place by making the right choices and not falling for the adornments of life.[66]

Tabātabā'i's commentary on the final narrative of this cluster, namely 67:2, expands on his ideas about the connection of *balā* and the notion of death. While he starts off with a brief explanation of the meaning of death – transfer from one state to another – his focus remains on the notion of *balā*. According to Tabātabā'i, man will go through the stages of life and death in order to be tested; the main purpose is to distinguish the virtuous from the non-virtuous. The final stage of this process will be the reward which man receives as the result of his conduct.[67]

Verses on Manifestation of Divine Trial in Man's Life

In this section we will review the exegetical sources and discuss the commentators' viewpoints with regard to the manifestation of *balā*. The selected narratives which represent the Qur'anic approach on means through which *balā* is realized in man's life are:

The nature of man is that, when his Lord tries him through honours and blessings, he says, "My Lord has honoured me", but when He tries him through the restriction of his provision, he says, "My Lord has humiliated me" (Q. 89:15-16).

> *When man suffers some affliction, he cries out to Us, but when We favour him with*
> *Our blessings, he says, "All this has been given to me because of my knowledge" – it is*
> *only a test, though most of them do not know it* (Q. 39:49).

Tabari's brief note on 89:15-16 can be considered more of an extended translation than a commentary. His explanation emphasizes how man reacts in these two situations, namely, time of wealth and when his provision is restricted. To this end he writes: "when man is privileged through God's grace, he feels honored, and when his provision is restricted, he feels humiliated; he is not grateful for his health and livelihood."[68]

Similarly, with reference to 39:49, Tabari's exegesis underscores man's responses in dealing with various circumstances.

> Man turns to God during calamity and hardship but when he receives God's
> mercy, and his hardship or sickness is replaced by goodness and health, he says,
> "the reason I have been given the blessings is because God is happy with me and
> that He knows I deserve His mercy due to my knowledge".[69]

Tabari then quotes a tradition in support of his comment and continues with his elucidation on the last part of the narrative. To this end he writes: "but God's mercy after hardship is, in fact, a trial so that they can be tested, however, most people don't realize this due to their lack of knowledge and ignorance."[70]

Zamakhshari offers a more in-depth explanation on 89:15-16. Below is the summary of his comments.

> And if they ask: how can abundance and inadequacy of wealth, both be means of
> *balā*? We will answer: because in both of these situations man will be put to the
> test; whenever God opens the doors of abundance and gives man much wealth,
> He is testing him and reveals him either as being grateful or as an ungrateful
> man. And if He restricts man's provision, again He is putting him to the test
> to show if he is patient, or if he will complain about his situation. Anyway, the
> underlying wisdom (*hikmat*) in both conditions is the same.[71]

As for his commentary on 39:49, Zamakhshari provides more details on the linguistics of several terms in this narrative, but offers very little on its *balā* aspect. According to Zamakhshari, God is telling man that the reason he was given the blessings and mercy was not for the reasons he has in mind, but rather as a test to find out whether or not he will be grateful.[72]

Mawdūdi's commentary of 89:15-16 begins with an explanation regarding man's perception of life on this earth. Furthermore, he sheds light on the contributing factors which mislead man to certain responses in various conditions of his life.

Man regards wealth, position, and power of this world alone as everything. When he has it, he is filled with pride and says God has honored me; and when he fails to obtain it, he says: God has humiliated me. Thus, the criterion of honor and humiliation in his sight is the possession of wealth and position and power, or the absence of it, whereas the actual truth which he does not understand is that whatever Allah has given anybody in the world has been given for the sake of a trial. If he has given him wealth and power, it has been given for a trial to see whether he becomes grateful for it, or commits ingratitude. If He has made him poor, in this too there is a trial for him to see whether he remains content and patient in the will of God and faces his hardships bravely within permissible bounds, or becomes ready to transgress every limit of morality and honesty and starts cursing his God.[73]

Mawdūdī follows a similar path in his analysis of 39:49, where he elaborates on why human beings reach out to God in time of distress, but remain ignorant of Him when there are blessings and peace in their lives. According to Mawdūdī, what contributes to man's failure in recognizing the Divine plan during both circumstances is his ignorance and wrong sense of pride.

People ignorantly think that whoever is being blessed by Allah in some way is being so blessed necessarily on account of his worth and ability and that the same is a sign or proof of his being a favorite in His sight; whereas the fact is that whoever is being given something here, is being given it for the sake of a trial by Allah. This is a means of the test, and not any reward for ability, otherwise many able and worthy people would not be living in poverty and many unworthy people would not be rolling in prosperity. Likewise, these worldly blessings arc not a sign of one's being a favorite with Allah either. Everyone can see that many good people whose goodness is unquestionable arc living in hardship in the world, and many wicked people whose evil-doing is well known are enjoying the pleasures of life, Now, can a sensible man take the affliction of the one and the life of ease and comfort of the other as an argument to say that Allah hates the good man and prefers the bad man?[74]

While the exegesis of our first Shi'ite commentator, Rāzi, provides a brief explanatory note on 89:15-16, nevertheless he sheds light on an important aspect of the narratives not commented on by the first group of exegeses. According to Rāzi, man mistakenly makes an assumption that Allah has an obligation to grant him health and wealth, therefore, does not realize that he is put to the test.

And when Allah bestows a favor on man by way of granting him health or wealth, he takes it for granted and believes it to be his right to receive the blessings. In other words, he thinks it is Allah's responsibility to provide him with the favor, hence, it is a mandatory act on the part of Allah. But when he is tested by way of restriction on his provision, he complains, and interprets the situation as Allah's way of humiliating him. Therefore, through these verses, Allah is describing man's ingratitude during prosperity and lack of patience during hardship.[75]

Rāzi's observation of 39:49 emphasizes a similar aspect as he points out that man's self-centered character limits his ability to recognize the root of hardships and blessings in life.

Allah shows the true nature of man in this verse; he calls on us in time of distress and hardship, but when we grant him prosperity he attributes it to his own abilities or efforts, and claims "they have given me this favour because they knew I am worthy of receiving it due to my knowledge." Man does not realize that the favour is in fact a test.[76]

Kāshāni's commentary on 89:15-16 begins with an explanation regarding man's perception of life on this earth.[77] According to Kāshāni, man's inability to recognize his life's mission is indeed the fundamental reason for not recognizing the source and value of Divine trials. The purpose of man's creation is for him to make the best use of his limited time, serve in the cause of Allah, and prepare himself for the next life. However, man engages in worldly activities, invests his precious time in following unlimited materialistic ambitions, and forgets his responsibilities towards Allah. Kāshāni further observes that man mistakenly views financial means and social status as signs of a favored life; therefore, he complains as soon as Allah tests him by limiting his provisions. Kāshāni concludes by reminding his readers of a Qur'anic narrative whereby the only criterion for attaining an elevated status is to live in accordance to Allah's path: *"In God's eyes, the most honoured of you are the ones most mindful of Him"* (Q. 49:13).

In reference to 39:49, Kāshāni begins by shedding light on man's response when he is faced with various circumstances of his life, namely, distress and prosperity. What follows is the synopsis of his commentary. According to Kāshāni, while unbelievers did not express any sign of happiness when Allah's name was mentioned to them, they responded favorably and joyfully when engaged in conversations about their gods and goddesses. However, during a time of affliction they prayed to Allah in the hope of obtaining relief from the hardship; once adversity was replaced with goodness and health, they attributed the blessings received to themselves, i.e., their knowledge or being worthy of the blessings. Kāshāni concludes by highlighting that the bestowed blessing was in fact a test; hence, man must recognize Allah as the source of blessing, offer his utmost gratitude to Him, and plan his actions to best serve His cause.[78]

We will now turn to Tabātabā'i to find out what this contemporary commentator of the Shi'ite school of thought has to offer. What follows is the summary of his viewpoints on 89:15-16.

According to Tabātabā'i, this narrative acts as the concluding remarks of the previous verses and expounds upon man's response in two different conditions, namely, prosperity and adversity. While Allah puts man through a test in both of the above circumstances, man, on the other hand, is totally ignorant of this plan. Consequently, at the time of prosperity, he is proud of the fact that he has been selected to receive wealth, feels worthy to have been granted the blessings, hence, can spend it according to his desires with no limit or consideration. However, if the divine plan is to test him by restricting his livelihood, he feels Allah is against him and has humiliated him, hence, starts to complain and express his anguish. He further observes that the test is to place man in a situation where he expresses gratitude in prosperity and spend his wealth in the path of Allah. However, ignorant of this reality, man's wrong attitude towards Allah's blessing transforms that which was intended for man's spiritual growth and the key to his salvation into a cause of pain and sorrow in the life to come. Moreover, Tabātabā'i asserts that as the result of man's failure in realizing the Divine plan, he wrongly attributes an elevated status to himself in comparison to others, and assumes his prosperous condition is guaranteed and will last forever; therefore, he is entitled to act as he desires.[79]

Tabātabā'i concludes by drawing attention to three points. First, the significance of repeating the word *ibtilā* in both verses confirms that *balā* may in fact be manifested in both prosperity and adversity. Second, that granting man wealth is considered an honor and mercy from Allah, is due to the fact that this well-off condition is the key to man's salvation; and will remain a blessing only if man makes use of it in Allah's path and according to His guidelines. Thirdly, these two narratives maintain that man incorrectly assumes that possession of wealth and power is a sign of being honored by Allah, and lack of it is an indication of not being favoured by Allah; however, only good deeds are the criterion of being close and dear to Allah.

With reference to 39:49, Tabātabā'i's elucidation starts off by a general statement which shows the link between this and the previous narratives, and then provides a brief note on the *balā* aspect of the verse. According to Tabātabā'i, the fact that this narrative begins with the letter f/*fā* (denoting consequence), implies the connection to the previous verses – evildoers' lack of belief about the Hereafter – which results in their hearts shrivelling with aversion when they hear the name of Allah, but full of joy when other gods are mentioned. However, this turning away from Allah is not only the acts of the evildoers of the era of the Prophet, but it can be applied to any man whose heart pursues worldly causes and the pleasures of life.[80]

Tabātabā'i continues with his discussion and explains how this same person turns to Allah in time of distress and asks for the relief of hardship or adversity. However, due to lack of true belief in Allah, he is totally ignorant of Allah when a mercy from Him is bestowed. His failure to recognize that the true and only source of all goodness is Allah misleads man to trust that his own doing or knowledge is the source of this favor. Tabātabā'i concludes his commentary on the narrative by emphasizing the *balā* aspect of the verse, and illustrates that the bestowed favor is in fact a test from Allah; however, man does not realize it.[81]

Verses on Objects of Divine Trial

We will now turn to our third category and discuss the viewpoints of the exegetical works on the following selected narratives, in which tangible objects of *balā* are discussed:

> *We shall certainly test you with fear and hunger, and loss of property, lives, and crops; but, [Prophet], give good news to those who are steadfast* (Q. 2:155).
>
> *It was not you who killed them but God, and when you [Prophet] threw [sand at them] it was not your throw [that defeated them] but God's, to do the believers a favor God is all seeing and all knowing* (Q. 8:17).
>
> *Your wealth and your children are only a test for you. There is great reward with God* (Q. 64:15).

Tabari offers an in-depth elucidation of 2:155 by first offering a general discussion regarding *balā*, followed by his thoughts on the specified means of *balā*. What follows is a summary of his discussions.

He starts off by pointing out that the narrative contains a message from Allah particularly for the early Muslim community and the followers of Prophet Muhammad. The significance of *balā* in this verse, according to Tabari, is the fact that the true and dedicated followers of the Prophet needed to be distinguished from the rest of the population; therefore, the objects of *balā* are clearly defined in the narrative. Tabari points out that there were other occasions, such as when the direction of prayer (*qiblah*) was changed from Jerusalem to Mecca, whereby the followers of the Prophet were put to the test. He then offers a brief explanation about other nations and communities who were tested by Allah, and references the following narrative as an example: *"Do you suppose that you will enter the Garden without first having suffered like those who passed away before you? They were afflicted by misfortune and hardship"* (Q. 2:214). Tabari continues by narrating a tradition from Ibn Abbās who said: "Allah has informed the believers that this world is the place of *balā* as it was for His prophets, so that they can be purified; they should exercise patience."[82]

On the second section of his commentary on this narrative, Tabari starts explaining the meanings of tangible items of *balā* as set forth in the verse. According to Tabari, *khawf* implies fear from the enemy, and *jū`* means lack of food or hunger. Therefore, as Tabari observes, this verse is a forewarning to Prophet's followers in order to prepare them for a range of hardships that will afflict them by way of tests; hence, they should endure the difficult times with serenity. Tabari, once again, emphasizes that through these tests, sincere believers will be distinguished from the hypocrites and the sick-hearted.

In examining Tabari's commentary on 8:17, it becomes evident that, for him, the focal point of this narrative is the direct action of Allah, and not the actions of the Muslims, which resulted in a victory. A summary of his thoughts is as follows.

According to Tabari, this verse discloses a vital message to Prophet Muhammad and his followers by highlighting the events of the battle of Badr. Firstly, it reveals that Allah is He who destroyed the enemy and brought the victory. Secondly, throwing dirt into the eyes of the enemy as a symbolic act of humiliation performed by the Prophet is attributed to Allah. Tabari further argues that this narrative clearly rejects the claims of those who mistakenly believe their actions are independent of Allah. He also points out that *bala* in this verse may imply favour due to the fact that the word *hasanan* has been added to it; meaning Allah did a great favour to the Muslims.[83]

With reference to 64:15, Tabari's exegesis offers very little, making his note an extended translation rather than a commentary. To this end he writes: Allah is informing people that their wealth and children are means by which they will be tested; hence, if they disagree with what their families are asking them to do in favour of Allah's guidelines, they will be rewarded.[84]

Zamakhshari's commentary provides a brief note on 2:155; however, it sheds light on some of the details of the narrative which entails a broader scope. The following is the synopsis of his explanation.

Zamakhshari begins his explanation by pointing out that while this verse discloses some of the means by which man will be put to the test, the reason for the test is, however, to reveal man's true character, i.e., whether or not man is sincere in his faith and acts according to Allah's commands. He then sheds light on the significance of the word *bi-shay 'in* (little of something) and explains that to test someone with a little of something means that there could always be other tests of a greater magnitude; hence, man should always see the bigger picture and endure with patience. To support his argument, Zamakhshari mentions a tradition from Prophet Muhammad who upon losing light in his house said "we are from Allah and to Him we shall return." Surprised at the Prophet's response, somebody present asked "Was this a calamity?" To which he responded, "Anything that is bothersome to a believer is in fact a calamity." The Prophet then explains that the word *bi-shay 'in* means that in dealing with *bala*, we should know that there are always bigger *bala* and that Allah's mercy is always with us. Zamakhshari concludes by giving examples of various items of *bala*, and emphasizes that Allah's blessings is with those who are patient during *bala*.[85]

As for 8:17, Zamakhshari starts off by presenting some historical background about the previous battles between the *Quraysh* of Mecca and the Muslim community of Medina. As can be seen from the summary of his commentary provided below, Zamakhshari does not offer much on the *bala* aspect of this verse. According to Zamakhshari, in preparation to fight the enemy in the battle of *Badr*, Prophet Muhammad and his followers prayed to Allah for His assistance and support, and called on Him to grant them victory. Prior to starting the battle, as commanded by the Angel Gabriel, Prophet Muhammad threw a handful of sand at the opponent that struck the eyes of the enemy, and forced them to concentrate on getting the sand out of their faces and eyes. As the battle started, the Muslims were able to destroy the enemy and gain a remarkable victory.[86]

As Zamakhshari observes, Allah is informing the Muslims that they should not act arrogantly after achieving this victory, for it was Allah who sent the angels, bred fear in the enemy's hearts, and granted confidence in you to destroy the enemy. Zamakhshari further explains that the attribution of sand throwing to Allah is due to the fact that this action had a decisive impact on the enemy, whereas the Prophet's throwing sand without Allah's force would not be nearly as effective. Zamakhshari concludes his commentary by briefly mentioning that granting this extraordinary victory was a beautiful *bala* for the Muslims, in fact a blessing from Allah as He answered their prayers.[87]

Zamakhshari's view point on 64:15 outlined below is brief as he offers a general statement on children and wealth as items of *bala*. In his opinion this narrative is revealed during the time when many Muslim men were required to leave their families in order to support the cause of Allah. He mentions the case of Malik Ashja'i, whose wives and children used to beg him not to leave them to attend the battles, hence putting him under much emotional pressure. Zamakhshari further observes that this verse is warning the Muslims that their children may in fact be a *fitna* through which their fidelity and devotion to Allah will be tested. Zamakhshari ends his commentary by including a general statement from other exegetical works, without identifying the work, who said: "Love of wealth and children should not keep you from attending to your duty, i.e., obligation to fight in battles, or migrate to a new land."[88]

Mawdūdi does not offer any explanation on 2:155 and 8:17 in the form of commentary, but is content just to provide a translation of the narratives.

However, as far as 67:15 is concerned, Mawdūdi offers a short explanation and highlights the relationship of man's love for children in contrast to his love of Allah.

> Here one should also keep in view the Holy Prophet's saying which Tabarani has related on the authority of Hadrat Abu Malik al-Ash'ari, saying: "Your real enemy is not he whom if you kill there is success for you, and if he kills you, there is Paradise for you; but your real enemy may be your own child who is born of your own loins, or the wealth of which you are the owner." That is why here as well as in Al-Anfal: 28, Allah says: If you save yourselves from the temptation and allurements of worldly possessions and children, and succeed in keeping love of them subject to the love of Allah, there are rich rewards for you with Allah.[89]

The exegetical works of the Shiite school of thought will be examined next and their viewpoints regarding the three narratives of this category will be highlighted.

Rāzi's explanation on 2:155 begins by a quotation from Abdūllāh Abbās, one of the greatest scholars of the first Muslim generation[90] who said: "Allah has informed us that this world is the landscape for tests and trials."[91] He then provides a short note on the meanings of the five means of *bala* mentioned in this verse by cross referencing the viewpoints of other commentaries. To this end he writes: "Fear of the enemy during conflicts, hunger at the time of food shortage, reduction of wealth and financial bankruptcy, loss of life (self or a loved one), and sicknesses are all means by which man will be put to the test."[92]

Rāzi's commentary on 8:17 calls attention to the fact that man's self-admiration is the underlying cause for not recognizing the true source of this extraordinary victory. In Rāzi's opinion, this narrative emphasizes the fact that the attained victory at the battle of Badr was in fact due to Allah's support and mercy, and not the actions of the Muslims. He continues by illustrating the emotional dynamics of the followers of the Prophet who felt proud and overconfident of themselves. This egotistical behavior generated internal conflict whereby they started to argue with one another about their superiority. Rāzi explains that by utilizing the Arabic word *lākin*, Allah takes the attention off the people including the Prophet, and links the success directly to Him. Rāzi concludes by briefly mentioning that this was in fact a trial, to put the believers through a test with a blessing, in this case, the victory.[93]

In reference to 64:15, although Rāzi's comments are brief, nonetheless, he attempts to create a frame around the notion of children and wealth as items of trials. Here is a synopsis of his viewpoints. There are a number of reasons why this narrative points to wealth and children as objects of *balā*, i.e., means by which you will be tested. In case of children, they may prevent you from performing mandatory prayers, or encourage you to perform an act of sin; therefore, they will be your tests. As for wealth, you may obtain money through a prohibited means, or not spend on the path of Allah; both instances provide the stage for you to be tested.[94]

Kāshāni's elucidation on 2:155 starts off with an explanation regarding the rationale of the various trials which man will experience. What follows is a summary of his opinion. According to Kāshāni, this narrative, which is directed to Prophet Muhammad and his followers, informs us that although everyone's true character is well known to Allah, these trials are the only medium whereby man's disposition is revealed to him and to others. As a result of these tests, those who submit to the will of God and endure the hardship will in fact be known. Moreover, the true character of the intolerant people who are of a complaining nature will be revealed as well. He concludes by offering an explanation of the various means of *balā* as the other commentators have done.[95]

With reference to 8:17, Kāshāni begins by informing the reader of the battle of Badr and the superiority of the enemy's armed forces as compared to the Muslims. What follows is the summary of his commentary. According to Kāshāni, at the outset of the battle of Badr, Prophet Muhammad prayed to Allah, asked Him to fulfill His promise, and assist the Muslims in this battle. Subsequently, the Prophet followed angel Gabriel's commands and threw a handful of dust and at the enemy, striking their eyes. This act had a profound impact on the outcome of the battle, which resulted in an extraordinary victory for the Muslims. Kāshāni further observes that as the followers of the Prophet started to take credit for the victory, the narrative reminded them that all acts in this battle must be ascribed to Allah, i.e. Allah and His will in assisting you with His angels, is the sole reason for the victory. Kāshāni concludes by illustrating that this entire victory was in fact a favorable test for the Muslims as Allah heard the Prophet's plea for help and assisted them.[96]

As it pertains to 64:15, Kāshāni points out that man's true character is exposed by his level of attachment to wealth and children. In accordance with Kāshāni, children and wealth are the biggest and the hardest means by which man will be tested by. As Kāshāni observes, these trials will expose man's true character to show whether or not man's level of devotion to Allah and his love for Him takes precedence over his affection for these worldly adornments. Moreover, striving to achieve more financial prosperity, as well as higher level of attachment and involvement in the lives of the children, may cause man to move away from devoting his time to Allah and His cause. Kāshāni ends by reminding his readers that the more man invests his time and energy in these domains, the more he will forget his responsibilities towards Allah.[97]

Tabātabā'i begins his commentary of 2:155 by illustrating the link between this and the previous verses, whereby the believers were advised to seek out guidance and support by performing prayers and remaining patient.[98] According to Tabātabā'i, the early Muslims had to overcome many difficulties in order to safeguard their newly established community. Therefore, this narrative informs the followers of Prophet Muhammad that whatever difficulty they will face in the way of Allah must be perceived as a test from Him. Furthermore, the means of *bala* or the tangible items by which they will be put to the test are identified in this verse. These are: lack of security, hunger, and financial hardship, in addition to the possibility of their life or the life of their children being sacrificed.

Tabātabā'i starts his elucidation of 8:17 by reminding the reader that this narrative is about the accomplishments of the Muslims during the battle of Badr. The following is the summary of his commentary. As Tabātabā'i observes, the message of this narrative is to draw attention to Muslim's extraordinary victory of Badr, and to make known that this astonishing success was the act of Allah, and not the superiority of the Muslims. Tabātabā'i further explains it would have been impossible for the Muslims to win without Allah's support as they were at a disadvantage, i.e., lacking army equipment and enough warriors. Allah supported the believers because they called on Him; He heard their prayers and was aware of their position, hence, granting them the victory. Tabātabā'i emphasizes that this was, in fact, a mercy and a favor from Allah; putting them through a test by a gracious *bala*.[99]

With reference to 64:15, Tabātabā'i draws attention to an interesting point not mentioned by the other commentaries, namely, ascription of a prominent position to children. According to Tabātabā'i, the word *fitna* in this narrative corresponds to the challenges and obstacles through which man will be put to the test. While there are a variety of worldly affairs that can potentially serve as a means to test, the two most attractive and desirable of them are wealth and children. He further explains that, as a result of an emotional attachment and devotion towards offspring and possessions, man will begin to perceive them as equally important, or more significant, than his responsibility towards Allah. This attitude of attributing an elevated status to children and possessions, in as much as viewing them as the highest priority in his life, will cause man to defer his attention from accountability towards Allah, as well as life after death. Tabātabā'i concludes by emphasizing that this narrative is cautioning man that, since children and wealth are the means of test and trial in this life, he should not allow his affection for them overcome his loyalty towards Allah, i.e., submission to His will and strivings for the next life to come.[100]

Verses on Divine Trial Visited on Prophets and Their Communities

This section reviews the exegetical sources and throws light on the commentators' viewpoints regarding *balā* as it relates to prophets and their communities. To represent this category, we will discuss the following three narratives:

> *When they had both submitted to God, and he had laid his son down on the side of his face, We called out to him, "Abraham, you have fulfilled the dream". This is how We reward those who do good. It was a test to prove [their true characters]* (Q. 37:103-106).
>
> *"Remember when We saved you from Pharaoh's people, who subjected you to terrible torment, slaughtering your sons and sparing only your women – this was a great trial from your Lord"* (Q. 2:49).
>
> *"No messenger have We sent before you [Muhammad] who did not eat food and walk about in the marketplaces. But We have made some of you a means of testing others – will you stand fast? Your Lord is all seeing"* (Q. 25:20).

Our first Sunni commentator, Tabari, does not provide us with much explanation on 37:106, except to say: "This narrative illustrates that Prophet Abraham was put to a tremendous trial when Allah commanded him to sacrifice his son."[101]

With reference to 2:49, Tabari's elucidation is very short.[102] As he observes, while *balā* is mostly in hardship, it nevertheless can be in good and prosperity. This verse signifies the fact that slaughtering the new born baby boys by the people of the pharaoh was a *balā*, but when Allah saved the community the same *balā* was transformed to a blessing from Him.

Tabari's commentary on 25:20 attempts to demonstrate how the ordinary life styles of prophets was indeed a test for the addressee communities. According to Tabari, this narrative illustrates that social rank and financial differences between the people of a community are means by which people are put to the test. This *fitna* will reveal peoples' character, their level of gratefulness or patience, and whether or not they will follow Allah's path and strive to please Him regardless of their social rank and privileged circumstances. Tabari further observes that this is precisely the reason why Prophet Muhammad was not a wealthy person, but in fact, someone who had to work just as hard as any other ordinary member of the society. Therefore, a prophet who is living a simple life with no financial status is now the means by which his community is being tested, i.e.; God's message is conveyed through the messenger who is not an affluent member of the society and therefore does not offer any material attraction.[103]

Zamakhshari's commentary on 37:106 is very brief as he provides us with the following explanation. According to his observation, *balā* in this narrative corresponds to a test that differentiates the true character of people being tested. He further notes that, as the result of the *balā*, the genuineness and sincerity of faith is revealed; indeed both Abraham and his son submitted to the command of Allah, and proved their total devotion through this difficult *balā*.[104]

In his explanation of 2:49, Zamakhshari writes very little on the *balā* aspect of this narrative. In his opinion, if *balā* is related to acts of Pharaoh's people, it is a hardship and a test; however, if it is attributed to the release after the hardship, then it means a blessing.[105]

Zamakhshari provides an in-depth elucidation on 25:20, and argues that this narrative illustrates means by which both the Prophet and his community were put to the test. What follows is the summary of his commentary. In Zamakhshari's opinion, the fact that the monotheistic message of Islam was conveyed by a Prophet who was a regular member of society, someone who was engaged in everyday life activities, with no special powers or ability, is in fact a test. The extent of this test, however, encompasses not only the addressee community of Mecca, but also Prophet Muhammad himself.[106]

According to Zamakhshari, the social status and ordinary life style of the Prophet is a multidimensional test. On the one hand, due to lack of wealth and extraordinary abilities (magical powers), not only does society resist his prophecy and deny the prophetic message, but he is under constant pressure through verbal accusations and humiliation. As he further observes, the Prophet, therefore, is put to the test through these difficult times; he must remain dedicated in conveying the message while exercising patience and endurance in dealing with those who are making every effort to degrade him. On the other hand, the community is put to the test as their reasoning in refusing to accept the revelation is the messenger's ordinary position, lack of wealth and special powers. Therefore, since the Prophet did not offer any financial rewards, nor did he performed any magical acts, those who accepted the prophetic message did so because of its content and value, and to please Allah. Zamakhshari concludes by extending the impact of the test to all people at all times to point out that members of a society are the test for each other; the underprivileged are to exercise endurance, while the wealthy must show compassion and equity towards the deprived, as both conditions are in fact a trial from Allah.[107]

Mawdūdi's commentary on 37:106 calls attention to the fact that the ultimate goal of Abraham's dream in sacrificing his son was to expose the true act of submission.

That is, "We did not make you see in the dream that you had actually slaughtered your son and he had died, but that you were slaughtering him. That Vision you have fulfilled. Now, it is not Our will to take the life of your child: the actual object of the vision has been fulfilled by your submission and preparation to sacrifice him for Our sake.' 'We do not subject the people who adopt the righteous way to trials in order to involve them in trouble and distress and affliction just for the sake of it, but these trials are meant to bring out their excellences and to exalt them to high ranks, and then We deliver them also safe and sound from the dilemma in which We place them for the sake of the trial. Thus, your willingness and preparation to sacrifice your son is enough to entitle you to be exalted to the rank that could be attained only by the one who would actually have slaughtered his son for Our approval and pleasure. Thus, We have saved the life of your child as well as exalted you to this high rank. The object was not to get your son slaughtered through you but to test you to see that you did not hold anything of the world dearer than us."[108]

As for 2:49 and the hardship of the children of Israel, Mawdūdi writes the following: "It was a trial of their character. They were made to pass through the fire of the test to see whether they were pure gold or a base metal. Moreover, they were put to the test to see whether they would be grateful to Allah after their miraculous escape."[109]

In his commentary of 25:20, Mawdūdi begins by reminding his readers that all other prophets before Islam had a lifestyle similar to other members of society, hence, Prophet Muhammad falls within the same line.

> It is obvious that the Messenger and the believers were a test for the disbelievers as to whether they would believe even after hearing the Divine Message and seeing their pure character. On the other hand, the disbelievers were a test for the Messenger and his followers in the sense that they were a means of proving and trying their true Faith by their persecution. For it is this test alone which helps to discriminate the true Believers from the hypocrites. That is why, at first, only the poor and the helpless but sincere people embraced Islam. Had there been no persecution and hardships but prosperity, wealth and grandeur, the worshippers of the world and the selfish people would have been the first to embrace Islam. "Now when you have understood the wisdom of the test by persecution, it is hoped that you will endure all kinds of hardships without complaint, and willingly undergo the persecutions that are inevitable. It probably means two things: First, the way your Lord is conducting your affairs, is according to His will and nothing that happens is without His knowledge. Secondly, He is fully aware of your sincerity and righteousness in serving His cause under all kinds of hardships. You should therefore rest assured that you will have your full reward. He also sees the persecution and iniquity of the disbelievers; therefore they will not escape the consequences of their wickedness.[110]

We will now examine the viewpoints of the Shi'ite commentators on the above three narratives.

On 37:106, Rāzi does not offer much except to say, "This was a test that we brought on Abraham and his son Ismail; for sure this was an enormous hardship on both of them."[111]

With reference to 2:49, Rāzi provides a detailed explanation on the story of Pharaoh and his cruel behavior towards the people of Israel; however, he does not comment on the *balā* aspect of this narrative.[112]

Rāzi's discussion on 25:20 begins by drawing attention to the fact that this narrative is a reflection of the Meccans' criticism of the Prophet Muhammad's ordinary life style. Following is a summary of his commentary.

As Rāzi observes, this narrative is addressing those whose disapproval of the prophetic message is based on his ordinary life style, as well as informing the messenger that their criticism is not surprising, i.e., that other prophets had to face the same challenge. Rāzi further explains: the fact that all other prophets before Islam had to walk in the market place, consume the same food as others, and perform normal activities of the daily life, is a test for the community. He then expands on the content of this verse by giving examples of how people are the means by which others are put to the test, i.e., the healthy are the test for the sick, the one who has sight is the test for the one who cannot see, and the wealthy will be a test for the poor. How people perceive their circumstances and whether or not they submit to what Allah has provided for them is the test. Rāzi concludes by reminding his readers that, if Allah had so willed, He would have made the Prophets wealthy and with extraordinary powers in order to attract the addressee communities. However, the content of the revelation, not the social and financial class of the prophet, must be the sole drawing factor for people to accept the message.[113]

Kāshāni offers the following brief explanation on 37:106: "Certainly the trial of Abraham was a tremendous test and a clear ordeal by which the sincere man is distinguished from the untruthful one; due to its happy ending, some have referred to it as a blessing and a favor from Allah."[114]

With reference to 2:49, Kāshāni first presents a full explanation of the story of the Israelites and their harsh treatments by the peoples of Pharaoh, the birth of Musa, and his upbringing in the Pharaoh's household. He then comments on the *balā* aspect of this narrative which is summarized below. As Kāshāni observes, this narrative may be interpreted in multiple dimensions. On the one hand, the hardship of the Israelites - slaughtering of their sons and taking advantage of the girls- was a great ordeal from God to test their endurance. Conversely, the narrative may also mean that the Israelites' escape from Egypt and their liberation was truly a tremendous gift and a blessing from God to test their thankfulness. He concludes by reminding his audience that certainly God's trials can be both in good and bad; man should exercise gratitude in good times, and endurance in hard times.[115]

Kāshāni's commentary on 25:20 starts off with a brief note on the occasion of this revelation, and the fact that this narrative was a response to the unbelievers' objection to Prophet Muhammad due to his ordinary life style. The following is the summary of his viewpoints. According to Kāshāni the focal point of this narrative is the fact that man's life on this earth is designed to embrace various forms of trials and tests. Therefore, in this divine plan, members of society are put to the test through each other's financial status and health conditions. The rich and the poor, the healthy and the ill, are not only experiencing their trial and must act in charity and exercise patience, but their condition is in fact a trial for others. Consequently, those who are patient during hardship, as well as the person who is grateful in prosperity and helps the needy, will be distinguished from the self-centered. Kāshāni further explains that if indeed the Prophet was a wealthy man, the people of Mecca might have been attracted to him due to his financial assets and not the content of his prophetic message. He concludes by reminding the reader that Allah is most wise in the making of this world; hence, the various life conditions of the people are part of His plan and serve a purpose, namely, to provide the context for man's trial.[116]

Tabātabā'i begins his commentary of 37:106 by providing a connection between the previous narrative, "indeed we reward those who do right", and the narrative in discussion. What follows is the summary of his commentary. According to Tabātabā'i, this verse illustrates that rewarding the righteous people by Allah is a multi-step process: first We put them to the test through situations which are perceived as hardships and calamities; however, they are in fact painless and easy to deal with; when they have passed through the journey of their trial with success, we reward them with the best compensation in this world and the hereafter. He concludes his comments by emphasizing the trial of Abraham: that in fact this hardship was just a trial for Abraham, and although it was an extremely difficult situation to encounter, the object of the trial, i.e., sacrificing his son, was not the purpose but a mean by which he was tested.[117]

Tabātabā'i does not offer a detailed commentary on 2:49 but only expounds on its translation.[118]

As for 25:20, Tabātabā'i offers an in-depth discussion which is summarized below. According to Tabātabā'i, this narrative is the second response to the idolaters' disapproval of the Prophet; that this messenger is not the first messenger of God, but there were other prophets who had the same lifestyle as ordinary members of their society. Therefore, this prophet is exactly like the other prophets who had no extraordinary powers, no garden to consume from and no accompanying angel. Since Muhammad's ordinary life style is not any different than the previous messengers, why do you have expectations of him which were not expected of others?[119]

Tabātabā'i further observes that if the messengers had extraordinary abilities and divine powers, these faculties would have served as the validation base for the message being conveyed, resulting in submission and acceptance without a sincere belief in the content of the monotheistic message. Consequently, the ordinary lifestyle of the messengers serves as the means by which the addressee communities are put to the test; hence, the sincere believers will be distinguished from the contemptuous. Tabātabā'i concludes by elucidating on the last section of the narrative: *"Your Lord is all seeing"*; and affirms that in view of the fact that Allah's universal goal is for man to achieve his full potential in which ever path he chooses for himself, therefore, providing an environment in which man will be put to the test is essential in achieving that goal.[120]

Conclusion

An examination of the notion of Divine trial in the light of the two main scriptural sources of Muslim learning, namely, the prophetic traditions (*hadīth*) and the Qur'anic exegetical works (*tafsīr*), seems to suggest some concluding results.

An overall statistical appraisal of *balā* in major *hadīth* collections does not reveal a significant number nor does it undertake an all-inclusive discussion. With the exception of *Nahjol-Balāgha*, the conceptual theme of the *ahādith* appears to concentrate exclusively on one aspect of *balā*, namely, adversities, afflictions, and calamities. Whereas prosperity as a context of *balā* is clearly stated in the Qur'an, there is no evidence of this aspect of *balā* in the *hadith* collections. Furthermore, the idea of an afterlife reward, highlighted in many of the prophetic traditions, attempts to encourage man to accept hardship and demonstrate endurance. Conversely, *Nahjol-Balāgha* portrays a constructive role for *balā* in man's life. According to Imam Ali, one of the most beneficial aspects of *balā* is its effectiveness in eliminating some of man's most undesirable qualities, namely, self-admiration, egotism, and lack of consideration for others. He also underscores the significance of *balā* in providing opportunities for man to express regret for his past behavior and return to the path of Allah.

A scrutiny of the selected Qur'anic narratives in the exegetical commentaries reveals that, for the most part, the Sunnite and Shi'ite commentaries offer similar explanations. They all seem to comment on the nature of good deeds, and emphasize that obedience to Allah's commands is man's ultimate test. The exegeses draw attention to examples of good deeds, and further underscore the importance of sincerity and pure intention to please Allah.

The significance of *balā* within the creational structure of the cosmos was addressed, to some extent, by Mawdūdi, the Sunni contemporary exegesis and in greater detail by Tabataba'i, the Shi'ite commentary of the modern period. Mawdūdi is of the opinion that the purpose of Creation is the moral trial of man, to set the stage for man to freely exercise his delegated powers as Allah's vicegerent on this earth. The Shi'ite commentator, Tabātabā'i, demonstrates that *balā* is part of the Divine plan and an objective of Creation, to provide an excellent environment by which man's full potential can be actualized. Furthermore, he emphasizes that *balā* is the vehicle by which the pious and the sincere person will be distinguished from others, which ultimately provides the context for reward and punishment in life after death.

On the manifestation of *balā*, the exegeses are in convergence that both adversity and prosperity are means by which man is put to the test. While the *tafsīr* works criticize man's reaction to the different circumstances of life, they each provide a rationale for man's unwarranted behavior. Mawdūdi and Tabātabā'i point out that man views wealth, position, and power as the criteria for honor and humiliation; therefore, their deficiency misleads him to think he has been humiliated by Allah. Rāzi, one of the Shi'ite commentators, stresses that man incorrectly assumes it is Allah's duty to always accommodate his needs; therefore, he loses sight of the *balā* aspects of his life's circumstances.

As for the narratives on objects of *balā*, the commentators generally offer a similar explanation; however, each has a unique perspective on various parts of the verses. Both groups of exegesis seem to be in agreement that Allah is well aware of how man will ultimately act; however, trials will reveal man's true character for himself and others. Tabari and Zamakhshari both speak of man's true character being revealed through these tests; the sincere is distinguished from the untruthful person. This is especially true when wealth and children are mentioned as *fitna* as means by which man's love and devotion to Allah will be put to the test. Kāshāni points out that man's character is exposed by his level of attachment to life's adornments such as children and wealth. Tabātabā'i is of the opinion that due to an emotional devotion to children and wealth, man will begin to perceive them as life's highest priority; this will then become the primary reason for deflecting his attention from Allah.

With reference to trials of Prophets and their communities, while the exegeses offer somewhat parallel presentation, a difference of opinion does exist. They all seem to agree that *balā* in forms of adversity and suffering plays a central role in revealing the sincere believers from the rest of the addressee communities. Zamakhshari, however, further points out that certain circumstances may be a *balā* for both the prophet and the community. This multi-dimensional nature of *balā*, according to Zamakhshari, is evident in the case of Prophet Muhammad and the Meccan community. Although the Prophet's ordinary life style, lack of wealth and magical powers, was the test for society and the main reason for their resistance in accepting the message, this situation was in fact a major test for the Prophet himself, i.e., to test his dedication in conveying the message while maintaining the best moral behavior in dealing with his people.

Rāzi and Kāshāni are of the opinion that, while each member of a community may experience their unique trial at the individual level, that same condition will be a trial for the other members of society, i.e., the trial of the poor is to endure with patience, while that of the wealthy is to be thankful and assist the poor. Finally, Tabātabā'i underlines the importance of the belief in life after death, and the fact that ultimately the best reward awaits the person who remains a sincere believer through the journey of life and its many challenges and trials.

It can be concluded that both Sunnite and Shi'ite commentaries offer comparable elucidation on the notion of *balā* within the context of the selected twelve narratives. With the exception of Kāshāni who considers following the *imam* is a test and as such a good deed, there is very little evidence as to the sectarian viewpoints of the commentators. From the chronological perspective, the two exegeses of the Modern period, namely, Mawdūdi and Tabātabā', provide the most comprehensive explanation of the narratives under discussion, and illustrate a coherent link between the concept of *balā* and the responsibility of man as he goes through the journey of life. From the two modern exegetical works, Tabātabā' represents the most extensive *tafsir* and provides an all-encompassing elucidation of the narratives.

The next chapter of this study will provide an overview of Divine trial relating to the Qur'anic prophets.

When Abraham's Lord tested him with certain commandments, which he fulfilled, He said, "I will make you a leader of people"...

(Qur'an, 2:124)

3

The Qur'anic Prophets and Divine Trial

One of the central themes of the Qur'an is the doctrine of revelation (*wahy*) and the notion of prophethood (*nabuwwa*), whereby the communication between the Divine reality and human reality is made possible. The Qur'anic Prophetology reveals a historical continuity of prophets, and noticeably indicates that every nation was addressed by a messenger who conveyed the divine message in their own language. While each addressee community (*umma*) may have been given specific commandments and guidelines most appropriate for their historical context and circumstances, the monotheistic essence of the Divine message remained the same. As Renard observes, "God alone initiates the message and communicates it through prophets, without whom humanity would have very little chance of attaining to the ultimate truth."[1]

The Qur'an frequently reveals that the making of the universe as well as the creation of mankind is purposeful (Q. 38:27) and that upon completion of his life on this earth man will return to God (Q. 23:115). As the highest ranked creature of God's creation and His vicegerent on earth (Q. 2:31), man's inner-nature (*fitra*) is composed of the Divine Spirit (Q. 15:29), and he is the sole guardian of the Divine Trust (Q. 33:72). Furthermore, the ability to distinguish between good and evil has been ingrained into man's nature (Q. 91:8), empowering him to live a meaningful life and follow the path of righteousness. These primordial characteristics of man, along with the Divine message conveyed through the prophets, provide humankind with the necessary guidance (*hidāya*) to succeed in this life and earn an eternal life in paradise. Furthermore, God sends the messengers not only to communicate the Divine message but also to serve as exemplars for the community; to encourage and inspire people to follow in their footsteps. Indeed, "the prophet not only conveys; he reveals; he almost does unto others what God does unto him."[2] As Rahman notes: "God sends His messengers, for it is the moral aspect of man's behavior which is most slippery and difficult to control and yet most crucial for his survival and success."[3]

In this chapter the reader will be presented with a brief overview of the Qur'anic approach to the notion of Prophethood. Subsequently, a synopsis of the story of each selected Qur'anic prophet and their addressee community will be presented. In addition to a general discussion regarding many of the challenges and difficulties that the prophets encountered, by employing textual and historical analysis methods, special emphasis will be given to the Qur'anic pericopes which – whether directly or by implication – highlight the Divine trial (*balā*) aspect of the story. Through the above discussion, one of the hypotheses of this study, namely, the mainstream exegetes' inability to comprehend the all-embracing and foundational aspect of *balā* as the Qur'an seems to suggest, and their lack of intellectual engagement with the notion of "divine trial" as a universal phenomenon, will be discussed and further established.

The concept of Prophethood within the Qur'anic context is presented as a universal phenomenon whereby certain inspired individuals are divinely elected (*iṣṭafā*) and are charged with a prophetic mission (Q. 3:33). These extraordinary personages dedicate their life to God and His people. According to Heschel:

> In speaking, the prophet reveals God. This is a true marvel of a prophet's work: in his words, *the invisible God becomes audible*. The prophet's eye is directed to the contemporary scene; the society and its conduct are the main theme of his speeches. Yet his ear is inclined to God. He is a person stuck by the glory and presence of God, overpowered by the hand of God. Yet his true greatness is his ability to hold God and man in a single thought.[4]

This process of divine election, the Qur'an asserts, empowers the prophets with the knowledge of the unseen, an aptitude that is not shared with anyone else (Q. 72:26-7). In describing the concept of Prophethood, the Qur'an utilizes two terms: "the word for 'prophet' is *nabī*, plural *anbiyā* and *nabiyyūn*. A much more prevalent term, however, is *rasūl*, plural *rusul*, which denotes a 'messenger' or 'apostle'."[5] Some Muslim exegetes differentiate between a *rasūl* as one who is supposed to bring a revealed scripture and a *nabī* as a more generic prophet; however, these distinctions are not always consistent with the terminology used in the Qur'an for different prophets.[6]

As can be observed from the Qur'an, the history of prophethood begins with Adam and culminates in Muhammad as the final messenger or "seal of the Prophets" (Q. 33:40). According to Muslim tradition, God sent 124,000 prophets at different times and to every community; however, the Qur'an mentions only twenty-five prophets and messengers by name, most of whom are well known biblical personages.[7] The primary reason for revealing this information to Prophet Muhammad was, it is claimed, to "strengthen" his heart, present a historical continuity of the Divine message and His elected messengers, as well as providing an opportunity for the Meccans to learn from the previous addressee communities. As Wheeler observes: "among those mentioned by name are: Adam, Idris, Noah, Hud, Salih, Abraham, Ishmael, Isaac, Jacob, Lot, Joseph, Shuayb, Job, Dhu al-kifl, Moses, Aaron, David, Solomon, Elijah, Elisha, Jonah, Zechariah, John, Jesus, Muhammad."[8]

Muslims, the Qur'an asserts, must believe in all revealed scriptures and prophets and not make any distinction between the messengers (Q. 2:285). The Qur'an further emphasizes that true righteousness is based on the belief in God, the Last Day, the Angels, the Books and all God's messengers (Q. 2:177). The Qur'an, however, recognizes certain messengers and identifies them by the title of *ulū l-`azm* "messengers of firm resolve"[9] (Q. 46:35). Their importance lies in the fact that they all received revelations from God and that, whether in existence now or not, these revelations contained laws and that contributed to the long and progressive process of Divine revelation.[10] According to Rubin:

> A special group of God's messengers is mentioned in 46:35, being called 'those endowed with constancy (*ulū l-`azm*)'. The Qur'an says that they have borne patiently and Muslim exegetes are not unanimous as to who they were. Some say that they were those who established a law (*Shari`a*) among their nations, like Noah, Abraham, Moses, Jesus, as well as Muhammad. Others hold that they were those who suffered the hardest trials or the deepest remorse. In the later case, they include Jacob, Joseph, Job and David, in addition to the five prophets already mentioned.[11]

As noted previously, revealed scriptures are a major component of the prophetic mission; of the prophets mentioned in the Qur'an only those who are called the messengers (*rusul*) seem to have brought a new scripture. The Qur'an frequently refers to itself and other divinely revealed scriptures as a "book" (*kitāb*), and confirms that they are all "enlightening revelations" (Q. 35:25). Additionally, the Qur'an mentions scriptures revealed to Abraham, and points out the individual titles of the other scriptures: Torah (*Tawrāt*) of the Israelite prophets, David's Psalms (*Zabūr*) and Jesus's Gospel (*Injīl*).[12] While the Qur'an notifies Muhammad of previous prophets and messengers before him, it does confirm that only a partial list has been revealed to him (Q. 4:164 and 40:78); nevertheless, the stories of the prophets make up a significant portion of the Qur'an.

As already established, God sends His messengers to communicate the Divine message of monotheism, to act as the ultimate source of guidance, and to continue living as a prototype and the most excellent role model for the community. The Qur'an reveals that God makes "a special covenant" (*mīthāg*) with the prophets to ensure the prophetic mission is accomplished (Q. 33:7). As divinely guided and elected individuals, the messengers undertook a tremendous responsibility and tried every method to persuade their addressee community of the truth of their message, one of which is to give good tidings for those who believe and warn the unbelievers (Q. 6:48). According to Rahman, "The primary task of the prophets is to awaken man's conscience so that he can decipher the primordial wiring on his heart more clearly and with greater conviction."[13]

Overview of Divine Trial in the Lives of the Prophets

As mentioned previously, the stories of the prophets, which form a significant portion of the Qur'an, start with Adam as the first prophet, and culminate in Muhammad as the seal of the prophets. The majority of the twenty-five prophets mentioned in the Qur'an are well known figures within the Jewish and Christian traditions; nevertheless, the Qur'anic accounts might have slight variations form the biblical versions. With the exception of Yūsuf, whose account is fully presented in sūra twelve, the stories of the prophets appear throughout the Qur'an and not in chorological order. Moreover, all of the Prophets referenced in the Qur'an are men. As Esack points out: "While Mary was the recipient of revelation, nowhere do we get any indication that she was expected or did play the social role of Warner or the bearer of good tidings."[14]

As reformers of society, one of the prophets' primary responsibilities was to strive for social justice and increase communal awareness. Through acts of mercy and compassion, God's prophets are portrayed as having made every effort to magnify the otherwise slightest inequalities such as mistreatment of the deprived, and emphasize that all members of society are responsible for the moral state and well-being of the people; that while a few may be involved in actual acts of crime, all members of the community are responsible.[15] However, since the majority of people tend to be concerned with their self-interests and don't wish to be troubled by the miseries of others, they choose not to respond favorably to the prophets' message.

Therefore, a common theme among the prophetic tales, which is highlighted throughout the Qur'an, is peoples' disrespect for the prophets and lack of interest in the monotheistic message. While the Qur'an clearly indicates that the addressee communities were expected to acknowledge and believe the message of their prophets (Q. 4:64), the people's response was, for the most part, obstinacy and rejection. The main reason for this rejection was the fact that prophets were ordinary human beings with no extraordinary abilities and no worldly possessions. The Qur'an, time and again, sheds light on nations' harsh reactions and their wicked treatment of the prophets; not only were they mocked (e.g., Q. 15:11), they were also accused of being liars (e.g., Q. 35:25), magicians, poets, and madmen (e.g., Q. 51:52). As Rubin points out, "The Prophets have also suffered actual persecution, such as the threat of expulsion (e.g., Q. 14:13), and also death at the hand of their own peoples, as was the fate of the Israelite prophets (e.g., Q. 2:61, 91, etc.)."[16]

The next section of this chapter will present a brief discussion about the following Qur'anic prophets and their communities: Nūh, Ibrāhim, Lot, Mūsa, Yūnus, Ayyūb, Yūsuf, Suleimān, Davood, Zakariya, Isa, and Muhammad. This selection is based on the comprehensiveness of the Qur'anic representation of these prophets, with special emphasis on the *balā* (trial) aspect of the prophet's life both at a personal level and as the leader of the community. A section is devoted to each prophet whereby trials and challenges of their prophetic mission within their historical-cultural context are discussed. It should be noted that the story of Adam and his trial - the fall, and man's vicegerency on earth - will be discussed in the next chapter as part of the mystical interpretation of Divine trial.

Noah (*Nūḥ*)

Nūḥ, a well-known character within the Jewish-Christian traditions, is one of the major prophets of the Qur'an, with his name being mentioned in twenty-six different *sūras*.[17] These Qur'anic narratives reveal that Nūḥ's prophetic mission was to address a very obstinate community of disbelievers who rejected the divine message and insisted on practicing polytheism. Nūḥ's prophetic assignment is claimed to have lasted nine hundred and fifty years (Q. 29:14) during which time he preached and warned his people. The message was loud and clear: God's mercy is upon them if they repent and His wrath if they persist in disbelief. This long period of continuous teaching and warning produced very little success. While a small number accepted the monotheistic message, the majority mocked him, rejected the message and urged him to worship their pagan gods. The end result was destruction of the community through a devastating flood which eradicated the disbelievers, while the few who had believed in Nūḥ's message were saved in his ark and continued to live as the first monotheistic society (e.g., Q. 11:25-49).

Muslim exegetes provide lengthy discussions on the story of Nūḥ and expand on the Qur'anic narratives. The commentaries attempt to shed light on topics such as the duration of Nūḥ's mission; his age; construction of the ark; number of people in the ark; the Deluge; drowning of his son; safe arrival of the ark, and creation of the first monotheistic community.[18] While the exegetical discussion is heavily centered on the historical and phenomenological aspects of the story, there seems to be little interest in the trial aspects of Nūḥ's life. Therefore, the mainstream exegetes, for the most part, do not provide an in-depth presentation of the notion of trial as it relates to Nūḥ and the demise of his son.

In review of the Qur'anic narratives on various aspects of this story, Nūḥ's appeal to God and his effort in saving his son deserve some attention here. According to the Qur'an, God revealed to Nūḥ that since his addressee community had not accepted the Divine message and persisted in the practice of polytheism, a major catastrophe was in the Divine plan. The revelation clearly indicated that while the entire population of unbelievers would be annihilated, Nūḥ's family and the few who had accepted the message would be saved.[19] Upon God's command, Nūḥ constructed an ark and took his family and the followers with him when the deluge occurred. When he realized one of his sons was fighting for his life, Nūḥ asked him to believe in God and enter the ship as there was no other way to survive; however, he rejected his father's invitation and consequently drowned in the flood. At this point Nūh appealed to God that his son was a member of his family whose protection had been assured by Him. The Divine responded to his plea by letting Nūh know that his son was not part of his family due to his wicked conduct; advised him not to ask God about things which he has no knowledge of, and warned him not to be ignorant (Q. 11:25-49).

According to Zamakhshari, Nūh's plea to God illustrates that he was not aware of his son's disbelief in God and, that had he known this, he would not have cried out to God in an attempt to save him. While this was a major trial for Nūh, he immediately realized his weakness and asked God for his forgiveness.[20]

Abraham (*Ibrāhīm*)

The Qur'anic representation of the story of Prophet Ibrāhīm seems to appear in a wide variety of contexts positioning him amongst the highest recognized Qur'anic prophets. As the father of the Abrahamic religions: Judaism, Christianity, and Islam, Ibrāhīm is mentioned by "some two hundred and forty-five Qur'anic narratives in twenty-five *suras*."[21] According to Firestone, "Although the Islamic Abraham shares many characteristics with the figure in the Bible and later Jewish exegetical literature, the Qur'an especially emphasizes his role as a precursor of Muhammad and establisher of the pilgrimage rites in Mecca."[22] The connection between Ibrāhīm and Muhammad is established in the Qur'an through various contexts; however, identifying them both as *hanif*, "pure faith" (e.g., 10:105), seems to be at the core of the Muslim exegetical discussions.[23] The Qur'an reveals a contention between the Jews and the Christians as they claimed that Abraham belonged to them (Q. 3:67). According to the Qur'anic exegete, Baiḍāwī, when the dispute was presented to Prophet Muhammad the above narrative was revealed to clearly state that Ibrahim was neither Jew nor Christian.[24] Time and again, the Qur'an refers to Abraham as *hanif*, and a role model for Muhammad whom God commands to follow (e.g., Q. 2:135; 16:123).

Although the Qur'an includes descriptive narratives of individual prophets which, for the most part, shed light on the unique virtues and moral character of each and every prophet or messenger, Ibrāhīm seems to have been granted some of the highest designations and titles such as: "very truthful" (*ṣiddīq*, Q. 19:41); "kind and gracious" (*halīm*, Q. 9:114). Moreover, as Rubin points out, "Abraham is described in Q. 4:125 as the one whom God took as a friend (*khalīl*)."[25]

The prophetic mission of Ibrāhīm begins in his birth land during the time when he challenges his father in the practice of idol worshipping, and encourages him to follow Ibrāhīm to the straight path of monotheism (Q. 19:41-47). Ibrāhīm's strong belief in monotheism, along with his persistence in renouncing the popular practice of idol worshipping, caused hostility between him and the rest of the community. In an attempt to prove the ineffectiveness of the idols, him takes his mission to a higher level and destroys the idols. For this he was thrown into fire to be burnt alive; however, with God's command the burning fire becomes cool and a safe haven for Ibrāhim (Q. 21:51-69). The tale of Ibrāhim and his challenges continues after migrating to a new land; seeking and at times mildly challenging God to strengthen his heart (Q. 2:260); being visited by divine messengers and given the news of a son (Q. 11:69-76); constructing the house of God Ka`ba (Q. 2:125); and finally his ultimate trial to sacrifice his son (Q. 37:103-7).

The story of Ibrāhim in the Qur'an reveals a variety of challenges and hardships, all of which he patiently endured and proved his steadfastness and devotion to God. However, unquestionably, the pericopes regarding his dream and the sacrifice of his son illustrate Ibrāhim's perceived superior level of truthfulness in fulfilling God's commands. According to Tabātabā'i, Ibrāhim is aware of the authenticity of the dream and is committed to carrying out God's command; nonetheless, to test his son, he informs him of the nature of the dream and asks his opinion. Tabātabā'i further concludes that Ismā'il's response to his father's question, i.e., "do what you have been asked to do" illustrates Ismā'il's deep understanding of the nature of God's command and his willingness in submitting to it.[26] Mawdūdi is also of the opinion that, although Ibrāhim was committed to carry out God's command, he consulted with his son in order to find out if in fact his prayer for a devoted son had been answered.[27] Although the name of Ibrāhim's son is not mentioned in the Qur'an, the exegetes nonetheless engage in an extensive discussion in order to identify the son who was the subject of the sacrifice. While there is divergence amongst the Qur'anic commentaries, the majority are of the opinion that it was Ishmael and not Isaac with whom Ibrāhim was put to the test.[28]

The exegetes' efforts in identifying Ibrāhim's son, however, may be questioned, based on the simple fact that the Qur'an itself is silent about it – surely, if this piece of information had any impact on the essence of the message, the revelation would not have left it vague. The underlying principle for this ambiguity seems to be the fact that the pivotal point of the Qur'anic narrative is the actual "trial" of Ibrāhim and his unquestionable submission to God's command, and not the identity of his son. Attention needs to be drawn to the fact that, once a name is associated to this profound and inspirational event, a whole set of historical contentions between the Judeo-Christian and Muslim communities are highlighted; the result of which may shift the emphasis from the notion of trial to various other arguments which do not, even remotely, heighten the understanding of the concept of trial. Therefore, by not clarifying the name of Ibrāhim's son, the Qur'an illuminates the significance of the essential teaching of this profound experience, and not the irrelevant details. The fundamental lesson of the trial of Ibrāhim, which is to submit to the Will of God and sacrifice his son - let go of the most precious attachment of his life - includes a universal message that everyone is able to relate to and reflect upon. This important aspect of the sacrifice narrative, which transcends all barriers and supports the centrality of the notion of *balā* illustrated in various parts of the Qur'an, seems to have been overlooked by the majority of the exegetes. As a result of this shortcoming, the Qur'anic exegetes have engaged in prolonged discussions about irrelevant details of the story which not only fail to promote a deeper understanding of concept of *balā* but, more importantly, entirely shift the attention to historical and sectarian arguments.

Lot (*Lūt*)

The story of Lūt, a familiar biblical figure, is considered to be one of the most well-known prophetic stories in the Qur'an and Muslim exegesis. The primary reason for this recognition is due to the fact that Lot's addressee community, namely the people of Sodom, practiced sodomy; their continued sinful behavior ultimately resulted in God's wrath and annihilation of the entire community (Q. 7: 80-84; 11:69-83; 27: 54-8). Having been mentioned twenty-seven times in the Qur'an, the story of Lūt and his people is considered among the Qur'anic stories of "Divine punishment" and is second in terms of number of verses to that of Noah and the flood.[29]

According to the Qur'anic commentaries, Lūt was sent to his people to prohibit them from their practice of homosexuality. Despite Lūt's numerous efforts, the community continued with their sinful behavior, threatened to expel Lūt and his family from their home, and remained ignorant of Lūt's warnings of a major calamity. The story reaches its climax during the time when Lot's guests - two attractive men who later identified themselves as God's messengers – were approached by members of the community in an attempt to subject them to sexual relationship.[30] Having been embarrassed by this shameful attempt, Lūt prays to God to free him of these people; he is then told by the guest angels to depart the city as God's punishment will strike at dawn. Lūt and his family were rescued while the entire nation, including his wife whom the Qur'an calls a disbeliever, was annihilated by a devastating natural calamity resulting in a powerful rain of brimstone.[31] According to Muslim historian Tabari, God sent three of his angels, namely Gabriel, Michael and Israfil in the form of young men in order to test the people of Sodom and then afflict them with the calamity.[32]

Tabātabā'i offers an in-depth discussion of the story of Lot, his traits and qualities, and his encounters with the people of Sodom. What follows is the synopsis of his viewpoints. According to Tabātabā'i, Lūt was Ibrahim's contemporary and among the first to support and believe in Ibrahim's monotheistic message; he also accompanied Ibrāhīm in the migration to Palestine. Subsequently, he was charged with a prophetic mission to address the people of Sodom, a community recognized to be the first to practice sodomy – a practice adopted by all members of the society as the standard way of life. Tabātabā'i is of the opinion that Sodom's female population was also engaged in same sex activities. This, he argues, is due to the fact that women did not offer their support to Lot and that all of them were destroyed at the time of the natural disaster; that God's wrath and chastisement only comes to the evil doers.[33] However, it may be argued that Tabātabā'i's deduction seems to be purely conjecture; there is no indication in the Qur'an to support his conclusion that the women of Sodom also practiced same-sex relations.

Lot's mission was to remind the people of Sodom that human beings are "naturally" created to engage in matrimonial relationships through which the continuity of human race is made possible. Contrary to Lot's efforts in encouraging the community to put an end to this unhealthy lifestyle, the Sodomites not only rejected his guidelines and continued with their behavior, they also attempted to seek pleasure by approaching Lot's guests – two or three handsome male visitors who later introduce themselves as God's messengers. Not recognizing that his guests are no ordinary men, Lot makes every effort to protect them, inasmuch as offering his daughters to the aggressors and desperately asking them to stay away from his guests.[34] However, as with all his other attempts, Lot's last plea was rejected at once; out of helplessness and extreme anxiety, Lot cried out *"if only I had the strength to stop you or could rely on a strong support!"* (Q. 11:80).[35]

It can be observed from the Qur'anic narratives that Lot had faced many challenges and hardships in dealing with the community. However, his ultimate trial seems to be highlighted in the above mentioned narrative whereby, not realizing that God's support was already there, in desperation he is searching for a strong power to support him; as soon as the angels identify themselves he recognizes that indeed God's assistance has been there all along. While Muslim scholars have offered sympathetic explanations for Lot's minor shortcoming, there are nevertheless prophetic traditions in which Lot has been slightly criticized. In his tales of the Prophets, Mahallāti references a tradition from the sixth Shi'ite Imam, Ja'far al-Sādiq, who said: "when Lot was frantically seeking help and wished for a powerful support to lean on, Gabriel said: 'if only Lot would realize what strong aid he has at home'".[36] Furthermore, Tabātabā'i quotes a tradition in which Prophet Muhammad is reported to have criticized Lot for his lack of trust in God which resulted in him seeking other powers to support him.[37] Nevertheless, Tabātabā'i questions the authenticity of the *hadīth* and emphasizes that Lot was a noble prophet who constantly remembered God and was mindful of His sovereignty and support. Tabātabā'i further agrees that the reason for Lot's strong appeal for help was due to his lack of knowledge that God's angels were in his house, and not that he was searching for a strong support other than God.[38]

Moses (*Mūsā*)

The importance of Moses in the Qur'anic teachings becomes visible through more than 136 narratives of various lengths in both Meccan and Medinan periods of the revelation. Having been mentioned more than any other prophet, including Prophet Muhammad, Moses seems to be the most prominent prophet of the pre-Islamic period.[39] An overview of the Qur'anic treatment of Moses reveals various resemblances between the Qur'anic accounts and the Christian and Jewish exegetical tradition. However, the Qur'an and the Muslim exegetes present a new perspective on some of the themes associated with Moses, especially the older narratives. According to Schöck, "the essential feature of the allusions to the past is a typological interpretation of the earlier narratives, by which the biography of Moses is seen in the light of the biography of Muhammad."[40]

The story of Moses in the Islamic scripture is portrayed by revealing a wide variety of events which happened through the course of his life, some pertaining to an extended period of time. However, the large majority of the Qur'anic accounts seem to shed light on two common periods of Moses' life. The first group of pericopes illustrates Moses in Egypt which includes passages about his birth and growing up; his killing of an Egyptian; his departure to Midian; prophetic mission and Pharaoh; and migration from Egypt. The second group of narratives gives attention to Moses and his encounters with the Israelites after the exodus, including passages about wandering in the wilderness; Moses on the mountain; the golden calf; and the city by the sea where Moses meets with the servant of God.[41]

According to the Qur'an, Moses was born during the time that the Israelites were enslaved by Pharaoh and forced to perform extremely difficult physical labor. Having been informed about Abraham's foretelling – a boy who would destroy his kingdom – and fearful of the accuracy of this news, Pharaoh commanded the killing of all newborn Israelite males (Q. 28:1-6). God, in His divine plan, inspired Moses' mother to leave her baby in a box and cast it on the Nile river, only to be discovered by Pharaoh's wife who convinced her husband to let the baby boy live with them as their own child; hence, Moses is brought up in Pharaoh's household and under his guidance (Q. 28:7-13).

The Qur'an describes a series of events that happened after Moses reached maturity and was given "wisdom and knowledge" (Q. 28:14). Muslim exegetes have some disagreement about this narrative. For example, Zamakhshari is of the opinion that the narrative refers to the time which Moses reached forty years old, and that "wisdom and knowledge" means he was elected as a prophet.[42] Tabātabā'i, on the other hand, attests that the verse refers to when Moses must have been eighteen years old, which is the time a person reaches maturity.[43] The passage continues by informing the reader that Moses killed an Egyptian, an action which he blamed on Satan, and subsequently departed to Midian to escape the death penalty (Q. 28:15 - 22). Moses settles in Midian after helping two daughters of an old man, marries one of them, and agrees to work for a number of years for his father-in-law. Although the name of the old man who hires Moses is not mentioned in the Qur'an, commentators have consensus in identifying him as prophet Shu`ayb.[44]

Following the completion of his employment contract, Moses and his wife depart from Midian, the time which marks the beginning of his prophetic mission as Moses receives the first revelation. During a cold night of their journey, from a distance Moses sees a fire or a light, and as he anxiously approaches the area, God speaks to Moses and commands him to take off his sandals for he has entered the valley of Tuwā (e.g., Q. 20: 9-24, 28:29-35). Moses' mission is to invite Pharaoh to believe in God and request the release of the enslaved Israelites to Moses so they may depart Egypt. Moreover, to reinforce the prophetic mission and provide confirmation for Moses' claim of prophethood, Moses is given two signs which play a significant role as he approaches Pharaoh and his council;

namely the sign of Moses' rod which transformed into a serpent or snake, and the sign of his hand which glows white but which is unharmed[45]. Moses responds frightfully due to his killing of an Egyptian and Pharaoh's plan to make him pay for his act, and asks God to send his brother Aaron to support him in this difficult mission, a request which is fulfilled by God (Q. 20:17-23; 28:31-2).

The Qur'anic passages in which the confrontation between Moses and Pharaoh is presented appear in various parts of the Qur'an. A number of narratives present the details of dialogues between Moses and Pharaoh, whereby Moses openly rejects Pharaoh's claim of Lordship, and proclaims that God of the universe, who is the Lord of this world and the next, is the true God (e.g., 26:10-29). Other accounts illustrate the contest between the magicians of Pharaoh and Moses which resulted in the submission of a few defeated magicians to the God of Moses (e.g., Q. 7:103-26), and Moses' demands for the Israelites to be free to go with Moses (e.g., Q. 26:17-19). The final stage of this confrontation takes place when Moses and the Israelites exodus Egypt and are followed by Pharaoh and his army; Moses strikes the sea with his rod which by God's command divides the sea; the Israelites are saved while the Pharaoh and his army are drowned (e.g., Q. 44:17-33).[46]

The second group of Qur'anic narratives illustrates the tale of Moses and his encounters with the Israelites after the exodus. According to Muslim exegetes, God provided the Israelites with a number of blessings such as water, food, clouds to protect them from the sun, and fire to keep warm at night - so they might live as a faithful community and in accordance with God's guidance. Notwithstanding God's favors, the Israelites did not show any gratitude and thankfulness, rejected God's signs, and continually disobeyed His commands; their transgression resulted in a number of retributions during the course of their existence (e.g., Q. 2:47-61).[47] Other Qur'anic passages recount the story of Moses during the forty nights on the Mountain[48]; his request to see God; revelation of Torah; his disappointment upon his return and finding people worshiping the golden calf; his plea to God to separate him and his brother from the sinful Israelites; and finally Moses' encounter with a servant of God to elevate his knowledge and wisdom (e.g., Q. 7:142-150; 5:25; 18:60-82).

As can be seen from the above synopsis, the story of Moses in the Qur'an includes a variety of incidents which can be attributed to the notion of Divine trial. Firstly, Moses is tested by coming across two men in conflict – one belonging to his faction and the other to his enemies - with no prior knowledge of the cause of the argument and due to his lack of patience; Moses' anger takes over his reasoning which results in killing of the Egyptian. Moses immediately acknowledges that he allowed Satan to lead him to this dreadful act and asks God for forgiveness. According to Zamakhshari, although the man who lost his life was among the unbelievers, Moses did not have the liberty to take his life; his action was not a command from God and was due to his lack of self-control; hence, he committed a sinful act.[49]

Secondly, Moses is tested when – as commanded by God - he and a number of Israelites meet near the mountain during the time the Torah is going to be revealed. At this time, Moses asks to see God; while He reminds him that no human is capable of seeing God, He informs Moses that He will manifest in the mountain and that if the mountain can tolerate the glory of God, then, Moses will be able to see God as well. Upon God's manifestation, the mountain crashes into pieces and Moses falls down unconscious; once recovered, Moses repents for his request and proclaims he is amongst the first to believe.

While the Qur'anic exegetes have commented on these passages and provided elucidation on the incident, divergence does exist. Rāzi is of the opinion that Moses did not commit any wrongdoing by requesting to see God and that, indeed, as a prophet he had the wisdom to recognize that even prophets are not able to see God. Rāzi further observes that Moses' request was in fact the people's demand who wanted to see God to ensure the Torah was revealed truly by God himself; therefore, he did so due to the pressure of the people.[50] Conversely, according to Zamakhshari, the fact that Moses asks God's forgiveness and repents upon gaining consciousness reveals his acknowledgment that he was at fault. Zamakhshari also points out that prophets are the exemplars to the community, and even if he was under pressure from his people, he should not have been influenced by them to make such an imprudent request.[51]

Thirdly, Moses' response to people's worship of the golden calf, which made him react in such an infuriated fashion, deserves some attention here. The story recounts Moses' furious behavior to the point that he threw the Tablets down, held Aaron by the hair, and while pulling him accuses his brother of misconduct. In an attempt to calm Moses, Aaron anxiously defends himself by letting Moses know that he was overpowered by the community, that he almost lost his life trying to prevent them from this sinful act, and appeals to Moses not to make the enemy happy by mistreating him. It is only after Aaron assures Moses of his innocence that Moses realizes he has reacted excessively and asks God to forgive him and his brother (Q. 7:148-58; 20:80-98).

According to Zamakhshari, Moses' outraged reaction towards Aaron, accusing his brother of irresponsibility for his inability to prevent people from worshipping the cow, as well as blaming him for their sinful act, demonstrates Moses' temperament as impatient and at times intolerable. He further notes that the Israelites had a more favorable attitude towards Aaron than Moses due to his calm and peaceful personality. Zamakhshari concludes by reminding the reader that the fact that Moses repents and asks God's forgiveness illustrates that he acknowledged his wrong behavior towards Aaron; he also pleads with God to forgive Aaron to show the community that he is now pleased with his brother.[52] Furthermore, in Wheeler's opinion, one reading of Q. 7:154, in which the incident of Tablets being thrown down by Moses is revealed, draws attention to the fact that guidance and mercy may have been taken away from the Tablets at this time. He then refers to the following tradition: "Ibn 'Abbās states that when Moses threw down the Tablets, God recalled six of the seven parts and left only one seventh for the Israelites."[53] Wheeler further points out that early Christian exegesis also illustrate that Torah was imposed further on the Israelites as a punishment for their sinful act of worshipping the cow.[54]

Fourthly, the story of Moses comes to notice in Q. 5:25 when the Israelites refuse to enter the holy land as commanded by God; in desperation, Moses asks God to separate him and his brother from the disobedient people, the consequence of which was God's chastisement to make the Israelites wander in the wilderness for forty years. According to Wheeler:

> Moses' request to God that He separate him and his brother from the sinful Israelites in Q. 5:25 is understood by Muslim exegetes as his refusal to intercede on behalf of his people. Al-Tabarsi says that the request was equivalent to Moses asking God to take him and his brother to Heaven while the Israelites were damned to Hell. According to al-Zajjāj (d. ca. 337/949), Moses and Aaron enjoyed special privileges in the wilderness so that they suffered little while the Israelites were punished for forty years.[55]

The fifth and final episode of Moses' story relating to divine trial becomes visible in his meeting with an unnamed individual, whom the Qur'an refers to as "one of Our servants – a man to whom We had granted Our mercy and whom We had given knowledge of Our own". This fascinating parable demonstrates how Moses is put to the test and is challenged to overcome impatience by witnessing the actions of the "servant of God" – as paradoxical as they may seem. The Qur'anic account reveals that Moses and his companion are on a journey to find the location where the "two seas join" - this has been revealed to Moses as where he will find the "servant of God". Subsequent to traveling on foot for quite some time, in extreme tiredness, they stop for a little while to rest and consume their food – a fish which they had brought. The companion informs Moses that at some point he saw the fish swimming away in the sea but forgot to let him know; Moses immediately interprets the event as the sign, and realizes that the fish must have swum "where the two seas join". They go back to the path and by tracing their footsteps find the way to the designated location where Moses meets the servant of God, and the companion seems to depart from the scene (Q. 18:60-82).

The Qur'anic commentator, Rāzi, provides the reader with background information by reporting that during one of Moses' public preachings, a man from his audience asked him "Oh prophet, is there any one more knowledgeable than you on this earth? To whom Moses replies: "No"; Gabriel informs Moses that God is sending His greetings and questions you as how do you know if there is a more informed man than you or not; and why did not you say only God knows? God reveals to him that, indeed, a man to whom God has granted Mercy and knowledge is the most knowledgeable man; upon Moses' persistence in wishing to find him, he is instructed that the servent of God can be found at a place where the two seas join.[56] The servant of God who was endowed with knowledge is identified as Khiḍr, "the green", by the Muslim scholars, some of whom claim that he may have been a prophet.[57] It needs to be noted that neither Rāzi nor any other Qur'anic exegete makes any reference to the fact that Moses's response to the above question, was in itself a test for him.

During their initial meeting, Moses asks permission to accompany Khiḍr in his journey and shows eagerness to learn from him. Khiḍr does not respond positively to Moses's request and informs him that he does not have the patience to bear the events that he will be witnessing. However, upon Moses' insistence and assurance that he will be able to observe the incidents, Khiḍr allows Moses to accompany him so long as he does not demand any explanations from Khiḍr until he provides them. The Qur'an then reveals certain events and actions performed by Khiḍr which seem paradoxical and unwise to Moses; hence, failing to keep his promise, the impatient Moses challenges Khiḍr and demands an explanation for his actions. Throughout the journey, Khiḍr reminds Moses of his vow and informs him of his inability to continue on this journey due to lack of endurance. Finally, after granting Moses three chances, Khiḍr provides explanations for his otherwise controversial conduct, and makes him aware that all of his actions were done according to God's plan. The story culminates when Khiḍr departs the scene and Moses is left behind while he is saddened and remorseful.

The mystical dimensions of this fascinating parable will be dealt with in the next Chapter, where divine trial is discussed from the perspective of Muslim mystics.

Jonah (*Yūnus*)

Prophet Yūnus, whose story also appears in the Bible, is mentioned in the Qur'an five times; he appears with other prophets who have received revelations (Q. 4:163); as a righteous prophet who was divinely guided (Q. 6:86); and his people as the only community who escaped divine punishment (Q. 10: 98). These Qur'anic narratives present Yūnus' story in a concise format; however, the Muslim commentaries have discussed the matter in fuller detail, some continuing with the biblical teachings.[58]

According to the Qur'an, Yūnus, who is also referred to as Dhū l-Nūn ("the man of the whale"), is charged with a prophetic mission to lead his community on the path of righteousness and belief. During the course of his mission, Yūnus becomes frustrated; reacts wrathfully to his people's obstinacy; and finally decides to run away. Subsequent to his departure, and having been thrown to the sea and swallowed by a fish, he acknowledges his sinful behavior, and after praising God asks for His forgiveness. The continuation of the story appears in another passage where the Qur'an reveals that Yūnus's plea is accepted; he is released from the belly of the fish on to the shore where he settles for some time. The story concludes in a happy ending when Yūnus is returned to his people who had repented to God, and having been granted mercy, they escape divine punishment (Q. 21: 87-8; 37:139-48; 10:98).

In an attempt to demonstrate various aspects of Yūnus' story, in addition to shedding light on some of the theological questions rose by his actions, Muslim scholars have elaborated extensively on the above Qur'anic narratives. As illustrated in the Muslim tradition, Yūnus' is called to address the large pagan community of Nineveh to believe the monotheistic message he was preaching.[59]

It is reported that the people of Nineveh did not respond positively to Yūnus, called him a liar, and challenged him to bring about God's punishment if in fact his claim of prophethood was genuine. Having failed to guide the community in the path of monotheism, Yūnus is unable to tolerate the burden of prophetic mission; asks God to reprimand his people; furiously runs away and boards a ship as it is about to depart.[60] It is further understood that, although Yūnus was charged with a divine mission to guide a community, and was expected to practice a high level of tolerance, he nonetheless exercised impatience. He behaved wrathfully towards his people, so much so that he desires they be punished by God; to complete his unacceptable conducts, he decides to depart without having been granted permission to do so; hence, implying that God has no power over him. In summary, Yūnus seems to have illustrated the following shortcomings: impatience; wrathfulness; refusal to transmit divine message, and departing from the scene without God's permission.[61]

According to Muslim tradition, prophets are immune from wrongdoings, especially when it comes to conveying God's message and following His commands. Therefore, the Qur'anic exegetes have offered alternative ways to interpret the story. Zamakhshari is of the opinion that, since Yūnus did his best to convey the monotheistic message with no success, he rationalized his anger and frustration, which resulted in his departure; he regarded it as evidence of his dedication to God and a testimony to his objections to the pagan practices. Zamakhshari, however, acknowledges that Yūnus should have remained with the community, and continued his mission with a higher level of tolerance while awaiting God's command.[62] It may be noted that Zamakhshari does not comment on the fact that Yūnus' lack of patience which resulted in his departure may be viewed as a Divine trial where he was put to the "test".

Conversely, according to Tabātabā'i, Yūnus, whom the Qur'an identifies as rightly guided, and mentions him with Abraham and other prophets, did not commit any transgression: his wrathful behavior was not towards God; his departure was not due to his refusal to continue his prophetic mission, and that he did not get reprimanded by God when he was swallowed by the fish.[63] Furthermore, in Tabātabā'i's opinion there are two major elements that deserve attention: firstly, the narratives allude to Yūnus' actions and as such should not be taken literally but rather symbolically; secondly, Yūnus' supplication with God when he is captured by the fish, demonstrates that the reason for his repentance is for what his actions *may* have implied and not that he has committed those wrongdoings.[64] Tabātabā'i further emphasizes that, having been swallowed by the fish, Yūnus is granted an opportunity to reflect on his life, accomplish spiritual growth, and experience an extraordinary mystical experience which improved his status as a prophet and as an exemplar. Engaging in a prayer which shows his full submission to God's will, Tabātabā'i asserts, is the result of God's mercy which is plausible only by experiencing the divine trial. He concludes that Yūnus' desperation in turning to God, and God's favorable response in honoring his plea, is what every believer should follow in their individual life.[65]

Job (*Ayyūb*)

The story of Ayyūb, a well-known prophet in Jewish and Christian tradition, is revealed in the Qur'an only in four concise passages in which he is praised for his level of devotion to God, and is called "an excellent servant". Ayyūb is mentioned among the more famous prophets such as Abraham, Noah, and Jesus, those whom God has chosen and preferred over the rest of the people and guided them to serve as the best exemplar (Q. 6:83-90). Ayyūb is also listed among the prophets who have received revelation to convey God's message so mankind would have no excuse before God (Q. 4:163-165). The exceptional character of Ayyūb, namely his devotion to God, gratefulness both during healthiness and when afflicted with a serious disease, as well as his utmost endurance at the time of adversity, is what earns him the title of "excellent servant" (Q. 38:41-2 and Q. 21:83-4).[66]

The Muslim exegetical works have elaborated on the tale of Ayyūb in an attempt to shed light on some of the aspects of the story not mentioned in the Qur'an. According to Ibn Kathir, Ayyūb was a prosperous man who, due to his strong faith in God, constantly acknowledged God's blessings, attributed the sources of his wealth to God, and offered extensive appreciation to Him. Ayyūb had also been granted a big family, including a number of sons who were known for their bravery, and large amount of workers who managed his lands and cattle, all of which he was both proud of and grateful for. However, although Ayyūb remained in constant remembrance of God, his life changed drastically when his family and all of his belongings are taken from him; the calamity is worsened when he is afflicted with a painful disease which results in sores to appear all over his body.[67] Ibn Kathir further notes that after Ayyūb's illness continued for an extended period of time, people began to despise him and eventually drove him out of town. Ayyūb was left alone with his misery; his wife was the only one who did not abandon him. Ibn Kathir is of the opinion that during the time of his afflictions, "Ayyūb never lost his patience but remained steadfast and devoted to God, and that he is an example of a prophet who experienced various kinds of trial."[68]

Although there is divergence concerning the duration of Ayyūb's trial, Balāghi is of the opinion that this period lasted seven years;[69] nonetheless, the Qur'an illustrates a happy ending to the story. Ayyūb pleaded to his Lord that Satan was the cause of all his calamities, and that God was the "most merciful of the merciful". In Sūrābādi's opinion, Ayyūb's call on God came after he heard a few of his former students engaged in a conversation implying that God does not afflict anyone with such adversity unless the individual has committed a great sin and, therefore, deserved to be punished.[70] As is revealed in the Qur'an, due to his faithfulness and endurance, Ayyūb's cry was answered at once. God instructed him to strike the earth with his foot which caused a spring of cold water to gush forth; subsequently, he is asked to wash and drink from this refreshing water; hence his body is healed. Furthermore, God in His mercy restored his family and his wealth two-fold, and made this story a lesson for those with understanding and wisdom (Q. 38: 41-4). According to Johns:

In the light of this inter-text, the status and role of Job in the divine economy of prophetic guidance is clear. These two periscopes present Job's distinctive charisma, that of patience in enduring undeserved suffering without challenging God to explain his wisdom in putting him to the test. The story of Job in the Qur'an then is understood primarily as a reward narrative with an emphasis different from that of the story of Job in the Bible.[71]

Joseph (*Yūsuf*)

The story of Yūsuf, a prophetic personage common to the Jewish, Christian and Islamic tradition, is referred by the Qur'an as "the best of stories" (*aḥsan al-qaṣaṣ*), and is the only extensive prophetic tale reported in a continuous and systematic format in the Qur'an. While Yūsuf is mentioned in two separate Qur'anic passages: as a pious ancestor (Q. 6:84), and as a messenger with clear proofs (Q. 40:34), the twelfth *sūra* of the Qur'an is named after him and is exclusively devoted to an uninterrupted narrative of his life. The *sūra* sheds light on various episodes of Yūsuf's life starting from his youth when he is separated from his father Jacob (Ya`qub), and is thrown in the well and abandoned by his brothers. Upon freedom, he is accused of an unlawful relationship with his master's spouse and is imprisoned due to this false accusation. Finally, due to his extraordinary ability to interpret dreams, Yūsuf is released from prison, is appointed king's minister and, at last, is united with his family (Q. 12: 3-111). Furthermore, this long narrative illustrates that Yūsuf was an honorable man who, despite his virtuousness, is faced with some of the most difficult adversities; nonetheless, he remains in constant remembrance of God and asks for His guidance and protection. As Goldman observes; "Throughout the *sura*, there are interjections that exhort the believers to see the hand of God in human affairs and to recognize the power of true prophecy (Q. 12:7, 56-7)".[72]

The story begins by Yūsuf informing his father of a dream that he had whereby eleven stars, as well as the sun and the moon prostrated before him. Ya`qub replies: "My son, tell your brothers nothing of this dream, or they may plot to harm you – Satan is man's sworn enemy"; as well as letting him know that he has been divinely elected as a prophet (Q. 12: 4-6). Yūsuf's brothers collude to harm him as the Qur'an reveals a dialogue between Jacob and his sons in which they convince him to allow Yūsuf to journey with them to the countryside. Jacob's hesitation proved right as the brothers collectively decide to throw Yūsuf in the well, return home pretending to be heartbroken as they inform their father of an unavoidable accident – that Yūsuf was attacked by a wolf – and present him with his bloody shirt as evidence. Jacob responds by letting them know that he is aware of their wronged conduct; however, it is best to remain patient and that he will seek God's assistance to exercise endurance as he goes through this hardship (Q. 12: 7-18). As for the innocent Yūsuf who found himself at the bottom of a dark pit, he is assured of his wellbeing as the Qur'an speaks of God's revelation to Yūsuf, *"you will tell them of all this at the time when they do not realize who you are!"* (Q. 12:15).

The Qur'anic tale of Yūsuf continues when a caravan in need of water stops at this particular location; however, to their astonishment, instead of water a young boy is found in the bucket, to which they respond with joy as they sell him as a slave to an Egyptian household where he grows to be a young man in possession of extreme handsomeness. The wife of his master, not named in the Qur'an, attempts to seduce Yūsuf which he rejects at once. Failed in her first attempt, she arranges for a ladies' gathering whereby Yūsuf is faced with the same temptation from a number of women; while rejecting their invitation, Yūsuf desperately seeks God's assistance in preventing him from committing this sin, a prayer that is granted by God. Consequently, Yūsuf is imprisoned for not complying with the orders of his master's wife. The Qur'an reports a series of events during the time Yūsuf remains in prison, including dialogues with his companions about monotheism, and interpretation of two of his friends' dreams. A few years later he is requested to interpret the dream of the Egyptian king, which, due to much ambiguity, the kingdom's official dream interpreters were unable to explain; due to his extraordinary interpretation of king's dream the king orders the termination of his captivity. When he is given the good news of freedom, Yūsuf refuses to depart from prison until the King questions his wife about the events prior to his imprisonment, so his master is made aware that he did not betray him; upon questioning the wife, she admitted her wrong conduct, removed the accusations and attested to Yūsuf's innocence. At last, Yūsuf regains his freedom, and with his honesty and loyalty proven and his honor being restored, he is selected as the personal assistant to the king of Egypt (Q. 12:19-53).

The final episode of the story takes place when Yūsuf's brothers arrive in Egypt in search of provisions; upon entering at the kingdom Yūsuf recognizes them while they do not realize the identity of this generous king. The Qur'an reports of a series of events whereby Yūsuf provides the brothers with an excessive amount of food and encourages them to bring their brother to receive a bigger supply next time and engages them in a conversation about their father and the younger brother which eventually leads to his identity being revealed. Upon this recognition, the brothers express extreme shame and sorrow for their actions. To their astonishment, Yūsuf forgives the brothers and asks them to take his shirt and lay it over their fathers' eyes; as such, his father regains his sight and the entire family comes to the kingdom to be reunited. The story culminates when Yūsuf greets his parents with a warm welcome as they enter the city, praises them when at the kingdom and positions them at the highest seats of the palace; the parents and the brothers prostrate in front of Yūsuf, a scene that he had seen in his dream and once again shares with his father at this time (Q. 12:53-111).

Muslim exegetes have commented extensively on all aspects of Yūsuf's story; nevertheless, what is presented here is for the most part a synopsis of the discussions on the divine trial features of the story. In an attempt to shed light on what appears to be a father's unjust treatment of his children, namely, Jacob's excessive love of Yūsuf, Muslim scholars concur that Jacob had legitimate reasons for showing more affection towards two of his sons.

According to Balāghi, although Jacob had twelve sons, he expressed an enormous amount of attention and love towards Yūsuf and his younger brother Benjamin due to the fact that they were the youngest of the sons, and as they had lost their mother at a young age were in need of emotional support. Balāghi further observes that, while this eventually leads to his other sons' jealousy and resentfulness, Jacob had not committed any wrongdoing.[73]Tabātabā'i is also of the opinion that Jacob, who was a prophet himself, recognized the unique abilities and virtues of Yūsuf, was aware that Yūsuf will be a prophet, and as such, paid special attention to him and admired him for his qualities.[74] It may be argued, however, that Jacob's differentiated affections towards his sons may also be viewed as a test for him, a point that it is not referenced in any of the commentaries.

Furthermore, Tabātabā'i provides a detailed discussion about the centrality of dream in the story of Yūsuf as well as other prophetic dreams mentioned in the Qur'an. Through this presentation, Tabātabā'i references some of the scientific research on the validity of the notion of dreams, which grants authenticity to Yūsuf's story and his ability of interpretation. He further observes that God in his wisdom, through a dream, assured Yūsuf of his future, and as such, provided him with divine guidance. Moreover, Tabātabā'i emphasizes that God's Will always prevails; despite the fact that all odds seemed to be against Yūsuf – abandonment by his brothers, humiliation of slavery, false accusations and imprisonment - every circumstance of his life proved to be instrumental in leading Yūsuf to a prosperous life that was planned for him.[75] According to Esack: "By his participation in a government that was not 'fully believing', Joseph represents righteous political participation for just and noble purposes without insisting on absolute power."[76]

According to Al-Ghazāli, Yūsuf is a perfect example of a pious individual who while experiencing various trials, both in adversity and prosperity, nonetheless remained devoted to God, expressed utmost trust in His will, and showed patience during hardship and thankfulness at the time of power and abundance. Al-Ghazāli then comments on Yūsuf's behavior where he is looked after by a powerful Egyptian man and his wife, where a close relationship was formed between Yūsuf and his master; nonetheless, "he continued to uphold and observed the religious beliefs and traditions of his ancestors as well as their belief in the one God, preserving at the same time his personal virtue and upright conduct."[77]

David (*Dāwūd*) and Solomon (*Sulaymān*)

David and his son Solomon, two well-known biblical personages, are mentioned in the Qur'an amongst the prophets who are bestowed with kingship, power, wealth, and extraordinary abilities, generally not attributed to other Qur'anic prophets. David appears in sixteen Qur'anic pericopes while Solomon is mentioned in four extensive accounts. Although the uniqueness of each of the two prophets is demonstrated in the Qur'an at the same time, noticeable similarities are also apparent; therefore, the story of David and Solomon is presented here in a single section.

The Qur'anic story of David starts with his participation in a fierce battle between King Saul (Tālūt) and his long-term enemy Goliath (Jālūt). In facing the powerful army of the opponent, David offers a sincere prayer and asks God for His assistance in this brutal combat. David and his soldiers courageously defeat the powerful army of the enemy, Jālūt is exterminated by David, and an enormous victory is announced for King Saul. God in his mercy rewards David by granting him power, wealth, and wisdom; David is eventually selected as the next king and takes charge of Saul's kingdom where he remained in power as a popular emperor (Q. 2:250-1). In other Qur'anic narratives, David and Solomon are portrayed as God's prophets with David having been revealed a Scripture called Psalms (Q. 4:163; 6:84). Furthermore, as illustrated by the Qur'an, David and Solomon possessed some of the most extraordinary abilities not common to other Qur'anic prophets: understanding the language of birds and animals (Q. 27:15); mountains and birds joining them in praise of God (Q. 34:10); David being appointed as the deputy of God on earth (Q. 38:26); and David as the one for whom God melted iron in his hands (Q. 21:80).[78]

The Qur'anic account which sheds light on some of David's unique characteristics, and also reports of an incident in which David is put to the test, appear in chapter thirty-eight of the Qur'an and deserves some attention here. In Qur'anic phraseology, David is portrayed as *"Our servant, a man of strength who always turned to Us"*; as the prophet whom *"mountains joined in glorifying Us at sunset and sunrise"*; the one whom *"We gave wisdom and a decisive way of speaking"* (Q. 38: 17 -20). At the peak of this descriptive narrative we are told of the following incident:

> *The two litigants climbed into his private quarters. When they reached David he took fright, but they said: do not be afraid; we are two litigants, one of whom has wronged the other, judge between us fairly and guide us to the right path. This is my brother who had ninety-nine ewes and I just had the one and he said, "let me take charge of her", and overpowered me with his words. David said, "he has done you wrong by demanding to add your ewe to his flock. Many partners treat each other unfairly. Those who sincerely believe and do good deeds do not do this, but these are very few." David realized that We had been testing him[79], so he asked his Lord for forgiveness, fell down on his knees, and repented. We forgave him* (Q. 38: 21 -25).

The above narratives, alluding to David's wrong judgment, provided the context for Muslim scholars to comment on David's story, some of whose interpretation may have been influenced by Judeo-Christian traditions. The Qur'an, unlike the Bible, does not explicitly mention anything about Uriah, Bathsheba or any of David's marriages or children except Solomon. Nonetheless, the early Muslim literature relating the tales of the prophets linked the story of David, his appeal to God, and the divine forgiveness, to the biblical story of Bathsheba and Uriah; the later exegetical works represent David as completely purified of all wrongdoings.[80] As observed by Hasson, later Muslim scholars portray a different image of David according to sectarian viewpoints. While the canonical Sunnite *hadith* collections emphasize David's devotional practices such as prayers and fasts, the Shi'ite, on the other hand, maintain David's complete infallibility; and the Muslim Sufis who paint David's portrait as the symbol of asceticism and the best role model to follow.[81]

The Qur'anic exegete, Tabātabā'i, is of the opinion that the biblical interpretation of the story, namely that David was infatuated with Uriah's wife Bathsheba, planned his death by positioning him at the front line of his army, and consequently married Bathsheba, is pure human fabrication as God's prophets are immune from such accusations. Tabātabā'i further points out: the fact that the litigants mysteriously appeared in David's private room – without anyone coming through the door – proves that they were, in fact, angels sent by God to test David; to teach him best practices in providing judgment; and finally for him to get closer to God through repentance. Tabātabā'i, concludes by emphasizing that the narratives in discussion (Q. 38:21-5) must be understood symbolically and allegorically, not literally.[82] Furthermore, Ibn Kathir has the following opinion on David's judgment and piety:

> God addressed David with the intention of making him responsible for the matters and judgment of people. He ordered them with justice and following the truth which was sent down from God, not his own opinions and whims. David was known to be certain in his justice, abundant in worship, having performed many sacrifices, so that not a single hour passed of the night and the beginning and end of the day without the people of this house being in worship.[83]

The story of Solomon, David's only son mentioned in the Qur'an, is presented in the Islamic scripture through four concise and allusive narratives. Nevertheless, encouraged by Solomon's extraordinary abilities and traits, the commentaries have added details not mentioned in the Qur'an, transformed it to a colorful tale, and provided symbolic interpretation of his life.[84] Solomon is demonstrated in the Qur'an as a powerful ruler who inherited his father's kingdom (Q. 21:78-9); a prophet who received divine wisdom (*hikma*) and knowledge (*'ilm*), as well as a personage who possessed a number of supernatural powers, namely, the ability to comprehend the language of the birds and ants to communicate with them (Q. 27:15-8). Furthermore, Solomon is described by the Qur'an as being able to rule over the wind which allowed him to be transported to anyplace he so willed (Q. 34:12). This unusual power is also attributed to the *jinn* under his command – the *jinn* is able to travel to a far land, take the throne that belonged to the Queen of Sheba, and bring it to Solomon in the blink of an eye (Q. 38:42).[85]

The portrait of Solomon in the Qur'an is presented as a virtuous man who, regardless of his paranormal capabilities and being in charge of a glorified kingdom, remained devoted to God and grateful for all His blessings; nonetheless, he was not exempt from a challenge which would put his character to the test. The Qur'an reports of an incident which sheds light on Solomon's level of affection for horses. On one occasion, as he was inspecting the condition of his horses and admiring their beauty, the sun went down and Solomon missed the afternoon prayer; he then said: *"My love of fine things is part of my remembering my Lord"* (Q. 38:31-33). By and large, Muslim exegetes are in agreement that Solomon's attachment to his horses was, in fact, the reason for not remembering God which resulted in not performing the afternoon devotional prayer. Nonetheless, the commentators are divergent about the nature of his affections, and whether or not such behavior is acceptable from a Prophet. Furthermore, as can be noted from the discussion below, the exegetes fail to notice any reference to the Divine trial feature of this incident, and therefore fail to point out that Solomon was put to the "test".

According to Mahallati, horses played a crucial role in any army and were instrumental in bringing victory for Solomon; therefore, he paid much attention to them and admired their performance. Mahallati also points out that Solomon's army was engaged in battles for the sole purpose of the spread of monotheism, and as such, his devotion to the well-being of the horses was not a shortcoming on his part, that in fact this showed his devotion to God.[86] Zamakhshari, on the other hand, is of the opinion that Solomon expressed much affection towards his horses because he had inherited them from his father; however, once he realized he had missed the afternoon prayer, he sacrificed a horse which provided food for the poor; this was done as a sign of his devotion to God.[87] Tabataba'i seems to have offered the most comprehensive elucidation on this story as he demonstrates that Solomon's affections for the horses was not for any reason other than his love of God. He concludes by arguing that Solomon's attentiveness toward one prayer distracted him from performing another prayer; however, devotional prayer was of a higher rank to taking care of the horses, and as such, acknowledges that his love of the horses is, in fact, part of his love for God.[88] And lastly, Ibn Kathir quotes a tradition from Imam Ali that in Solomon's religion delaying a prayer was allowed for a good cause such as conquest or the inspection of horses; therefore, Solomon did not commit any sins.[89]

Jesus (*Isā*)

The story of Jesus, the prophet whom the Christians believed to be the Son of God, is reported in the Qur'an in more than twenty-five narratives. The Islamic scripture refers to Jesus as Isā, often in conjunction with his mother Mary (Maryam) - Isā b. Maryam - Jesus son of Mary; and addresses him with the unique title of "the Messiah". While the Qur'an reports of Jesus' miraculous birth and portrays him amongst the highest ranked Qur'anic messengers, it categorically denies his divinity. The Qur'an further attests that while Jesus had the ability to perform miraculous acts such as healing the sick and granting life back to the deceased, nonetheless, execution of these extraordinary acts was done according to God's Will and exclusively through divine permission.[90]

As noted above, the vast majority of the Qur'anic narratives regarding the story of Jesus refer to him as "the son of Mary"; hence, rejecting the Christian belief that Jesus was Son of God, as well as emphasizing Mary's eminent status. Furthermore, it can be observed from the Qur'an that Jesus' story is not only intertwined with that of Mary, but also with prophet Zechariah (Zakariyyā) and his son John (Yahyā); therefore, the following brief mentioning of these Qur'anic periscopes is both necessary and beneficial.

The story of Zechariah, the father of John the Baptist (Yahyā), appears in four Qur'anic passages (Q. 3:37-44; 6:85; 19:2-15; 21:89-90); he is portrayed as a devoted servant of God who has grown old without experiencing fatherhood. While Zechariah's faith is put to the test through the hardship of childlessness, he remained nonetheless a pious believer and endured the difficulty. In another pericope where Zechariah is chosen to serve as Mary's guardian, he prays to God for a descendant and - despite his old age and his wife's barrenness – his prayer is answered: *"God gives you news of John, confirming a Word from God"* (Q. 3:39). While Zechariah is pleasantly surprised, he is unsure of the validity of this news, and as such asks for a sign, to which the angels reply: *"Your sign is that you will not communicate with anyone for three days, except by gestures".* The story of Zechariah and his trial "is an encouraging example of how the believer should persevere through difficulties, trusting in God…that God will show them mercy in the midst of their difficulties."[91] Moreover, the Qur'an portrays John as an individual of dignified and distinguished character and a prophet who will *"confirm a Word from God"* (Q. 3:39); and commands him to *"hold on to the Scripture firmly"* (Q. 19:12). The Muslim exegetes are in agreement that "John confirms the Torah, not that he brought a new scripture."[92]

Zechariah and John are linked to Mary and Jesus through other pericopes which will be highlighted below. The third chapter of the Qur'an relates the story of `Imrān's family (Mary's father) whereby, under the assumption that she is carrying a baby boy and aware of the fact that service in the temple was a male privilege, `Imrān's wife dedicated her unborn child to God's service. However, to her astonishment, she gave birth to a baby girl, named her Mary, appealed to God to protect her and her offspring from Satan (Q. 3:35-6), and fulfilled her promise in devoting her to be at God's service. Contrary to the normal practice at the temple, God in His kindness accepted Mary and made it possible for her to grow up in a sanctified environment under Zechariah's guardianship. Zechariah looks after Mary and observes that she is the recipient of miraculous sustenance with which God had provided her – this exceptional treatment highlights Mary's superior status (Q. 3: 37).[93] Tabātabā'i is of the opinion that Mary's utmost devotion to God which resulted in God's special blessings, invoked Zechariah's sincere plea to God to favor him with a child.[94] Furthermore, in this pericope the story of Zechariah is introduced between the verses on Mary's birth and childhood, and the news of Jesus' miraculous birth and his Prophethood. The correlation involving these biblical personages has caused extended and, at times, controversial discussions amongst Muslim scholars. According to Stowasser:

> This close association between the figures of Zechariah and Mary on the one hand and those of John and Jesus on the other establishes a special place for May in the Qur'anic context of prophetic history. Some medieval Muslim theologians – especially of the short-lived Zāhiri School, such as Ibn Hazm of Cordoba (d. 456/1064) – even assigned the rank of "Prophethood" (*nubuwwa*) as opposed to "messengerhood" (*risāla*) to Mary and also the mother of Isaac and Moses and the wife of Pharaoh. They justified this classification on the grounds that these women receive knowledge from God through word or inspiration. Consensus-based Sunni theology, however, strongly rejected this position as heretical innovation.[95]

The Muslim exegetes, nonetheless, are in convergence about Mary's purified status and her superior rank as indicated in the Qur'an; *"Mary, God has chosen you and made you pure: He has truly chosen you above all women"* (Q. 3:42). Zamakhshari is of the opinion that the first "chosen you" refers to the time that Mary's mother dedicated her un-born child to be at God's service; God graciously accepted Mary; granted her a holy upbringing under Zechariah's supervision; and provided her with miraculous nourishments. The second "chosen you" in this verse, Zamakhshari attests, relates to God's exceptional favor and blessing when He elected Mary to miraculously experience motherhood without any human involvement and give birth to Jesus, a blessing and favor that God has not bestowed onto any other woman.[96]

An overall study of the Qur'anic narratives concerning the life of Jesus shed light on three major themes: Jesus' conception and infancy; his rank as a messenger and prophetic mission; and Jesus' death or crucifixion.

The events concerning the birth of Jesus are found in one of the longest pericopes about him, namely the Qur'anic Chapter called Mary. The news of Jesus' miraculous conception was announced to Mary while she was in seclusion: *"We sent Our Spirit to appear before her in the form of a normal human"*; Mary immediately asked God's protection and requested him to go away; he reassures her that: *"I am but a messenger from your Lord, come to announce to you the gift of a pure son"*. Astonished at this news, Mary questions the angel by asking him, *"how can I have a son when no man has touched me; I have not been unchaste"*, to which he informs her of God's message: *"It is easy for Me: We shall make him a sign to all people, a blessing from Us, and it was ordained: she conceived him"* (Q. 16-21). The narrative recounts that Mary withdrew to a remote location; when the pains of childbirth drove her to the trunk of a palm tree, she exclaimed, *"I wish I had been dead and forgotten long before all this!"*; but a voice cried to her from below: *"Do not worry: your Lord has provided a stream at your feet and if you shake the trunk of the palm tree towards you, it will deliver fresh ripe dates for you*"; Mary is instructed to eat from fresh dates, be joyful, and refrain from speaking with anyone (Q. 19:22-26). The narrative culminates at the time when Mary is returned to her people and is accused of un-chastity; however, she remained silent and pointed to the baby; when they asked: "*How can we converse with an infant?*" – Jesus spoke up in her defense and announced himself as: "*I am a servant of God. He has granted me the Scripture; made me a prophet; made me blessed wherever I may be. He commanded me to pray, give alms, and to cherish my mother*" (Q. 19: 27-33).[97] Furthermore, a similar version of this proclamation is included in other Qur'anic narratives such as Q. 3:42-7, while Jesus' ability to speak in his infancy is also alluded elsewhere in the Qur'an: Q. 3:46 and Q. 5:110.

The second theme within the story of Jesus pertains to his status as God's messenger and his prophetic mission. As mentioned previously, the Qur'an firmly rejects Jesus' divinity and refers to him as the "son of Mary" (e.g. Q. 5:17 &116).

The above point is further emphasized through other narratives in which both Mary and Jesus are identified as "signs of God" (Q. 21: 91; 23: 50); – perhaps an allusion to the virginal conception, which, similarly to the creation of Adam, points to God's power.[98] Furthermore, Jesus is referred by the Qur'an as the "word of God" (*kalima*) (Q. 3:45; 4:171); various interpretations on the meaning of *kalima* have been offered by the Muslim exegetes; however, the general consensus is that it connotes God's power in the Creation[99] – "*This is how God creates what He will: when He has ordained something, He only says 'Be', and it is.*" (Q. 3:47). Zamakhshari points out that both the Jews and the Christians misunderstood Jesus' status, to the point that the Jews viewed him as an impure and fatherless child, while the Christians exaggerated and attributed divine status to him; both claims are strongly rejected by the Qur'an.[100] In an attempt to shed light on the accurate status of Jesus, and decisively refute the divine sonship and demonstrate that Jesus was, in fact, God's messenger, the Qur'an directly addresses the People of the Book:

> *People of the Book, do not go to excess in your religion, and do not say anything about God except the truth: the Messiah, Jesus, son of Mary, was nothing more than a messenger of God, His word directed to Mary, and a spirit from Him. So believe in God's messengers and do not speak of a "Trinity" – stop [this], that is better for you – God is only one God, He is far above having a son, everything in the heavens and the earth belongs to Him and He is the best one to trust* (Q. 4:171).

As Robinson observes, "the polemical context and the insistence that Jesus is *only* an envoy, word and spirit, should caution Christian apologists from interpreting *kalima* in the light of orthodox Christian *logos* theology."[101] The Qur'an confirms that Jesus' prophetic mission was to the Children of Israel[102], and that in preparation for this undertaking, God educated Jesus in the teachings of the Torah and the Gospel (Q. 3:49; 43:59). In addressing the community, Jesus conveyed God's monotheistic message; and while he attested the truth of what was in the Torah, made modifications to some of its rulings and removed a number of past restrictions; he also clarified some of the issues that the people were not in agreement about (Q. 3:50; 5:46; 43:63). Jesus is described by the Qur'an as a prophet who performed some extraordinary acts such as: enabling a blind person to see; creating birds from clay and granting them the ability to fly; and informing people of their whereabouts and what they ate, i.e. personal affairs which are otherwise unknown to others (Q. 3: 49; 5:110). It is, however, emphasized in the Qur'an that the purpose of these miraculous acts was to serve as authentic proofs of Jesus' prophethood, not to attribute divinity - Jesus never claimed his self-dependency in the performing of these acts which were done according to the Will of God.[103] It is also clearly stated in the Islamic scripture that Jesus was a sincere servant of God who never instructed people to worship him or his mother; he continually conveyed monotheism and the worshipping of God alone (Q. 5: 116-9).

The concluding Qur'anic theme concerning Jesus, and one which has raised extensive discussions amongst the Muslim scholars, is Jesus' death and the notion of crucifixion. The crucifixion narrative, which appears only once in the Qur'an, is revealed within the wider historical context of the Jews; and indicates certain examples of this community's unfaithful behavior. The pericope leading to the "crucifixion verse" provides such examples as: Jews when they broke their pledge and rejected God's revelation; unjustly killed their prophets; and uttered a terrible slander against Mary (Q. 4: 155-6). The "crucifixion verse" then follows:

> *They said, we have killed the Messiah, Jesus, son of Mary, the Messenger of God; they did not kill him, nor did they crucify him, though it was made to appear like that to them; those that disagreed about him have no knowledge…they certainly did not kill him – No! God raised him up to Himself; God is almighty and wise (Q. 4:157-8).*

While Muslims in general deny the crucifixion of Jesus, the Qur'an itself merely states that "they" (Jews) did not crucify him.[104] According to Muslim tradition, as Jesus' prophetic mission gained popular support, the leaders of the Jewish community along with the Romans sought to end his life; however, the Jews did not succeed as God raised Jesus up, and projected his likeness onto another person whom they crucified; therefore, Jesus is alive and will return at some point in the future.[105] The Qur'anic exegetes are in agreement that Jesus was neither killed nor crucified on the cross by the Jews, and that God raised him up to himself; hence, the claims of both Jews and Christians are rejected. However, various interpretations concerning the circumstances of Jesus' death have been offered. The Qur'anic commentaries have attempted to shed light on some of the most ambiguous points of the story such as: was there in fact a physical body on the cross that appeared to be Jesus?; and if so, who was he?; or was this just an illusion that God willed in order to discredit the Jews and cause confusion amongst them?

Zamakhshari is of the opinion that a man who pretended to be one of Jesus disciples led the Jews to Jesus' hiding place; however, at the time of capturing Jesus, God raised him up and made the hypocrite look like Jesus; the Jews then crucified that person.[106] Tabataba'i emphasizes that the significance of this verse rests upon the fact that the Jews themselves are unsure of what exactly happened to Jesus; therefore, their boast that they killed and crucified Jesus should not be taken seriously. Tabataba'i also attests that Jesus was, in fact, raised by his physical body and disagrees with the viewpoint of those who maintain that Jesus ascended by his soul; he argues that at the time of death everyone's soul is raised to God, and that the significance of Jesus' ascension was physical.[107] According to Mawdūdi, however, while the Qur'an explicitly states that Jesus was not killed by the Jews, it is silent on the nature of his death and, therefore, does not illustrate whether or not he was raised by body or soul. Mawdūdi further emphasizes that, whatever the nature of being raised may be – body, soul, or both – the fact that the narrative ends by *"God is almighty and Wise"* indicates that this incident was an extraordinary event.[108]

Although the Muslim commentaries have attempted to shed light on various aspects of Jesus' death, nonetheless, the Qur'anic teaching about this theme is not very lucid. According to Lawson:

> The Qur'anic exegesis of verse 4:157 is by no means uniform; the interpretations range from an outright denial of the crucifixion of Jesus to a simple affirmation of the historicity of the event. The first and by far the most frequent interpretation is that God rescued Jesus from the crucifixion in a miraculous manner and that someone else was substituted for Jesus on the cross.[109]

We will conclude this section by highlighting the divine trials and hardships in the life of Mary and Jesus. As discussed previously, Mary is celebrated in the Qur'an as the most prominent female figure, the recipient of divine favors, and a perfect exemplar for the believers. While Mary's exceptional status began before birth, when her mother dedicated her for God's service, nonetheless, Mary's devotion to God progressed as she constantly made a choice to remain on the straight path of righteousness and to purify herself. The Qur'an particularly points to the time that she was approached by the angel in the form of a man; in remembrance of the divine, she sought refuge with God from this handsome man, and requested him to leave; hence, "through the appearance of the angel in this manner, Mary had undergone a test and her modesty was made certain."[110] Mary's devotion to God was also put to the test during her pregnancy, giving birth to Jesus, the false accusations she received from her people; and finally her son's departure, through which she remained a sincere and pious servant of God.

As for Jesus, the most important challenge of his life seems to have been the unpopular reputation of the fatherless child which positioned him at the center of undesirable attention and exposed him to mistreatment. Not only Jesus had to exercise a high level of tolerance to deal with this constant cruelty, he was also obliged to defend his mother and protect her from the false accusations surrounding his conception and birth. Jesus remained a humble servant of God all through his life and continually urged people to worship the God that his mother and he worshipped; although in possession of extraordinary abilities, he attributed superior power to God and did not claim to be of a divine entity. Jesus lived an ascetic life-style with no materialistic attachment and is portrayed as a symbol of compassion and love with total devotion to God.[111]

Muhammad

As stated previously, according to the Qur'an, God's monotheistic message is conveyed to humankind through the history of Prophethood, a process which began with Adam and culminated in Muhammad whom the Qur'an calls "the seal of the prophets".[112] The Islamic scripture also attests that the history of revelation is concluded by Muhammad as the final Book, "The Qur'an" is revealed, the religion of "Islam" is established, and the process of making the Abrahamic religions, Judaism, Christianity, and Islam, is completed.

The story of Muhammad appears in the Qur'an through countless pericopes which highlight events from the time he was called to prophecy, his challenges and hardships, and the creation of the Muslim community. Except for a short narrative which represents a period of Muhammad's life before prophecy, his early life is not reflected in the Qur'an: *"Did your Lord not find you an orphan and shelter you, find you lost and guide you, find you in need and satisfy your needs?"* (Q. 93:6-8). However, an extended description of Muhammad's story, including his birth and early life in Mecca, his personal and communal life in Mecca and after migration to Medina, and his teachings during the making of the Muslim community, are recorded in his biography (*sīra*), the earliest and most recognized of which is the work of Ibn Ishāq (d. 218/833).[113]

Although Muhammad became an orphan at any early age, he grew to be a well-respected member of the community and due to his wholehearted character and honesty became widely known as al-Amin, "the trusted one".[114] While the Bedouin Arabs lived a nomadic lifestyle, Muhammad's own life centered on the urban environment; he was a merchant by profession and successfully managed Khadija's business – a forty year old widow whom he married at the age of twenty five – he never took another wife while he was married to her and not until she passed away.[115] As Armstrong points out: "this was no marriage of convenience: Muhammad gave a large proportion of the family income to the poor and made his own family live very frugally."[116]

It has been reported by the Muslim tradition that Muhammad had a reflective nature which caused him to spend an extended amount of time in seclusion. He regularly retreated to cave Hirā at the Mountain of Light close to Mecca where he worshipped God and continued his inner search. During the month of Ramadan and at the age of forty, he has an extraordinary experience where he is visited by angel Gabriel who brings the first Qur'anic revelation. Muhammad is called to serve as God's final prophet; the Divine revelation continues for the next twenty three years.[117]

A broad thematic approach to the story of Muhammad in the Qur'an may be viewed in light of the scope and purpose of his prophetic mission, as well as in relation to other prophets, scriptures, and communities.[118] A quick review of the Qur'an shows that Muhammad is not always referred to as "Muhammad" and that depending on the context of the verse he is addressed by various names and appellations. If the focus of the narrative is to address him in his relation to God the titles of *rasūl* "messenger", *al-nabi* "prophet", and *'abd* "servant" of God are used (e.g. Q. 3:144; 8:64; 17:1; 25:1). He is also referred to as *nadhīr* "warner", *bashīr* "announcer", and *mudhakkir* "reminder", all of which allude to the prophet's mission (e.g. Q. 2:119; 88:21).

Muhammad's prophetic mission, which is grounded in the notion of monotheism (*tawhīd*) and emphasizes the eschatological future, begins at the local level: *"Warn your nearest kinsfolk"* (Q. 26:114); then the larger audience of Mecca: *"So We have revealed an Arabic Qur'an to you, in order that you may warn the Meccans"* (Q. 42:7). However, the Qur'an also demonstrates that Muhammad was sent as a messenger to all humankind, therefore, his message includes a universal aspect: *"We have sent you [Prophet] only to bring good news and a warning to all people"* (Q. 34:28); *"Say [Muhammad], 'People, I am the Messenger of God to you all…there is no God but Him…so believe in God and His Messenger…and follow him so that you may find guidance"* (Q. 7:158); and *"We sent you [Prophet] only as a mercy to all people"* (Q. 21:107).

As discussed previously, a large portion of the Qur'an is devoted to the tales of the prophets and their addressee communities; therefore, the Muslim community is reminded that their prophet is a link in the chain of preceding prophets: *"Muhammad is only a messenger before whom many messengers have been and gone"* (Q. 3; 144). The Muslims are also advised to believe in all God's prophets and not make any distinction between them:

> So [you believers], say, "We believe in God and in what was sent down to us and what was sent down to Abraham, Ishmael, Isaac, Jacob, and the Tribes, and what was given to Moses, Jesus, and all the prophets by their Lord. We make no distinction between any of them, and we devote ourselves to Him" (Q. 2:136).

By establishing the affinity between Muhammad and the other prophets, the Islamic scripture confirms that all prophets experienced the same process of revelation; that, in essence, the message revealed to all of them is one and the same; therefore, the goals of revelation are also common to all the prophets.[119] The universality of Muhammad's mission, then, is further emphasized: *"We have sent revelation to you [Muhammad] as We did to Noah and the prophets after him"* (Q. 4:163). Furthermore, The Qur'an asserts that the monotheistic religion conveyed by Muhammad was revealed in the previous Scriptures; however, "whether through ignorance or by deliberately distorting the message, many

Jews and Christians had fallen into disagreement, each claiming to have the truth".[120] The evidence of the relationship of the Qur'an and previous divine Books is clearly stated in the following verse: *"This is a blessed Scripture that We sent down to confirm what came before it"* (Q. 6:92).

Muhammad is described by the Qur'an as a noble messenger for whom God and the angels pray (Q. 33:56); a prophet who is compassionate, gentle, and *"an excellent role model for those who put their hope in God"* (Q. 33:21). In another narrative the Qur'an informs the community that: *"A Messenger has come to you from among yourselves. Your suffering distresses him: he is deeply concerned for you and full of kindness and mercy towards the believers"* (Q. 9:128).

Notwithstanding Muhammad's efforts, the first few years of his undertaking did not produce much success; with the exception of a small group, the larger Meccan community refused to accept the Prophet's message of monotheism.[121] Many of Muhammad's encounters with the community, including those that throw light on his relationship with the unbelievers, are described in the Qur'an and occupy a major portion of the Book. The unbelievers are portrayed as those who are stubborn and persistently refuse to listen to the Prophet's message (Q. 21:36); disrespect the Prophet and act contemptuously towards him and his followers (Q: 6:7); and forcefully try to expel the Prophet from his homeland (Q. 9:13). Furthermore, the Qur'an speaks of the various reasons that the unbelievers presented in justifying their positions against Muhammad: his social and financial status was not good enough (Q. 43:31); he is only a human and not an angel (Q. 17:94); and that he was not able to bring a sign from the heaven, i.e. perform a miracle (Q. 7:203; 11:12). Since Muhammad is not able to produce proofs of his divinity, he is accused of being a sorcerer (Q. 10:2); a poet possessed by *jinn* (Q. 37:36); therefore, his message is not divine and is more of a "fairy-tales of the ancients" (Q. 25:4-6).[122]

The Qur'an demonstrates that, notwithstanding the unbelievers' attempts to question Muhammad's mental fitness and the truth of his monotheistic message, God supported the Prophet by revelations that validated his Prophethood, confirmed his psychological integrity, and established the divinity of the message: *"Your companion [Muhammad] has not strayed; he is not deluded; he does not speak from his own desire; the Qur'an is nothing less than a revelation that is sent to him"* (Q. 53:2-4). Other narratives reminded the community that the fact that Muhammad has not asked for any financial reward proved that he was conveying a divine message (Q. 25:57); while other pericopes challenge the disbelievers to produce similar passages to the Qur'an if they claim that this revelation is not authentic (Q. 52:33).

The story of Muhammad in the Qur'an further points to a number of occasions where the Prophet seems to have experienced sadness and a sense of failure for not being able to persuade the unbelievers to believe in his message.[123] Through this difficult time, God encourages his messenger and reassures him that his responsibility is to communicate God's message, and that he is not accountable for the unbelievers as he is not their guardian (e.g. Q. 6:107; 17:54). God's support further comforts Muhammad when he is told that God is aware that the accusations of the unbelievers have caused him much suffering, and advises him not to let his soul be wasted in regret for these people; not to let the unbelievers cause him anguish with their actions (e.g. Q. 15:97; 35:8; 5:41; 27:70); and encourages him to endure this hardship through proclamation of Lord's praise in the morning and at night (Q. 42:48-9). In addition to the encouragement narratives, the messenger is advised not to give in to the pressure of the unbelievers and remain firm in his path (e.g. Q. 45:18); at other occasions he is commanded "not to obey" the unbelievers and the "hypocrites", and only follow what has been revealed to him (Q. 33:1-2).[124]

While God's support for the prophet and the believers is repeatedly reinforced in the Qur'an, nonetheless the integrity of the message was preserved through a direct divine protection. To this end, the Islamic scripture reveals an occasion when the unbelievers almost succeeded in their temptation of Muhammad to falsify the revelation in return for their friendship; by divine protection the messenger remained firm:

> [Prophet], the disbelievers almost tempted you away from what We had revealed to you, so that you would have invented some other revelation and attributed it to Us and then they would have taken you as a friend. If We had not made you stand firm, you would almost have inclined a little towards them. In that case, We would have made you taste a double punishment in this life, and a double punishment after death and then you would have found no one to help you against Us (Q. 17:73-4).

The story of Muhammad and the early Muslim community is filled with hardship as they struggled to survive in Mecca and overcome the devastating conditions which the unbelievers imposed on them. These trial times eventually lead to success as the Prophet and the early followers migrate to Medina where they, despite numerous enemy attacks, with God's support, defend the newly established religion, and after the final victory which led to the fall of Mecca, are able to unite Arabia under the banner of Islam (e.g. Q. 9:40; 48:1).[125]

We will conclude this section by a short discussion regarding the divine trials in the story of Muhammad. As it is illustrated in the Qur'an and summarized in the above discussion, Prophet Muhammad's life is occupied with many challenges and hardships such as: growing up as an orphan; living in a polytheistic and unjust society with no moral values; after prophecy being called a liar, a mad man, and a poet; forced to leave his homeland to escape assassination; as well as the battles and struggles of leading a community. In addition to some of the most difficult adversities in which he was tested personally, the Qur'an also mentions a few particular trials concerning his prophetic mission; one of these we discussed above whereby with God's intercession the Prophet is saved from altering the revelation. However, the Qur'anic chapter of `Abasa "He Frowned" reports of an episode that deserves some attention here:

> *He frowned and turned away when the blind man came to him – for all you know, he might have grown in spirit, or taken note of something useful to him. For the self-satisfied one you go out of your way – though it is not your responsibility if he does not attain purity – but from the one who has come to you full of eagerness and awe you are distracted. No indeed! This is a reminder – whoever wishes will remember it – inscribed in honoured scrolls, exalted, pure, by the hands of novel and virtuous scribes* (Q. 80:1-16).

The review of some of the major Qur'anic commentaries reveals that the Muslim exegetes are generally not in conformity about the identity of the person who "frowned". However, they are in agreement that the occasion of revelation relates to an important meeting between the Prophet and some of the most influential leaders of the Meccan community. While the Prophet is hoping to persuade his audience to accept the new religion, a blind Muslim man interrupts the meeting and repeatedly calls on the Prophet to attend to him. In his eagerness to attract the disbelievers, the Prophet frowned at the blind man, and received the revelation which condemned such behavior.[126]

The point of contention is whether or not the Prophet, who is referred to by the Qur'an as a mercy for humankind, is in fact the direct audience of the aforementioned narratives. Tabarsi is of the opinion that the narrative under discussion does indeed address Prophet Muhammad. To ground his argument, Tabarsi provides the following rationale: that this natural response was due to his extreme concern for losing the opportunity to win the hearts of his audience and not out of ignorance or disrespect for the blind. He further argues that while the messenger was known for his gentleness towards the poor and disadvantaged members of the society; nonetheless, he was still a human, therefore, expressing a humanistic emotion for the Prophet does not confirm he had a shortcoming or that he committed a sin. Upon receiving this revelation, Tabarsi continues, the Prophet was reminded that he should not be overly concerned with the disbelievers' lack of acceptance due to their high social and financial status, and that the honor is with those who have already believed in the message of Islam. Tabarsi's concluding remarks inform the reader that, subsequent to this event, the Prophet extended his attention to the blind man, and on numerous occasions, engaged in conversation with the him letting him know that the fact that God reprimanded the messenger is the testimony to this man's sincere and pure heart.[127] Zamakhshari is also of the opinion that the narrative is directed at the Prophet and is of a disciplinary nature to further encourage the messenger not to concern himself with the wealthy disbelievers.[128] Conversely, in Tabātabā'i's viewpoint, the Prophet whom the Qur'an calls the best role model and a mercy to humankind is not capable of such mistreatment. Furthermore, Tabātabā'i refers to Tabarsi's discussion in his Al-Mizan and totally rejects the possibility of such undesirable behavior on the part of the Prophet.[129]

The above exegetical elucidations of the aforementioned narratives seem to suggest that the Muslim exegetes, for the most part, attempt to demonstrate that the Prophet was blameless and did not commit any fault. In establishing the innocence of the Prophet, they take a "defensive" approach and make a serious effort to demonstrate two main points: firstly, that the revelation is in fact addressing one of the attendees of the meeting – one of the wealthy unbelievers who acted egoistically towards the blind man; therefore, the Prophet is not the one who frowned at the blind man and is not the audience of the narrative; secondly, even if the Prophet did frown he did it for a good cause; i.e., for the sake of Islam – in Tabātabā'i's case, he employs an all-embracing tactic which implies that the dignity of the Prophet has been compromised by these verses and as such his status must be restated as firmly as possible.

However, it may be argued that, clearly, this was not the only occasion that an influential member of Meccan society looked down at the followers of the Prophet; and secondly, of the participants in the meeting, who may have been so important to be addressed by the revelation? Furthermore, undoubtedly, God was aware of the importance of the meeting which the Prophet was engaged in, as well as his good intentions and selfless reasons for disliking the interruption caused by the blind man; nevertheless, the revelation came and addressed the Prophet – one may ask, what would be the point of the narratives if in fact no fault had occurred? It may further be argued that, the Prophet was a "human" being with humanistic emotions and concerns, and naturally, as he is put to the "test" he may not have been able to act flawlessly at all times. These narratives, therefore, seem to illustrate that as eager as the Prophet was in promoting the message of Islam, he should practice compassion and empathy and lead by example – that this model of behavior is not to be compromised even by the Prophet and not even when God's message is being promoted. However, the apologetic approach employed by the exegetes indicates that they may have entirely overlooked the possibility of this event as a "trial" for the Prophet.[130]

Conclusion

The notion of Prophethood which provides the indispensable connection between God and man is presented in the Qur'an as a universal phenomenon. The divinely elected prophets, whom the Qur'an calls *nabi* and/or *rasūl*, hold exceptional faculties and are the true manifestation of God's mercifulness. Their mission is to communicate God's monotheistic message to man, as well as to serve in an exemplary role to inspire and guide people in the path of righteousness. The concept of Prophethood is also linked to the creation of the cosmos. The Qur'an, time and again, asserts that the making of the universe as well as the creation of man is purposeful, and that man will ultimately return to God; therefore, his guidance and salvation is at the center of the Qur'anic teaching. Man's primordial characteristics, which God has ingrained into his creation (*fitra*), as well as divine guidance, which is conveyed through the prophets and lived by them as best role models, are the fundamental means by which man's guidance (*hidāya*) is ensured.

The stories of the prophets and their addressee communities which occupy a major portion of the Qur'an illustrate the historical continuity of Prophethood, and provide a major source of guidance for the Muslim community. The Qur'anic prophets, whose stories were discussed in this chapter, demonstrate that each and every one of the prophets experienced a similar process of revelation. This progression further develops the prophetic mission which leads to addressing an obstinate community. While the prophets engage in conveying God's message and attempt to guide their people to live an honorable life, they patiently endure some of the most difficult challenges of their life. Furthermore, by virtue of their conduct and behavior – such as steadfastness and trustworthiness – the prophets lead by example and, as such, are the most excellent role models to be followed.

In the context of their responsibilities in relation to God and their people, therefore, the prophets are put to the test, and as such, their trial is of type one which was discussed in the first chapter of the study, *balā* as a pillar in the creation of the cosmos. Furthermore, as the prophets are tested both in adversity (e.g., Yūnus and Ayyūb), and prosperity (e.g. Solomon and David), their trial is also of type two, manifestation of *balā*. Additionally, due to the fact that the prophets were tested by tangible means such as wealth, social rank, family members, etc., their trial is also of type three of the defined categories. It goes without saying that both the prophets and their addressee communities are the exclusive means of trial for the fourth category.

The review of the tales of the Qur'anic prophets, including their challenges and sacrifices, provides sufficient examples of various types of *balā* which some of the most virtuous men of God had to encounter. God's messengers, whose lives were centered on pleasing God and leading the way for the community, have indeed experienced multiple layers of divine trials. This of course is due to their higher status and level of responsibility as means by which mankind is guided towards God's monotheistic path which ultimately ensures his salvation.

According to the exegetical literature presented in this chapter, the mainstream Muslim exegetes generally fail to engage in an intellectual and in-depth discussion of the notion of *balā* in its most complete form; i.e. as a fundamental component of the structure of the universe which the Qur'an seems to suggest. As mentioned at the beginning of the chapter, it appears that the Qur'anic exegetes are mostly concerned with the historical facts and irrelevant details of various events in the lives of the prophets. Hence, by emphasizing the otherwise insignificant elements of the prophetic tales, they seem to pass on opportunities to promote the universal message relating to the notion of *balā*, and the importance of an in-depth understanding of the concept which can fulfill the intellectual minds of their audience.

In an attempt to gain a deeper understanding of concept of *balā*, the following chapter of this study will discuss the perspectives of the Muslim mystics, and sheds light on their elucidation of this important Qur'anic concept.

We have adorned the earth with attractive things so that We may test people to find out which of them do best.

(Qur'an, 18:7)

4

Divine Trial from the Muslim Mystical Perspective

As the first chapter of this study - typology of *balā* narratives in the Qur'an - demonstrated, the notion of Divine trial occupies a significant position in the Qur'an because it is regarded as a fundamental component of the structure of the universe, and plays a purposeful function in the Divine plan. Nevertheless, according to the exegetical literature presented in the previous chapter, the mainstream exegetes, for the most part, do not engage with the notion of *balā* in a comprehensive manner and fail to effectively illustrate its impact and the all-embracing aspect which the Qur'an seems to emphasize. Being set forth as the "reason for the creation" (Q. 11:7), affirming that "everything" on this earth is designed to put man to the test (Q. 18:7), and that you will be tested in "good and bad" (Q. 21:35), are but a few examples whereby the centrality of the concept of *balā* in the Qur'anic teaching is signposted; nonetheless, by and large, the exegetical literature seem to lack an in-depth analysis of this concept – an inquiry which might otherwise be expected of the Qur'anic commentaries.

Contrary to the exegetical literature, however, in the opinion of the writer, the mystical and Sufi literature encompasses an all-inclusive investigation of the notion of Divine Trial which accords with the significance and import that appears to have been emphasized in the Qur'an. The objective of the current chapter, therefore, is to examine the perspectives of the Muslim mystics and explore the meaning of *balā* in a more didactic manner. To achieve this objective, the universal definition of the term "mysticism" and its various connotations will be discussed first, followed by an overview of the mystical tradition of Islam with special attention to the distinctions between the terms "Sufi" and "Muslim mystic". Subsequently, by employing a critical analysis approach – as a tool in the form of deconstructionist method – the all-inclusive meaning of *balā* portrayed in the Qur'an and its implications with respect to trial in the context of Adam and his "fall", trial as means of self-knowledge, self-purification and God-awareness, and trial in suffering, will be discussed in light of the teachings of a Muslim mystic representative.

What is "Mysticism"?

"Mysticism" is a difficult term because historically it has been utilized to identify a broad spectrum of practices and experiences across various cultures; therefore, providing an all-inclusive definition which can signify its true meaning is a challenging task. The difficulty arises from the "mysterious" element embedded in the term "mysticism" which carries certain ambiguity and implies imprecise thinking or vagueness. W.T. Stace calls the term an "unfortunate" word as it suggests something of a secretive nature, confused and uncertainty, miracle mongering, and claims "it would be better if we could use the word "enlightenment" or "illumination" which are used in India for the same phenomenon; but it seems that for historical reasons we in the West must settle for mysticism".[1] The entrenched mysterious feature of the term is understood from its Greek root *muein* "to remain silent"; but later the "mystical silence came to mean wordless contemplation".[2] Moreover, the etymological lineage of the word shows its usage in Christianity first to signify the hidden meanings of the scripture, but later developed to include the Greek connotations of silence and secrecy, and eventually "the formulation of the modern usage of a state of consciousness that surpasses ordinary experience through the union with a transcendent reality".[3] According to Evelyn Underhill, mysticism is "the science or art of the spiritual life" and may be defined as:

> Broadly speaking, I understand it to be the expression of the innate tendency of the human spirit towards complete harmony with the transcendental order; whatever be the theological formula under which that order is understood. This tendency, in great mystics, gradually captures the whole field of consciousness; it dominates their life, and in the experience called "mystic union", attains its end. Whether that end be called the God of Christianity, the World soul of Pantheism, the Absolute of Philosophy, the desire to attain it and the movement towards it - so long as this is a genuine life process and not an intellectual speculation - is the proper subject of mysticism. This movement represents the true line of development of the highest form of human consciousness.[4]

Although Underhill's elucidation provides an overall definition of mysticism, the means by which an experience may be justified as a "mystical experience" must still be clarified.

As Dupré observes, the commentators are not in agreement regarding the characteristics of the mystical experience; however, William James's description is extensively accepted.[5] In James's opinion, the word "mystical" is often used to convey a mere approach which is thrown at any unclear and sentimental attitude; therefore, in an attempt to restrict its usage, he suggests four characteristics which, when they occur, may be called "mystical experience".[6] According to James, the four marks of an authentic mystical experience are: *Ineffability*, which underscores the secretive and incommunicableness of the experience and that "no adequate report of its contents can be given in words"[7]; *Noetic* quality, which emphasizes the fact that mystical states are states of knowledge; "they are states of insight into depths of truth unplumbed by the discursive intellect"[8]; the *Transiency* characteristic indicating that, for the most part, the duration of the mystical states tends to be short and not sustainable for a long period; and finally the *Passivity* of the mystical experience emphasizes that while the subject may have been engaged in certain meditative techniques, "once the characteristic sort of consciousness has set in, the mystic feels as if his own will were in abeyance, and indeed sometimes as if he were grasped and held by a superior power".[9] James is also of the opinion that to overcome all barriers between the individual and the Absolute and to become aware of the oneness with that Absolute is the common nature of all religious experiences that is "hardly altered by differences of clime or creed".[10]

This concept of the intrinsic tendency of the human soul which, according to Underhill, yearns to be in complete harmony with the transcendental element of the cosmos, the Reality or Absolute as the source of the universe, and awareness of the oneness with that Reality, by means of reaching a higher level of consciousness, which is described by James as authentic mystical states, is therefore the primary concern of mysticism. The foundation of mysticism, then, is grounded in the fact that human beings - mortal as they are and limited as they may be in their comprehension of that Reality – have the potential, due to the divine element of their inner nature, to see past the surface of things to understand the reality beneath. Hence, it is a common theme for all religions.

The review of various religious traditions demonstrates that, although the traditions which are based on a revealed scripture are presented in a formal structure or exoteric framework which emphasizes the practice of the religious Law; nonetheless, within the context of that structure, esoteric doctrines eventually develop to engage with the essence or inward meaning of those practices. Esotericism, therefore, is that mystical or inward element of the religion which breaks through the forms and offers the most comprehensive range of spiritual prospects.[11] Hence, in the words of Schuon, for the science of religions, esoterism comes after dogma and, at times, may be considered an artificial development which may have been influenced from foreign sources.[12] On the other hand, it should be noted that it is the "development" of the esoteric doctrine which comes later as the erudite component is intrinsic in the nature of religion itself. Consequently, Schuon emphasizes that "the sapiential element must precede the exoteric formulation since it is the former which, being a metaphysical perspective, determines the form; without a metaphysical foundation there can be no religion."[13]

That the esoteric dimension is an eternal wisdom which is shared across various religious traditions and cultures, is shown by the study of perennial philosophy.[14] The perennialist scholars shed light on the fact that the world's religions – diverse as they may be – share a transcendental feature which makes it plausible to overcome religious differences. Yet, according to Schuon, while there is a transcendent unity between all religions, true unity pertains only at the esoteric level; that with God at the apex, there is a horizontal line dividing esoteric and exoteric dimensions of all religions: divergence exists below the line, the exoteric level, with convergence above the line, the esoteric level.[15] Additionally, it may be stated that although the mystical aspect of the world's traditions share a deep affinity, nonetheless, distinctions do exist in the way by which the practitioners of each tradition approach the mystical world, a point which is discussed by Rudolph Otto in his comparative analysis of mysticism in the context of the eastern and western traditions.[16]

Considering the ambiguous nature of the topic under discussion, how then, may human beings discover and nourish their spiritual potential and tendencies to become in tune with transcendent reality? As Huxley observes, "the nature of this one reality is such that it cannot be directly and immediately apprehended except by those who have chosen to fulfill certain conditions, making themselves loving, pure in heart and poor in spirit".[17] To meet the conditions mentioned by Huxley, the human consciousness must be elevated to a higher state of consciousness which is achievable only in certain types of personalities. The mystics, therefore, are those whose character has been, through certain practices and attainment of higher knowledge, developed to search for that truth or reality which is the fountainhead of the universe. Driven by this passionate quest, the goal of the mystics, then, is to "establish communication with that only reality, that immaterial and final Being, which some philosophers call the Absolute, and some theologians call God."[18]

In concluding the above brief discussion as it relates to mysticism and esotericism, Stoddert's observation may be pointed out: "terminologically one may regard esoterism and mysticism as synonymous; mysticism is known to be the inward or spiritual dimension within every religion and this is precisely what esoterism is."[19] Therefore, religious mysticism[20]– in the case of "revealed" religions– is the esoteric dimension of the religion which flourishes from its own tradition to which is inseparably attached, sheds light on the total "truth" of the exoteric framework, and paves the way for journeying towards God and realization of the Divine Presence.

Muslim Mysticism

Historically, the mystical dimension of Islam is presented through Sufism, a branch of Muslim thought which deals with the esoteric understanding of the teachings of the religion, and is systemically structured in what may be called "Sufi practices and rituals".

The word Sufism is the translation of the Arabic word *taṣawwuf* which refers to the action of being a *Sufi*, and encompasses two possible meanings: the first signifies purification and is derived from *ṣūfiya* "it was purified", while the other is derived from the word *ṣuf* "wool" to denote wearing a wool garment as a sign of spiritual poverty (*faqr*).[21] The development of Sufism may be traced back to a century or two after Prophet Muhammad's death as the sincere practice of Islam's original teachings and the simple life style of the Prophet gave way to the extravagant and luxurious life style of the caliphs, and the original practices of Islam seemed to have been reduced to the letter of its law or the exoteric framework.[22] Consequently, those disturbed by the worldliness that had captured Islam "sought to purify it from within, recover its liberty and love, and restore to its deeper, mystical tone...externals should yield to internals, matter to meaning, outward symbol to inner reality."[23] That Islam encompasses both external (*ẓāhir*) and inner (*bāṭin*) aspects, is understood from the Qur'an (57:3), therein God is presented as both the Outward (*al-ẓāhir*) and the Inward (*al-bāṭin*); hence, the rationale for a profound spiritual understanding of the cosmos.

Sufism, while it adheres to fulfillment of the laws of Islam (*ẓāhir*), nevertheless, emphasizes the more in-depth meanings of those practices (*bāṭin*), and motivates direct contemplation of the Divine. Although the early Sufis were simply ascetics, by third century (ninth century C.E.) asceticism was regarded only as the first requirement of this spiritual journey, and other methods and practices deemed indispensable. As a result, a systematic approach was developed whereby, under the guidance of a spiritual master (*sheikh*), Sufis assumed heavier disciplines that proved instrumental as the aspirant – with God's grace – strived in their spiritual quest, and climbed the ladder to achieve direct knowledge of God. As Sufi orders (*silsilah*) were established, these particular practices and disciplines became part and parcel of the Sufi "path". Although there are variations of Sufi practices as defined by different Sufi orders, according to Nicholson, however, the oldest Sufi treaties mention the following seven stages: repentance, abstinence, renunciation, poverty, patience, trust in God, and satisfaction.[24] The seeker must cross all the stages and any other state which may have been bestowed onto him by God before he is "permanently raised to the higher place of consciousness which Sufis call "the Gnosis" (*ma'rifat*), where the seeker (*tālib*) becomes the "knower" or "gnostic" (*'ārif*), and realizes that knowledge, knower, and known are One."[25] Hence, the doctrine of Divine Unity (*tawḥīd*) – the solid essential of Islam which according to the Islamic Law (*sharī'ah*) all Muslims affirm– is now realized by the Sufi.

In summary, the Sufi doctrine and method of exploring the spiritual realities of the universe is based on the Qur'an and the *Sunna* of the Prophet, and is manifested through double folded aspects of the teachings of Islam: the exoteric framework (*sharī'ah*); and the esoteric path (*tarīqah*). Through certain practices and under the guidance of a spiritual master, the aspirant will journey through various stations on the Sufi path, and ultimately reach the state of the Divine presence, that hidden treasure (*ḥaqīqah*), which is not obtainable by those who concern themselves only with the dogmatic formulations of Islam.[26]

As mentioned previously, the mystical dimension of Islam is primarily represented through Sufism; however, as Geoffroy points out, it must be emphasized that "not all Islamic spirituality and esotericism is represented by Sufism."[27] Considering the fact that the core principles of both Sunnite and Shi'ite traditions of Islam emerge from the fundamental sources of the religion – Qur'an and *Sunna* of the Prophet – it is not surprising that both traditions engage and expound upon esoteric wisdoms. According to Nasr, "'Alī, who is the representative par excellence of Islamic esoteric teachings, is not only the first Imām of Shī'ism, but also at the origin of the initiatic chain of nearly all Sufi orders."[28] It should also be noted that the first eight Shī'ite Imāms are highly regarded as central spiritual authorities or poles of Sufism.[29] Furthermore, it must be noted that the term "Muslim mystic" is a comprehensive term encompassing all those who have engaged with the esoteric dimension of Islam; hence, while every Sufi may be called a mystic, every mystic is not a Sufi.[30]

The following section aims at introducing the Muslim mystic representative whose teachings, relating to the all-inclusive meaning of *balā*, will be investigated. However, it may prove beneficial to first restate what has already been established: the framework of this study is centered on the Qur'anic narratives relating to the notion of Divine Trial (*balā*); while the major commentaries of the Qur'an provide a general understanding of this concept, by and large, the classical exegetical literature seem to present a clear deficiency when it comes to an all-encompassing engagement with the topic. Alternatively, the mystical and Sufi literatures seem to engage with the concept of *balā* in all its dimensions, and offer a deeper understanding which concurs with the importance of this concept presented in the Qur'an. However, in order to shed light on the esoteric understanding of the concept of *balā*, clearly, an exhaustive scrutiny of all major works in the field of Muslim mysticism is not conceivable. Therefore, to represent the views of the mystics of Islam on *balā*, the teachings of one of the most influential Muslim mystics and Sufi, namely, Jalāl al-Dīn Rūmī, will be studied, and particular attention will be paid to his *magnum opus*, the *Mathnawī*, which may be considered an esoteric commentary to the Qur'an.

Jalāl al-Dīn Rūmī: A Brief Historical Background

Jalāl al-Dīn Rūmī was born in Balkh – in the Persian province of Khorāsān, present day Afghanistan – in the year 604 A.H. / 1207 A.D.[31] His father, Bahā'Walad, was a well-respected jurisprudent and Sufi. His adherence to the more esoteric dimensions of Islam gained him popularity and put him in conflict with some of the more legalistic minded intellectuals of his time. According to Este'alāmī, Bahā'Walad's book of the *Ma'ārif* (Divine Science) demonstrates the depth of his devotion to Sufism which clearly was not tolerated by some of his contemporaries including Fakhr al-Din Rāzī, the well-known theologian and Qur'anic commentator who also lived in Balkh.[32] As this hostile situation escalated and in anticipation of the attack by Mongol army, Bahā'Walad, his family, and many of his followers left Balkh to make the pilgrimage to Mecca. During this journey, they visited

Nīshāpūr and were received by ʿAttār, the prominent Persian poet and Sufi master who recognized Rumi's exceptional intellectual ability at the age of thirteen. Attār presented the young boy with his book of *Asrārnāmeh* (The Book of Mysteries), telling his father, "Your son will soon light a fire to the souls of God's lovers".[33] Upon completion of the pilgrimage, BahāʾWalad set out for Asia Minor, decided to settle in Konya (present day Turkey) where he was admitted among the highest ranked scholars, and given the title of *Sulṭān al-ʿulamā*, "Sultan of the men of knowledge."[34]

Under the guidance of his father and at a relatively young age, Rumi started to learn the various exoteric aspects of the religion of Islam, and soon became proficient in the Qurʾan and *Hadith* studies: jurisprudence, philosophy, and theology. According to Humāʾī, at the time of his father's death, the twenty-five year-old Rumi not only was familiar with spiritual teachings of Sufism, but also had established himself amongst the highest jurisprudents of the Ḥanafi law school; thus, he was asked to assume the responsibilities of his father.[35] Rumi's acquaintance with Sufism was elevated to mastery level after he took formal training under Burhān al-Dīn Tirmidhī, one of the most distinguished Sufi masters of the time, and a disciple of Rumi's father. At the age of thirty-nine, Rumi was a well accomplished Sufi master who had gained widespread recognition in both exoteric and esoteric dimensions of Islam, and continued to educate the students of the spiritual path as well as the traditional students of religious sciences.[36]

It is the third period of Rumi's life – from the age of thirty-nine to sixty-eight – that has attracted the attention of many scholars in the field of Muslim mysticism. A mysterious personage by the name of Shams al-Dīn Tabrīzī, generally referred to as Shams, suddenly appeared in Konya in the year of 642/1244, and Rumi was transformed. In the words of Zarrinkub, the short visit between Rumi and Shams marks the beginning of a new experience for Rumi; its lasting influence is manifested in Rumi's outward behavior, where this serious jurisprudent and charismatic Sufi master unexpectedly became a poet who was intoxicated with Divine Love.[37] As a result of his companionship with Shams, Rumi realized that his preoccupation with his selfhood, all of his accomplishments, was preventing him from reaching the top of the spiritual ladder; that in order to make room for the love of the Beloved, he needed to detach from all his attachments. In Soroush's view, Shams strengthened Rumi's will power, to find the courage to risk losing it all in the hope of attaining the One, an enormous undertaking which, without any reservation, Rumi accepted and succeeded in; its fruitful outcome was the religious experience: union with God.[38] From this point on, Rumi's religious knowledge – including theology and philosophy – was expressed through poetry and music "*samāʿ*", as they proved to be his preferred form of expression and perhaps, the key to his universal appeal. According to Shafiei Kadkani, Rumi is considered one of the greatest intellectuals of the world, whose widespread influence is largely due to his mystical interpretation of some of the most difficult theological concepts expressed in a poetic and inspirational language.[39]

Rumi's overall worldview and his mystical elucidations of various concepts, within the context of Muslim tradition, are presented in his works: *Dīwān-i Shams-i Tabrīzī* (Collected Poems), *Mathnawī* (Couplets), *Fīhi mā fīhi* (Discourses), *Majālis-i sab'ah* (The Seven Sessions), and *Makātīb* (Letters). However, as Halabī observes, *Dīwān* and *Mathnawī* are considered as Rumi's major works.[40] Moreover, in Zamāni's opinion, *Mathnawī* is ranked as one the most influential mystical literary works in the world.[41] In order to shed light on Rumi's teachings as it relates to an all-inclusive meaning of the Qur'anic notion of Divine trial "*balā*", all of his work will be examined; however, for the reasons that will be explained below, this study is particularly concerned with the teachings of Rumi's *magnum opus*, the *Mathnawī*.

Allusion has already been made to the fact that Rumi was considered amongst the highest ranked Muslim scholars of his time, a major authority in Islamic law, and served as a prominent teacher for most of his life. It is not surprising, therefore, that many of the Qur'anic teachings and Prophetic traditions become visible in all of Rumi's works. However, according to Zarrinkub, the comprehensive representation of various themes of the Qur'an, and Rumi's mystical interpretation of its narratives, is mostly visible in the *Mathnawī*.[42] In support of this notion, Ighbāl argues: "*Mathnawī* was hailed as a unique revelation of esoteric truth long before Jāmī called it 'the Qur'an in Persian', and said of the poet, 'though he is not a Prophet, he has a Book'."[43]

In Zarrinkub's opinion, there is no doubt that much of Rumi's teachings presented in *Mathnawī* are heavily influenced by the Qur'an, and clearly indicate the significance of the Qur'an in shaping Rumi's overall worldview, as well as his mystical outlook.[44] Zarrinkub further concludes that understanding the *Mathnawī* is not possible without constant help from the Qur'an; likewise, a deeper analysis of many of the Qur'anic concepts becomes possible through *Mathnawī*. Therefore, for Zarrinkub, *Mathnawī* is considered an esoteric commentary of the Qur'an, which illustrates Rumi's deep understanding of some of the most difficult epistemological concepts of the revealed text.[45] Khoramshāhī also supports this notion and states that, while *Mathnawī* may not appear in the list of the formal Qur'anic exegesis, nevertheless its content sheds light on much of the hidden and mystical truth of the Qur'an; therefore, he argues, identifying it as a gnostic Qur'anic commentary is well justified.[46]

Reaffirming the overall importance of *balā*, Divine trial, and its various connotations discussed in the typology chapter, in the Qur'an; and by drawing particular attention to the narratives where *balā* is portrayed as the central pillar in the creation of the universe, Rumi's teachings will now be examined to investigate how the concept of *balā* may be understood from his mystical perspective. To achieve this objective, several key Qur'anic themes pertaining to mankind's creation, as well as the purpose of his life on earth, which seem to implicitly relate to the all-inclusive meaning of *balā*, will be studied. Accordingly, the Qur'anic concepts such as: the "purpose" of man's creation and how this purpose may be "actualized", man's awareness and acknowledgment of both the mission and the "challenges", and finally, man's salvation and the return to his original Source will be examined, and their connections to the notion of *balā* will be emphasized in light of Rumi's teachings.

God and the Cosmos

From the Sufi perspective in general, and Rumi's world view in particular, the Universe and the multiplicity of forms that appear in it, is the product of God's Acts (*af'āl*), and His Acts are the manifestation of the Divine Names (*asmā'*) and Attributes (*sifāt*).[47] This understanding, of course, is in accordance with the Qur'anic teachings where God is made known through His creation and frequently invites man to contemplate on His signs (*āyāt*): *"The night, the day, the sun, the moon, are only a few of His signs."* (Q. 41:37). According to Rahman, while the Qur'an includes voluminous references to creation of the world and ways by which God is revealed through His Names and Attributes, God's essence (*dhāt*), however, is not a topic of discussion in the Qur'an.[48] This debate, nevertheless, is a major discussion in the field of Muslim theology where God's Essence, Attributes, and Acts appear as concepts of primary concern for the Muslim thinkers.[49] However, as Schimmel points out, Rumi does not engage in theological questions as they relate to God's essence (*dhāt*), and is primarily concerned with God as the Creator who never ceases His creative process.[50] To this end, Rumi seems to have followed the prophetic tradition where the Prophet advises the community to engage in conversations about God's creation, yet prohibits them from seeking to investigate the essence of God.[51]

Expounding upon the importance of Divine Names and Attributes in the creation of the Cosmos, Rumi draws a strong distinction between "form" (*sūrat*) and "meaning" (*ma'nā*), and reminds his audience that while there are tremendous multiplicities in this world, they are all manifestations of the One:

> Know that the world of created beings is like pure and limpid water in which the attributes of the Almighty are shining.
> The whole sum of pictured forms is a mere reflection in the water of the river: when you rub your eye, (you will perceive that) all of them are really He.[52]

Having established the fact that everything in the universe points to the One Reality- the Creator and Sustainer – Rumi, then, attempts to answer man's existential question: what was God's purpose for creating the world? The answer to this question, Rumi informs us, is in the famous "sacred" *hadith* (*hadith ghodsi*) where God said: "I was a Hidden Treasure, I wanted to be known; thus, I created the world that I might be known".[53] According to Chittick, for Rumi, the goal of the creation is to make God manifest.[54] The result of which is an increase in the effects of His Attributes which is how His Acts may become visible.

The creation of these creatures of the world is for the purpose of manifestation, to the end that the treasure of Divine providences many not remain hidden.[55]
God was not increased by bringing the world into existence: that which He was not formerly He has not become now.
But the effect (phenomenal being) was increased by bringing created things into existence; there is a great difference between these two increases.
The increase of the effect is His manifestation, in order that His attributes and action may be made visible.[56]

From the Rumian perspective, man is the fruit of the Creation and plays a profound role in the manifestation of the Divine Attributes. To emphasize the significance of man as God's final created being, Rumi employs an analogy – as it is the case with many other themes of *Mathnawī* – of tree and its fruit: the only reason that the gardener plants a tree is for the sake of the fruit. Since man is the goal of creation, the fruit of the tree, he is the last creature that comes into existence; yet, in reality, he is the first.[57] Therefore, if the Qur'anic narrative where *balā* is stated as the reason for the creation, to test man,[58] is viewed from Rumi's point of view – that the goal of the creation is to manifest God and man is the fruit of the creational tree – it becomes clear that Rumi is referring implicitly to the positive aspects of Divine trial outlined in the typology.

That man's ultimate responsibility is to live according to the potentials of his inner-nature, capable of fully manifesting the Divine attributes, and yet, realize that the key element in actualization of these potentials is his "free volition and choice" may be understood from numerous verses of *Mathnawī*, as well as other works of Rumi. This inclusive understanding of *balā*: seeing all aspects of life as trials and tests and means by which man is able to overcome those challenges to best fulfill his mission, and man's intrinsic capability of free will, with its initial manifestation in the story of Adam and the fall, is what the following sections of this chapter will investigate.

Creation of Adam: The "Fall" as Context for Divine Trial

The creation of Adam and the "fall" appears in several Qur'anic accounts; however, the following two accounts seem to represent a comprehensive description which provides the context for discussing Rumi's teachings:

[Prophet], when your Lord told the angels, "I am putting a vicegerent on earth," they said, "How can You [Lord] put someone there who will cause damage and bloodshed, when we celebrate Your praise and proclaim Your holiness?" but He said, "I know things you do not". He taught Adam all the names [of things], then He showed them to the angels and said, "Tell me the names of these if you truly [think you can]." They [the angels] said, "May You be glorified! We have knowledge only of

what You have taught us. You are the All Knowing and All Wise." Then He said,
"Adam, tell them the names of these." When he told them their names, God said,
"Did I not tell you that I know what is hidden in the heaven and the earth, and
that I know what you reveal and what you conceal?" When We told the angels,
"Bow down before Adam," they all bowed. But not Iblis, who refused and was
arrogant: he was disobedient. We said, "Adam, live with your wife in this garden.
Both of you eat freely there as you will, but do not go near this tree, or you will both
become wrongdoers." But Satan made them slip, and removed them from the state
they were in. We said, "Get out, all of you! You are each other's enemy. On earth you
will have a place to stay and livelihood for a time." Then Adam received some words
from his Lord and He accepted his repentance: He is the Ever Relenting, the Most
Merciful (Q. 2:30-37).

Your Lord said to the angels, "I will create a man from clay. When I have shaped him
and breathed from My Spirit into him, bow down before him." The angels all bowed
down together, but not Iblis, who was too proud. He became a rebel. God said, "Iblis,
what prevents you from bowing down to the man I have created with My own
hands? Are you too high and mighty?" Iblis said, "I am better than him: You made
me from fire, and him from clay" (Q. 38:70-76).

As it may be observed from Sufi literature, the mystics of Islam have extensively taken advantage of the rich symbolism which is illustrated in the Qur'anic story of Adam. Concepts such as God created Adam with "His hands"[59], breathed from His Spirit into him, and taught him the Names; Iblis's arrogant behavior and disobedience, along with his seductive role in misleading Adam; and freedom of choice exercised by Adam to eat the forbidden fruit which resulted in the fall are reflected in various parts of *Mathnawī*, and seem to appear at the core of Rumi's thought. According to Chittick, familiarity with these Qur'anic allusions, particularly the statement that Adam was "taught the Names", provides a sound foundation for many of Rumi's teachings concerning man's original state and his life on earth.[60] According to Rumi, Adam – the prototype of humankind in the state of spiritual perfection – became the mirror for God's Attributes by virtue of his knowledge of the Names. The Qur'anic commentaries provide a number of interpretations to explain what exactly the "knowledge of the names" corresponds to, such as the names of the plants, animals, mountains, and the like.[61] However, in Zamāni's view, for Rumi, the knowledge of the names does not pertain to the outward letters which identify things; but, rather, to the truth and reality of the mysteries of the Creation.[62] Therefore, for Rumi, the potential, creative ability, and power of imagination, which guide man to understand the endless possibilities of God's creation, are what make man the master over all created things.

The critical question, then, is why the news of creating Adam as God's vicegerent (*khalīfa*), with this high-ranking spiritual state, was not received well by the angels at first and later was totally rejected by Iblis? For Rumi, the initial reaction of the angels, and Iblis's disobedience rooted in pride and envy, was due to inability to distinguish between "form" (*ṣūrat*) and "meaning" (*maʿnā*). The angels, Rumi points out, were concerned with the material with which Adam was created and his outer appearance, and not the potential hidden in his inner-nature. Consequently, he repeatedly comments on this life-long trial, and encourages people to see meaning beyond forms:

> In an Adam who was without like or equal, the eye of Iblis discerned, naught but a piece of clay.
> He that regarded Adam as a body fled, while he that regarded him as the trusty Light, bowed.
> Bandage your Satanic eye for one moment: how long, pray, will regard the external form? How long, how long?[63]

This differentiation between "form" (*ṣūrat*) and "meaning" (*maʿnā*) which, according to Zarrinkub, is a fundamental theme in Rumi's thought, becomes clearly identified in the comparison analysis between the universe and man[64]. In this mystical worldview, while man appears to be a being among other beings in the universe, in actuality, the universe is in man; hence, Rumi says: "Therefore in form thou art the microcosm, in reality thou art the macrocosm."[65] It may be noted that while Rumi does not mention a particular Qur'anic verse about the similarities of man and the universe, nonetheless, that man and the cosmos are means by which God reveals the hidden treasure may be understood from the following narrative: *"We shall show them Our signs on the far horizons and in themselves, until it becomes clear to them that this is the Truth"* (Q. 41:53).

Furthermore, it may be argued that Rumi's description of man as the macrocosm in "meaning" seems to allude to the significance of the Qur'anic notion of Divine trials discussed in the typology. Once again, drawing attention to the Qur'anic narrative stating that the purpose of the creation is to provide an "acting stage" for man as he faces the challenges of his life (*balā*); the question is: what is this unique characteristic of man which not only distinguishes him from all other beings, but more importantly, makes him the goal of creation, and in Rumi's vision, the macrocosm? Furthermore, what is the relationship between that exceptional attribute of man with the notion of *balā* which the Qur'an refers to as the purpose for the creation of the cosmos? It is in light of this inquiry – and the lack of engagement with it in the exegetical works – that Rumi's teachings will be examined for the remainder of this section.[66]

As is true with many aspects of Rumi's mysticism, the origins of what makes man the macrocosm in his view, seem to be rooted in the Qur'an. The following three Qur'anic concepts – man is created as God's vicegerent (*khalīfa*); the *Alast* (pre-existence) covenant between God and man; and man as the accepter of God's Trust (*amāna*) – are noticeable not only in *Mathnawī*, but also in *Fīhi mā fīhi* and the *Dīwān*. As Zarrinkub observes, the relationship between the *Alast* covenant - which according to the Qur'an every member of human community has acknowledged – and the fact that man accepted the divine offer to carry the Trust (*amāna*), is vital to an in-depth understanding of why man, in Rumi's view, is the macrocosm.[67] The Qur'anic account relating to man as the divinely assigned vicegerent on earth appears in 2:30 and has already been cited above; the narratives concerning the *Alast* covenant and the Trust, appear once in the Qur'an and are as follows, respectively:

> *When your Lord took out the offspring from the loins of the Children of Adam and made them bear witness about themselves, He said, "Am I not your Lord?" and they replied, "Yes, we bear witness." So you cannot say on the Day of Resurrection, "We were not aware of this"* (Q. 7:172-3).
>
> *We offered the Trust to the heavens, the earth, and the mountains, yet they refused to undertake it and were afraid of it; mankind undertook it – they have always been very inept and rash* (Q. 33:72).

Prior to shedding light on Rumi's viewpoint as it relates to these three concepts and their connection to *balā*, two critical questions must be answered: when, or in what state did man entered into the covenant with God? And, what exactly is the Trust? There seems to be convergence amongst Muslim scholars concerning the *alast* agreement: the symbolic contract was signed when man was in proximity with God, and not yet been created in his form or physical being, man's state in "pre-existence"[68]. With reference to *amāna*, nonetheless, the classical Muslim exegetes have offered diverse interpretations such as adherence to religious duties as set forth by Islamic law, the intellect, belief in the Oneness of God, and knowing God.[69]

From the Rumian perspective, as Zarrinkub asserts, the central element in man's creation that makes him the perfect mirror, capable of manifesting the Divine Names and Attributes, is the ability of "free will" which is divinely embedded in man's inner-nature, and is what the Qur'an calls *amāna*, the Trust.[70] According to Humā'ī, contrary to the Ash'arite school of thought which believed human acts are predestined, Rumi is of the opinion that man has been granted free will.[71] However, as Schimmel points out, Rumi was not interested in the mere speculations of this theological issue, but rather, that its importance rested upon the practical implications of free will in everyday life.[72] As for Rumi, the fulfilment of the viceregal role – which in its most complete form is probable by the prophets and the saints – is conceivable only if man is able to exercise free will, for man to choose to become *muslim*. Rumi's interpretation seems to be supported by Rahman when he affirms that, according to the Qur'anic message: "The fundamental difference between man and the nature is that whereas natural command disallows disobedience, commands to man presuppose a choice and free volition on his part."[73] Nevertheless, making this "choice" is contingent upon man's awareness of the Divine, both within himself, and his surroundings. As Zarrinkub notes, for Rumi, man's inner quest in seeking God, and the desire to get to know Him, is initiated by God's love enabling man to make the "choice".[74] It is in light of this interconnectivity – and in accordance with the Sufi interpretation of the Trust – that occasionally Rumi refers to *amāna* as knowledge of God (*ma'rifat*).[75]

The two interpretations of the meaning of the Trust (free will and knowledge), therefore, may appear as a contradiction within Rumi's vision. However, as Zarrinkub points out, it seems justifiable to regard each meaning in relation to the other where, as a result of this complementary role, a more in-depth understanding is brought to light.[76] Hence, one may argue that this gnostic knowledge not only appears to be in close association with free will, but in fact, seems to flourish as a result of it. In other words, it is through his intrinsic ability of free will (*ikhtiār*) that man encounters life's challenges, Divine tests and trials, *balā*. It is through his choices, and how he responds to various circumstances of life, both good and bad, as well as the level of commitment in his spiritual development, that man's knowledge of the Divine grows and becomes fruitful. When seen from this perspective, it becomes clear that Rumi is implicitly referring to the instrumentality of the notion of *balā* and its various positive connotations outlined in the typology. As for Rumi, this divinely inspired gnostic knowledge with the attraction of God's love at its center, and the responsibility of free will, is the burden that no other creature has the potential to choose to accept and succeed in its fulfillment.[77] According to Furūzānfar, in Rumi's view, humans have been bestowed with the ability to "know" God and constantly be aware of His presence; however, how successful they are in actualization of this potential depends on the level of their yearning and effort.[78]

Finally, the *Alast* covenant revealed in Q. 7:172 – human beings testify that God is their Lord and Master (*Rabb*) – appears often in the *Mathnawī*. From the Rumian perspective, as the goal of the creation, man has agreed that his mission on earth is to display the attributes of his hidden substance i.e. God's attributes.[79] Therefore, as Chittick observes, in Rumi's vision, the primordial covenant further signifies that man accepted the Trust fully aware of responsibilities and consequences.[80] How well man remembers the covenant depends on how well he acknowledges that he is displaying the hidden treasure of God and not his own; this understanding is manifested through his actions as he is faced with various conditions of his life – good and bad. Consequently, according to Chittick, for Rumi, "the idea of the Covenant thus combines the purely metaphysical perspective of the manifestation and theophany of God's Attributes with the more religious and moral perspective of man's awareness and responsibility of his duties toward his Creator."[81] It may be argued, therefore, that Rumi's interpretation of the primordial covenant implicitly reveals the overall emphasis of the Qur'an concerning *balā* and its various aspects discussed in the typology. Moreover, Schimmel's observation seems to support one aspect of *balā*: "The Sufis have invented a beautiful pun on the human answer to this Divine address: the word *balā* 'Yes' was interpreted as meaning *balā* 'affliction.'"[82] Rumi further emphasizes that the inspiring and appealing cause for man's acceptance of the Trust – including the duties and hardships (*balā*) of serving as God's vicegerent on earth – was the sweetness of the Divine love which he had experienced during the time of "non-existence":

> The lover's ailment is separate from all other ailments; love is the astrolabe of the mysteries of God.[83]
> Love makes the sea boil like a kettle; Love crumbles the mountain like sand.
> Love cleaves the sky with a hundred clefts; Love unconscionably makes the earth to tremble.[84]

Moreover, as it can be seen from the *Dīwān*, in Rumi's vision, man freely chose to carry the *amāna* knowing that the fulfillment of this mission is made possible only through God's grace and His guidance:

> I took the Trust which heaven did not accept with the firm belief (*iʿtemād*) that Thy kindness would support me.[85]

Time and again, Rumi sheds light on man's imperative task: to see beyond his physical and material needs and realize the true meaning of his essence. It may be argued that Rumi is referring indirectly to *balā* and the Qur'anic narrative of *"everything on earth is beautified to test you"*; therefore, man should pay attention to his essence:

> Man's bodily senses are infirm, but he hath a potent nature within.
> This body resembles flint and steel, but intrinsically it is a striker of fire.[86]
> The material form of this twain – flint and steel – is vanquished by a hammer and anvil, but intrinsically they are superior to the mine of iron ores.
> Therefore Man is in appearance a derivative of the world, and intrinsically the origin of the world. Observe this![87]

As Humā'ī points out, by engaging in a comprehensive discussion relating to man's essence and his inner-nature, Rumi attempts to respond to man's most fundamental existential questions such as: where have I come from; where am I going; and what is my mission?[88] While continually reminding his audience of the purpose for man's creation and his abilities in manifesting the Names, Rumi illustrates that man's ultimate trial is to strive on the path of spiritual development so that he might best fulfill his responsibilities as God's vicegerent. In Schimmel's opinion, for Rumi, the key to unlock the mysteries of the hidden treasure in man's innermost essence is to recognize his position within the creational tree.[89] By stating the prophetic tradition that "God created Adam in His own image"[90], Rumi represents man as the perfect mirror with the ability to manifest all God's attributes:

> God created us in His image: our qualities are instructed by – are molded upon
> – His qualities.[91]
> Adam is the astrolabe of the attributes of Divine Sublimity: the nature of Adam
> is the theatre for His revelations.
> Whatever appears in Adam is the reflexion of Him, just as the moon is reflected
> in the water of the river.[92]

In other words, while the whole creation is manifestation of God's attributes and acts, man has been bestowed with the capability (the knowledge of the *asmā'*) and the choice (*amāna*) to actualize his potential, and therefore fulfill the viceregal role. In his *Fīhi ma fīhi*, Rumi directly refers to the Trust narrative, and alludes to the all-inclusive meaning of *balā*, the point that seems to be absent from the exegetical literature.[93] For Rumi, man's supreme *balā* is to be mindful of his most important task and mission on earth: strive in fulfilling the Trust by using the ability of free will "*amāna*" in ways, which is in accord with his divine essence:

> There is one thing in this world which must never be forgotten. If you were to forget everything else, but did not forget that, then there would be no cause to worry; whereas if you performed and remembered and did not forget every single thing, but forgot that one thing, then you would have done nothing whatsoever.... So man has come into this world for a particular task, and that is his purpose; if he does not perform it, then he will have done nothing. *"We offered the Trust to the heavens but they were unable to accept it"* (Q. 72:33). Consider how many tasks are performed by the heavens, whereat the human reason is bewildered...yet that one thing is not performed by them; that task is performed by man. *"And We honoured the Children of Adam"* (Q. 70:17); God did not say, "And We honoured heaven and the earth." So that task which is not performed by the heavens and the earth and the mountains is performed by man. When he performs that task, "sinfulness" and "folly" are banished from him.[94]

Restating Rumi's interpretation of the Trust as the ability of free will, with the two elements of knowledge of God and love of God, as its implementing instruments, one may note that the very first initiation of free will is symbolically illustrated in the story of Adam and further extends to the symbolic role of Iblis, insofar as man and his *balā* is concerned. Adam is the archetype of human race, and from the Rumian perspective, the fact that he followed Iblis's temptation and ate the forbidden fruit is evidence of man's ability to choose his path. For Rumi, Adam's regret validates his realization of free choice.

> He (Adam) cried, *"O Lord, we have done wrong"* (Q. 7:23), and 'Alas, that is to say, "darkness came and the way was lost."[95]

According to Lewis, Rumi is well aware of God's decree (*qazā*) in relation to the divine plan and man's destiny on earth; nonetheless, he makes a conclusive effort to demonstrate that man is free in his acts, and as such, accountable for his choices.[96]

> Our humility is evidence of necessity; our sense of guilt is evidence of free will.
> If there were not free will, what is shame? And what is this sorrow and guilty confusion and abashment?[97]

In one respect, man is free to submit to the demands of his animal-self and desires of his ego (*nafs*) – which reduces him below the animals –; on the other hand, he can choose to submit to the demands of his inner-most nature (*fitra*) which has been created in God's image– in which case he will raise above the angels. As Zarrinkub points out, both choices are considered as the two sides of the same coin: the ability of free volition (*ikhtiār*); Rumi emphasizes that submitting to the divine Will is what human beings are expected to choose.[98] In Schimmel's words, in comparison with angels who worship God in perfect obedience, man enjoys– or suffers from – the choice between obedience and rebellion.[99] It may be argued that this unique situation of man, his freedom in making choices that may or may not accord with the divine will and true to his nature, is the message of Q. 11:7, creation for the purpose of *balā*. Man's choices and how he selects the path of his life, then, are means by which his potentialities transform to actualities, which in turn is how he becomes the mirror that manifests God's Names and Attributes. Considering Rumi's view, then, the second part of Q. 11:7, "*to test which of you does best*", may be understood as: mankind is provided with the ability to best fulfill the viceroy role and manifest God's hidden treasure; yet, he is free in making that choice. As Rumi points out in his Discourses, mankind is faced with an enormous undertaking:

> The situation of man is like this. They took the feathers of an angel, and tied them to the tail of an ass, that haply the ass in the ray and society of the angel might become an angel. For it is possible that he may become of the same complexion as angel.[100]

Recapitulating Rumi's interpretation of the Qur'anic story of Adam's creation as well as narratives concerning the *Alast* covenant, the Trust, and the viceroy of God, one may conclude that every human being– in his perfect spiritual state– can become the perfect mirror in which the divine names and attributes are manifested. However, the ultimate question is: how can man achieve this goal? According to the Qur'an and, by extension, Sufi teachings, to accomplish his mission on earth, humankind must embark on the path of spiritual development to cultivate and actualize his inner potentials. The next section of this chapter will discuss the three stages of man's spiritual development as highlighted in Sufi literature: Self-knowledge (*ma'rifat al-nafs*); Self-purification (*tazkiyat al-nafs*); and God-awareness (*ma'rifat Allah*);[101] and will shed light on Rumi's teachings as it relates to these stages. The main focus of the section is to scrutinize Rumi's viewpoints as he portrays a spiritual road map to illustrate how can man best encounter the many challenges (*balā*) of his life and fulfill the viceregal role. In other words, our task is to find out: what are Rumi's guiding principles to assist man in "becoming" what he "is"?

Human Life as a Divine Trial: The Spiritual Development

Humankind's situation in this world, as described by the Qur'an and interpreted by the Muslim mystics, clearly shows that man's innermost nature is made of the best stature (*aḥsan taqwīm*); however, once separated from his divine origin and sent down to earth, he was reduced to the lowest state (*asfal sāfilīn*): *"We created man in the finest state; then reduced him to the lowest of the low; but those who believe and do good deeds will have an unfailing reward"* (Q. 95:4-6). Sufi commentator, Rashīd al-Dīn Maybudī, sheds light on the meaning of the Qur'anic term *aḥsan after taqwīm:* God created man in the perfect and most complete nature, capable of loving God and becoming the friend of God.[102] However, the actualization of these perfect possibilities of man's innermost nature can happen if he is placed on earth which is the world of natural passions and desires of the ego; hence, the state of *asfal sāfilīn.* From the Muslim mystical perspective, man who has been created in God's image, of the best stature, and then reduced to the lowest of the low, must realize that he has been separated from his divine origin for a purpose: to choose to become what he "is". In other words, man's outmost challenge or *balā* is to pay attention to his inner nature impulses, i.e. mystical quest, which poses three crucial questions: who he is, where he has come from, and where he is going. To these questions, the Qur'an explicitly replies *"...we belong to God and to Him we shall return"* (Q. 2:156). Notwithstanding the many attractions of the material world, as well as weaknesses, difficulties, and afflictions associated with the mortal life, man's supreme mission is to strive in the path of this mystical quest which ultimately leads him back to his original state. As Yasrebī points out, this spiritual journey, which is founded on the intimate relationship between man and his Lord, is a multi-dimensional process and requires man's ultimate determination and effort, sincerity, and reliance on God's assistance and Mercy.[103]

Self-knowledge (*ma'rifat al-nafs*)

The Muslim mystical literature includes a wealth of material relating to man's spiritual quest which is based on the teachings of the Qur'an and the traditions of the Prophet. This perennial mystical search is the journey of the soul from the outward to inward, from the periphery to the center, or as Rumi explains, from the form to the meaning; its apex is none other than getting to know one's self. That Self-knowledge (*ma'rifat al-nafs*) is the most significant goal of the spiritual path is affirmed by a well-known prophetic *hadith:* "He who knows himself knows his Lord" *(man 'arafa nafsah faqad 'arafa rabbah).*[104] While the major

Sufi treaties and practical manuals identify self-knowledge as the most important step in the spiritual development, clearly the depth and scope of this knowledge goes above and beyond the psychological level. As Michon observes, the human personality, the psyche, creates an incomplete entity that veils the vision of the total Reality or the Divine Self; yet, "the very existence of this veil allows, on its own level, for a seizure of the source of existence."[105] Nonetheless, through man's knowledge of his shortcomings and by making a sincere effort to eliminate whatever might be displeasing to God, the veil can be purified, making it transparent enough for God's light to shine through. Moreover, self-knowledge also has a positive aspect which enables man to recognize his virtuous qualities, to acknowledge that these virtues are originated from a divine source; therefore, he must attribute all glory to Him. Consequently, both aspects of self-knowledge will result in man's spiritual growth where he can experience a more intimate relationship with his Lord.[106]

From the Rumian perspective, the most significant step in getting to know oneself is to recognize that the self has been separated from its original Source, and further realize that this separation is the underlying cause of man's dissatisfaction – albeit his sophisticated life style and material possessions. In Zarrinkub's opinion, that Rumi's *Mathnawī* is the story of mankind longing to get reunited with his Source is understood from the first eighteen verses of the *Mathnawī*; and is further discussed in various contexts throughout the six volumes of this work.[107]

Listen to the reed how it tells a tale, complaining of separations
Saying, ever since I was parted from the reed-bed, my lament, hath caused man and woman to moan.
Everyone who is left far from his source wishes back the time when he was united with it.
The reed is the comrade of everyone who has been parted from a friend: its strains pierced our hearts.[108]

For Rumi, the reed symbolically represents mankind who has been separated from his source, and reports of the pain and suffering which he has to encounter due to this separation. Rumi asks his audience to listen to "this reed", himself, as the story he is about to share is, indeed, the story of humankind and his loneliness in this world, with trials and tribulations, as well as desires and attractions, pulling him in different directions. As Musafā points out, having understood the reality of man's situation, Rumi sketches two contrasting portraits of humankind.[109] The first portrait illustrates man in the state of *asfal sāfilīn*, an existence without a root and the slave of the material world, wondering around with no clear direction. The second portrait represents man in his original condition, the state of *aḥsan taqwīm*: peaceful and calm in the state of serenity as he is connected with the Divine, same as a drop of water in union with the ocean.[110] According to Rumi, man's ultimate trial, his *ibtilā*, is not to be deceived and distracted by the impermanent fascinations and attractions of this world, and to realize that true gratifications and contentment is achieved only by following the quest of his inner nature and striving to get re-united with his divine Source:

> We have come to know that we are not this body: beyond the body we are living through God.
> Oh, blest is he that has recognized his real essence and built for himself a palace in everlasting security.[111]

From the Rumian perspective, according to Zamāni, man has only one major predicament: knowing his self; if he is able to understand the mystery of the self, all other barriers and obstacles will be removed from his path.[112] However, the majority of people, as Rumi declares in *Fīhi mā fīhi*, dedicates their whole life searching and gaining various kinds of knowledge, and fails to recognize that lack of self-knowledge (*ma'rifat al-nafs*) is their prevalent *ibtilā*.[113] The point is also stated in the *Mathnawī*:

> He knows a hundred thousand superfluous matters connected with the various sciences, but that unjust man does not know his own soul.
> He knows the special properties of every substance, but in elucidating his own essence he is as ignorant as ....
> Thou knowest what is the value of every article of merchandise; but if thou knowest not the value of thyself, 'tis folly.
> Thou hast become acquainted with the fortunate and inauspicious stars; thou does not look to see whether thou art fortunate or unwashed (spiritually foul and ill-favoured).[114]

Rumi then reminds his audience that all other knowledge is contained in the knowledge that pertains to humankind's essence and true original state:

> This, this, is the soul of all the sciences – that thou shouldst know who thou shalt be on the Day of Judgment.
> Thou art acquainted with the fundamentals (*uṣūl*) of the religion, but look upon thine own fundamental (*aṣl*) and see whether it is good.
> Thine own fundamentals are better for thee than the two fundamentals[115], so that thou mayst know thine own fundamentals (essential nature), O great man.[116]

Moreover, for Rumi, the mission of getting to know the self is grounded in an already discussed concept, the notion of form and meaning, a theory which is the mainstay of Rumi's teachings and becomes visible in various contexts. According to Hakim, in Rumi's view, "...the transcendental self of man, which is his real and lasting essence, is uncreated and in so far as it is uncreated and real it is divine."[117] Therefore, as Chittick explains, in

Rumi's opinion, man will succeed in the attainment of self-knowledge only if he is able to see beyond his fictional individuality and understand his divine origin.[118] Additionally, so long as man remembers that the material world is but an impermanent and passing stage intended for actualization of his potentials, and so far as he does not consider this world his home, then he will prosper in this endeavor. Man's sincere efforts and struggle in search of self-knowledge (*ma'rifat al-nafs*), Rumi informs us, results in God-awareness (*ma'rifat Allah*), which is the essence of the primordial covenant, and ultimately leads him back to his original home where he belongs, untied with his *aṣl*, the Divine Source[119].

Notwithstanding the teachings of the Qur'an and the Muslim mystics which continually invite man to listen to his inner nature and set foot in the spiritual journey, man, for the most part, has not responded positively to this call and neglected the responsibility of the viceroy role. The underlying cause for man's behavior, we are told by the Qur'an and the mystics, is due to the fact that he has forgotten the purpose of his creation, which consequently attracted him to the false temptations of the mortal life. According to Nasr, "The cardinal sin in Islam is forgetfulness. It is negligence (*ghaflah*) of who we really are."[120] As Zamāni points out, in Rumi's view, due to not knowing the remarkable secrets of his own nature, man will continually search for extraordinary and astonishing things within the outer world. In other words, as a result of forgetting the high rank that God bestowed upon him, man will sell himself cheaply:

> The snake-catcher catches snakes in order to amaze the people – behold the foolishness of the people!
>
> Man is a mountain: how should he be led into temptation? How should a mountain become amazed at a snake?
>
> Wretched Man does not know himself: he has come from a high estate and fallen into lowlihood.
>
> Man has sold himself cheaply: he was satin, he has sewn himself on (become attached) to a tattered cloak.[121]

While negligence has been identified as mankind's existential problem, a substantial portion of the teachings of the Qur'an is dedicated to remind man of his true essence and to guide him to become who he is; in fact, one of the names that the Qur'an attributed to itself is "*dhikr*", "reminder". Furthermore, the exemplification of the Prophet whom the Qur'an calls the "best role model",[122] along with the mystical teachings and practice of Sufism, function to remind man of who he really is, to awaken him to see beyond his ordinary life and be attentive to his spiritual needs. According to Nasr, as a result of not knowing who he is man creates an illusory prison for himself and seeks to fulfill his needs outwardly; hence, man's utmost challenge "*balā*" is to recognize that, what he is in search of, actually resides within his soul which has its roots in the Divine Nature.[123]

Self-purification (*tazkiyat al-nafs*)

A significant amount of literature has been written by Muslim mystics to demonstrate the stages of the path to spiritual development.[124] The practical means by which man travels through the mystical journey to purify his soul is generally referred to self-purification (*tazkiyat al-nafs*). This concept is directly related to the all-inclusive meaning of Divine trial "*balā*" emphasized in the Qur'an as it illustrates the practical ways by which man's inner potentials are actualized. According to Nasr, Sufism is one such path which "removes man from his lowly state of *asfal sāfilīn* in order to reinstate him in his primordial perfection of *aḥsan taqwīm* wherein he finds within himself all that he had sought outwardly, for being united with God he is separate from nothing".[125] It may be noted, however, that while *tazkiyat al-nafs* is traditionally discussed in reference to Sufi practices; nonetheless, this spiritual journey is not exclusively limited to one being affiliated with a particular Sufi order.[126]

The notion of self-purification (*tazkiyat al-nafs*) is of primary importance for the Muslim mystics as it is considered the foundation of Muslim spirituality, means by which man becomes the perfect mirror wherein the most beautiful Names of God are manifested. As already mentioned at the beginning of the chapter, the underpinning of all essential themes relating to man's spiritual development is rooted in the Qur'an and exemplified by the Prophet; the same affirmation is true for the notion of *tazkiyat al-nafs*.

> *By the sun in its morning brightness and by the moon as it follows it, by the day as it displays the sun's glory and by the night as it covers it, by the sky and how He built it and by the earth and how He spread it, by the soul and how He formed it and inspired it [to know] its own rebellion and piety! The one who purifies his soul succeeds and the one who corrupts it fails.* (Q. 91:1-11)

Although the aforementioned narratives are the only series of the Qur'anic accounts that mention both terms of *tazkiya* and *nafs*; they are, nevertheless, of primary significance. As Picken observes, this is due to the fact that, not only these narratives reveal the nature of the soul (*nafs*), but more importantly, the possibilities of its purification or defilement.[127] Therefore, these verses implicitly point to the notion of *balā*, i.e. actualization of soul's potentials, and form the foundations of man's spiritual development. To this end, Muslim scholars, including the classical Qur'anic exegetes and the mystics, have discussed the importance of these narratives from various perspectives. The first significant point of discussion seems to be the fact that these narratives all begin by swearing of an oath which, according to the exegetes, denotes special emphasis in order to draw attention to the importance of the subject being presented.[128] That the narrative concerning the soul appears after six oaths referencing great creations such as the sun, the moon, the day, the night, the sky, the earth, and in conclusion the seventh oath relating the soul (*nafs*) further implies the significance of the final oath. Furthermore, in Bāzargān's view, this narrative states the nature of the soul and emphasizes the One who proportioned it, made it even and balanced, as well as having the capability to receive inspirations from the One.[129] It may be noted that while the narratives explicitly reveal that the subject of inspiration is soul's iniquity (*fujūr*) and its righteousness (*taqwā*), the ability to discern between right and wrong, virtuousness and immorality; nonetheless, these verses implicitly refer to the notion of Divine trial *balā* which, as discussed in the typology chapter, the Qur'an refers to as the purpose of the creation. Additionally, in Tāleghānī's opinion, the verse in discussion makes allusions to man's responsibility and accountability due to the fact that the soul has been bestowed with the ability of free will and therefore is capable of choosing one course of action over the other.[130]

The final two verses of this Qur'anic account deserve our utmost attention as they directly relate to our area of inquiry, namely, the process of spiritual progress through purification of the soul, and as such, need to be discussed prior to the examination of Rumi's teachings. The significance of these verses (Q. 91:9-11) is primarily due to the fact that they speak to the consequence or the fruit of man's informed choices. Therefore, we are told salvation (*falāh*) is achieved by "he who purifies the nafs (*zakkāhā*)"; in Picken's words: "more precisely to mean he who has caused his soul to grow, be augmented, be reformed, developed and purified has indeed attained true success, prosperity and salvation."[131] Alternatively, failure (*khāba*) is indeed the consequence for the one who selects the path of immorality and corrupts his soul (*dassāhā*) – the meaning of this verb is "to hide or conceal", implying that by choosing the path of disbelief, man will submerge his soul in his actions to the extent that his soul would be buried; hence, illustrating how the failure of human soul is instituted[132]. One may conclude, as Bāzargān points out, that these Qur'anic narratives reveal the nature of human soul and it's comparability to a seed: nurturing the planted seed will result in actualization of its potential, i.e. to become a strong and fruitful tree; similarly, neglecting its capabilities will lead to its gradual degeneration and the waste of its abilities, i.e. defeating the whole purpose of the seed's creation.[133]

Furthermore, in addition to the nature of the soul and its dual potentialities presented in the above account, the Qur'an reports of certain "qualities" and "states" of the soul which sheds light on the notion of man's spiritual development. According to Picken, from the overall portrayal of the qualities of *nafs* illustrated in the Qur'an the following features may be noted: *nafs* has desires (*hawā*) which act as emotions and drive the *nafs* to fulfill its needs such as pleasures and appetites (*shahwa*); *nafs* prefers ease over hardship and as such dislikes the burden of difficult tasks; while *nafs* has the ability to endure hardship, it tends to act impatiently at the time of adversity; *nafs* has the tendency to incline towards miserliness (*shuhh*), and that *nafs* may illustrate envy and jealousy (*hasad*), pride and arrogance (*kibr*).[134] Likewise, the *nafs* also has the potential to be described by positive counter-qualities. It may be pointed here that, once again, we are presented with an all-encompassing meaning of

Divine trial, *balā*, and the Qur'anic statement that *balā* is the purpose for the creation. For, by identifying the tendencies and numerous characteristics of human soul, as well as soul's ability to comprehend and differentiate between righteousness and immortality, the Qur'an clearly illustrates that every human being has the ability to attain good and bad deeds. In Bāzargān's words, man's ingrained abilities, inspirations, will serve as his guide; as long as he pays attention to his inner inspirations, he will actualize his potentials and ultimately find the way back to his Lord.[135]

As mentioned above, the Qur'an also reveals various states or types for the *nafs*, which are closely related to the qualities of the human soul: the inclined to evil soul (*nafs ammāra*); the self-reproaching soul (*nafs lawwāma*), and the tranquil soul (*nafs muṭma'inna*).[136] According to the Qur'an, the process of spiritual purification assumes a transformation of the soul which, depending on man's intentions and deeds, travels through three levels or degrees. The lowest state of the soul (*nafs ammāra*) which continually incites to evil to fulfill the temporal needs and desires of the human body, must gradually give way to the self-reproaching soul (*nafs lawwāma*). In this higher state, the soul begins to blame itself for its actions, regrets its past behavior, and inclines towards repentance. According to Geoffroy, as a result of this continued inner struggle, man's soul will reach its highest degree: the tranquil soul (*nafs muṭma'inna*), which is content and pleased with God, and likewise, God is pleased with the soul.[137] Consequently, from the Qur'anic perspective, man's ultimate challenge, life's ongoing trial, *balā*, is to remain cognizant of the qualities of his inner nature, and strive to move forward, through personal effort and free will, with the spiritual development of his soul. This process will ultimately lead man in a journey to "become" who he "is".

Rumi on Self-purification (*tazkiyat al-nafs*)

Keeping in mind the Qur'anic notion of Divine trial "*balā*", i.e. the underlying purpose for the cosmic creation, and its inference with the concept of *tazkiyat al-nafs*; as well as various qualities and dual potentialities of the human soul, and the significance of faculty of free will discussed previously, we will now scrutinize Rumi's teachings and highlight some of the practical guidelines that he offers in the path of self-purification. As already discussed, in Rumi's thought, humankind has been created in God's image and is the most distinguished creature of the whole Creation. However, as observed by Humā'ī, for Rumi, man's awareness of his divine nature and self-worth is the precondition for setting foot in the path of spiritual development.[138] The guiding principle in this path, Rumi reminds us, is to see beyond the surface of this world, to choose actions which accord with the essence and the true meaning of the world, and in fact, serve the purpose of man's creation. In Zarrinkub's opinion, Rumi's guidelines which are primarily in the form of inspirations– not resembling religious manuals wherein contains a list of permissible and prohibited acts for the sake of rewards and punishment of the other world– are meant to encourage the traveller to experience the sweet outcome of the spiritual path in this life.[139] In Rumi's view, man's spiritual advancement is a constant upward movement which he often articulates by the image of a journey. However, as Schimmel points out, in addition to the symbol of journey, which is also used by many other mystics, Rumi often refers to the path as the spiritual ladder or staircase; climbing every step of the ladder results in getting closer to the top, and eventually to the roof where the union between the lover and the Beloved takes place.[140]

For Rumi, similar to other Sufi masters, adherence to religious obligations and rituals of Islam as set forth in the Islamic Law (*shari'ah*) is essential for entering the spiritual path (*Tarīqah*). For, as Nasr observes, "according to a well-known Sufi symbol, Islam is like a walnut of which the shell is like the *shari'ah*, the kernel like the *Tarīqah*, and the oil which is invisible yet everywhere present, the *Ḥaqīqah*, the Truth"[141]. Therefore, the external support and the solid structure for the spiritual path of Islam is indeed the *shari'ah*, without which, the journey in the spiritual path will not be possible. According to Ashraf, from the Muslim mystical perspective, the inner meaning of the obligatory rituals of Islam is to lead man towards a closer relationship with God, to motivate him in the battle against the temptations of *nafs ammāra*, and the gradual transformation of the soul to its elevated state of tranquility.[142] As such, the required rituals, which are at the core of the *Sunna* of the Prophet, are viewed as the minimum that all Muslims are obligated to observe; yet, the spiritual development awaits those who adhere to the Substance of the Prophet. According to Schuon:

> Outwardly the Prophet is the legislator, and he can easily be grasped as such; inwardly, in his Substance, he represents esoterism at every level…a concrete and quasi-sacramental presence that prefigures the state of salvation or of deliverance and that invites one not to legality or to the social virtues but to self-transcendence and transformation – hence to extinction and to a second birth….Being a spiritual beatitude and thus a state of consciousness, the prophetic Substance remains independent of all formal conditions, even though the formal practices can be rightly considered as paths toward participation in this Substance.[143]

Consequently, the life of the Prophet, in both its external manifestations which forms the Islamic law, as well as, its inner reality which serves as the fountainhead for Islamic spirituality, is at the center of Rumi's teachings. In other words, the inclusive meaning of *balā*, the actualization of man's inner potentials is made possible through the example of the Prophet. Furthermore, as Zamāni observes, while for the Muslim mystics, including Rumi, Prophet Muhammad is the perfect role model whose state of perfection is unattainable by anyone else; there are, nonetheless, those who have followed the Prophet very closely and reached the state of sainthood.[144] These saints are able to serve as the spiritual guide, *shaykh*, a role that is crucial in the success of the mystical path. In support of this notion, Humā'ī points out that Rumi, not only discusses the importance of finding a spiritual guide, but also emphasizes total dedication and obedience to the guidelines of the *shaykh*.[145] However, according to Chittick, Rumi also warns against those who claim to be a true *shaykh* but in reality are not, and should not be followed. He further concludes that for Rumi, selecting such a person to guide the way and trusting one's spiritual advancement to him, will not only produce any success, but on the contrary, will prevent the seeker from climbing the first steps of the spiritual ladder, and may even result in much damage.[146]

Returning to our discussion about the significance of the rituals of Islam, such as daily prayer and fast of Ramadan, Rumi invites his audience to contemplate on the following suggestions: first, to pay close attention to the distinction between the form of the rituals and their inner meanings; second, he encourages the devotees not to limit themselves with what has been requested by the obligatory ritual practices, *shari'ah*, and to perform other complementary practices which are essential in the spiritual development.[147] An example of Rumi's interpretation regarding the inner dimension of the religious rites appears in *Fīhi mā fīhi*. Responding to a question from one of his disciples who asked "is there any way nearer to God than prayer?" Rumi said "Also prayer!" Then he elaborates:

> But prayer which is not merely this outward form. This is the "body" of prayer... everything which is expressed in words and sounds and has a beginning and an end is "form" and "body"; its "soul" is unconditioned and infinite, and has neither beginning nor end. Hence we realize that the 'soul' of prayer is not this form alone. Rather it is a complete absorption, a state of unconsciousness excluding and not finding room for all these outward forms.[148] Purpose of the prayer is that the spiritual state which possesses you visibly when you are at prayer should be with you always. Whether sleeping or walking, whether writing or reading, in all circumstances you should not be free from God's hand, so that "they continue at their prayers" will apply to you.[149]

It may be noted here that Rumi's interpretation of the ritual prayer stated above is rooted in the Qur'an where God's awareness is the foundation for the obligatory formal prayer. And, in fact, remembering God and constantly being aware of His presence is more significant than the actual ritual itself (Q. 29:45). Hence, as Shah-Kāzemi observes, one of the most essential practices of the mystical path of Islam and a key component in purification of the *nafs* is "remembrance of God" (*dhikr Allah*).[150] Michon supports this notion and points out, "doctrinally speaking, the *dhikr* is the becoming aware by the creature of the connection that unites him for all eternity to the Creator"[151]. Understood in this sense, both exoteric and esoteric dimensions of a religion are constructed in and around remembrance of God, *dhikr*. At the practical level *dhikr* may be viewed from within the frame of the *shari'ah* as is manifested through the obligatory ritual practices; next it is part of the virtuous practices that most dedicated Muslims perform such as reading the Qur'an; still at its highest level, it becomes a unique spiritual exercise in form of repetition and thoughtful penetration of God's most beautiful Names[152].

In Rumi's view, *dhikr* is an indispensible spiritual exercise as he clearly affirms in the following statement of *Fīhi mā fīhi*: "the remembrance of Him provides strength, feathers and wings to the bird of the spirit".[153] Moreover, throughout much of his teachings, Rumi speaks of a number of concrete and tangible benefits of the *dhikr* wherein contains the solution to some of the most difficult obstacles in the path of spiritual development. It may be argued that Rumi's interpretation of *dhikr*, when seen from the overall meaning of *balā*, seems to suggest that *dhikr* empowers man in overcoming some of the difficulties which may prevent him from realizing his inner abilities. An example of this becomes visible in his *Dīwān* where he informs us that *dhikr*, when invoked in sincerity, serves as the remedy for heedlessness, deliverance from negative and vicious thoughts, immunity from Satanic temptations, and cultivating human thought to be productive and positive:

> The cry of the ghouls is the cry of an acquaintance– an acquaintance who would lure you to perdition.
> It keeps on crying, "Oh caravan! Come towards me, here is the track and the landmarks".
> The ghoul mentions the name of each, saying "O so-and-so," in order that it may make that personage one of those who sink.
> When he reaches the spot, he sees wolves and lions, his life lost, the road far off, and the day late.
> Tell us, then, what is that ghoul's cry like? It is "I desire wealth, I desire position and renown".
> Prevent these voices from entering your heart, so that spiritual mysteries may be revealed.
> Invoke the name of God, burn the cry of the ghouls, close your narcissus-eye to this vulture.[154]

Furthermore, by nurturing and humbling the heart, *dhikr* prepares the human soul to quest for God's love and enjoy its company in various stations of the path. According to Rumi, as the seeker climbs the spiritual ladder, love for the Beloved grows deeper and intensifies to the point that he experiences His presence and unites with Him.[155] We may mention here that while remembering God is the ultimate act of worship for every Muslim, the more systematic forms of it appears to be practiced in organized Sufi gatherings. As Chittick observes, "remembrance or invocation is the central spiritual technique of Sufism, but always under the guidance of a *shaykh*, who alone can grant the disciple the right and the spiritual receptivity to invoke the Name of God in a systematic fashion"[156].

In addition to prayer and *dhikr*, Rumi makes a number of references to other practices which are considered among the first steps of the spiritual ladder, and as such, implicitly refer to the all-inclusive meaning of *balā*. These practices are essential in the process of self-purification or disciplining the *nafs* due to the fact that they target the base instincts of the *nafs*. Hence, from the Rumian perspective, in order to succeed in the battle against the sensuality of the ego, or to use the Prophetic tradition, "the greater war (*jihad*)"[157], one must reduce the amount of food intake as well as the time spent in sleep. Thus, concerning the obligatory practices of Islam, Rumi regards the fast of Ramadan the greatest pillar, and one of the best means by which the sensations of the *nafs* may be controlled.[158] As Schimmel notes, Rumi "kept the practice of fasting very strictly, even beyond the prescribed measure.., as he knew well the alchemy of hunger which the early ascetics had practiced and preached."[159] By the same token, Rumi makes numerous references to the importance of nightly vigil, a practice which he is well known for. In Rumi's view, night time provides the best opportunity for spending time alone with the Beloved:

> The Prophet said, "The night is long, so shorten it not with your sleep; the day is bright, so darken it not with your sins." The night is long for you to voice your secrets and ask your needs without the disturbance of people. When friend and enemies are not around to annoy you, you can achieve privacy and contentment. God pulls down this veil so that your acts may be protected and guarded from hypocrisy – so that they may be accomplished sincerely for Him alone. In the dark of night, the hypocrite is distinguished from the sincere believer and is disgraced. Things are hidden by night and become disgraced only by daylight. But the hypocrite is disgraced by the night.[160]

It is worth mentioning that while Rumi engages the seeker to firmly strive in the path of spirituality and contemplate on the goal of this journey, i.e. to control the sensualities of the ego and live according to the guidelines of the intellect, he nevertheless is well aware of the difficulties of the path. To this end, Rumi sheds light on a number of practices that assists the seeker in overcoming some of the obstacles. According to Humā'ī, one of the most important elements in succeeding in the path, in Rumi's view, is the companionship with other sincere friends, travellers, and the saints.[161] To Rumi, Religion is, in fact, finding and recognizing the proper companions[162] and that sitting with God, i.e. experiencing His presence, is conceivable through spending time with the saints:

> Whoever wishes to sit with God let him sit in the presence of the saints.
> If you are broken off, divided from the presence of the saints, you are in perdition, because you are a part without the whole.
> Whosoever the devil cuts off from the noble saints, he finds him without any one to help him, and devours his head.
> To go for one moment a single span apart from the community is a result of the devil's guide. Hearken, and know this well![163]

From the mystical perspective, man begins the spiritual journey by repentance (*towba*) through God's remembrance (*dhikr*); constant attentiveness to his actions (*murāqabah*); and by keeping track of his inner states (*muḥāsabah*), he will move up the spiritual ladder.[164] Moreover, according to Zamāni, concurring with this general Sufi model, Rumi emphasizes that patience (*ṣabr*), constitutes one of the most important stages of the path.[165] In Rumi's spirituality, detachment from the desires of the lower self, i.e. attractions of the material world, takes time and requires patience; a quality that eventually is build up within the soul. According to Schimmel, the significance of patience becomes visible in Rumi's spring-poems where he describes how the birds and trees are rewarded with lovely colors and aromas, after they patiently waited during the harsh times of the winter.[166] A related concept to patience is gratitude (*shukr*), which Rumi expounds upon and sheds light on its various connotations in the *Mathnawī*. From the Rumian perspective, Zamāni affirms, gratitude results in God's blessings and more favors, and leads man out of heedlessness, while ingratitude brings hopelessness and sorrow.[167] To this end Rumi writes: "ingratitude is the rule followed by the ape, while thankfulness and gratitude is the way of the Prophet."[168] In the third book of *Mathnawī*, he criticizes those who enjoy God's bounty; do not appreciate all that He has granted them; yet, they complain as soon as the slightest misery befalls them. Since the concluding section of this chapter will deal with the notion of suffering in Rumi's thought, it suffices us to reference one example here.

> Those bad-natured ones rendered no thanks for that bounty: in fidelity they were less than dogs.
> When to a dog there comes from the door a piece of bread, he will grid up his loins at the door.
> He will become the watcher and guardian of the door, even though violence and hard treatment befall him.[169]

Finally, from the Sufi perspective, an important dimension of self-purification, which is directly related to *balā* particularly in its manifestation in adversity and hardship, has to do with the concept of trust in God (*tawakkul*). Yasribī is of the opinion that *tawakkul* is considered one of the highest stages of the spiritual path; however, to reach the apex level of *tawakkul*, the seeker must remain firm and strong during trials and tribulations, "*balā*", which he faces.[170] While the Muslim mystics are in agreement with regards to the meaning of *tawakkul*, total trust in God Who is Wise, Kind, and Loving; at the practical level there seems to be some degree of divergence. As Schimmel notes, "*Tawakkul* in its interiorized sense means to realize *tawḥīd*; for it would be *shirk khafī*, 'hidden associationism', to rely upon or be afraid of any created being...resulting in perfect inner peace."[171] One of the implications of *tawakkul*, stated in the expression of *ḥusn aẓ-ẓann*, "to think well of God", was widely used in reference to daily needs such as food and clothing; to be certain that your provisions, *rizq*, will reach you. While this positive attitude with regards to total trust in God has been a source of strength, its exaggerated form, however, resulted in acceptance of a blind fate, the idea of predestination, and passivity[172]. For Rumi, God's will actualizes through and in connection with man's exertions and actions; hence, *tawakkul* is viewed as the dynamic force and the positive motivation, reassuring man that his efforts will produce results, either in this world or the hereafter. One may note that Rumi's interpretation of *tawakkul* implicitly refers to man's *ibtilā* both in its all-inclusive meaning, i.e. actualization of inner potentials, and its manifestation in adversities. As Zamāni notes, though Rumi mentions *tawakkul* in various contexts in his teachings; he fully expounds upon this topic in two stories of the *Mathnawī*.[173] In the first book, Rumi uses two animals to represent the two contrasting views: a beast as the symbol of passivity and indifference, those who are of the opinion that efforts on man's part conflicts with trust in God; and a lion to represent those who find no contradiction between their works while fully trusting in God. By reading this dialogue between the animals, the reader is left with a clear understanding of the importance of *tawakkul*, and Rumi's view on the topic: that man's efforts are indeed within the frameworks of God's Will.[174]

Furthermore, it must be mentioned that while Rumi inspires his reader to fully utilize his abilities in this spiritual journey: to get to know himself and realize the great potential of his inner nature, to commit to purification and augmentation of his soul and its transformation to tranquil level, and ultimately try to reach a close proximity with God to experience his presence; by the same token, he points out that these inspirations should not lead to overestimation of the importance of man's own efforts. For, as already discussed previously, in Rumi's view, man's biggest challenge, *ibtilā*, is to make a serious effort in detaching from all that occupies the self. Therefore, he continuously reminds the reader that, although man with his free volition embarks on this path and his aspirations (*himmat*) must remain at the highest level; yet, it is God's grace (*'ināyat*) that has granted him the aspiration in the first place. As Chittick points out, in Rumi's view, all success in the spiritual development, as well as everything that mankind owns and enjoys, is attributed to the Source and none to his own self.[175] Consequently, as it may be concluded from the above discussion, through various stages of the spiritual combat, man's struggle in self-knowledge (*ma'rifat al-nafs*), and self-purification (*tazkiyat al-nafs*) will lead to God-awareness (*ma'rifat Allah*). Through his sincere efforts and God's grace, this spiritual journey will lead to transformation of the *nafs* to its highest level of serenity, i.e. the tranquil soul. In combination of love of God, which occupies a major portion of Rumi's teachings, following this spiritual re-birth, man has become who he is. According to Chittick, for Rumi, one of the ways by which the newly born self is manifested is by fully giving up his will and asking God to do as He pleases, for man's ego, I-ness, and self-hood, no longer exists.[176] This brings us to our final analysis of Rumi's teachings and a recap to our previous discussion pertaining to the notion of free will and its relation to *ibtilā*.

Once again we will investigate Rumi's thought further as he unveils the concept of the Divine Trust (*amāna*), or free will. Rumi takes the matter to a higher level by engaging in a paradoxical discussion about free will which adds an important perspective to our understanding of the notion of _balā_. According to Rumi, prior to man being entrusted with free will, he was living in peace and harmony; however, acceptance of the divine trust, i.e. free will and the responsibility of choosing between one act over the other, caused a major disturbance to man's worry-less and serene situation. This constant predicament of having to decide between two opposite paths, with doubts and uncertainties on both sides, causes much anxiety and conflict in man's soul to the extent that he may desire not having the capability of free will. Rumi holds this situation to be the ultimate _balā_, the real test of man; the difficulty of which is the reason for the heavens and the earth not to have accepted this responsibility. Rumi, then, pleads to God not to place him in situations that he must decide between two or more choices:

> Who am I? Heaven, with its hundred mighty businesses, cried out for help against this ambush of free will; Saying, "Deliver me from this pillory of free will, O gracious and long-suffering; Lord!
> The one-way pull on _the straight Path_ is better than the two ways of perplexity, O gracious One.
> Although Thou art the entire goal of these two ways, yet indeed this duality is agonising to the spirit.
> Although the destination of these two ways is unto Thee alone, yet the battle is never like the banquet."
> This perplexity in the heart is like war: when a man is perplexed he says, "I wonder whether this is better for my case or that".
> In perplexity the fear of failure and the hope of success are always in conflict with each other, now advancing and now retreating.
> From Thee first came this ebb and flow within me; else, O gracious One, this sea of mine was still.
> From the same source whence Thou gavest me this perplexity, graciously make me un-perplexed likewise.
> Thou art affliction me…How long will this affliction continue? Do not afflict me, o Lord! Bestow on me one path; do not make me follow ten paths![177]

The above verses of the _Mathnawī_, however, as Zamāni observes, appear to be in conflict with Rumi's interpretation of the ability of free will, which is what makes man the fruit of the creation and means by which he becomes the mirror for God's attributes.[178] If according to Rumi's elucidation stated previously, free will is an indispensable component in the fulfillment of the viceroy role, then, pleading to God not to be placed in situations where free volition is put into practice seems to raise a significant inconsistency, and a paradox which needs to be dealt with.

Zamāni is of the opinion that the origin of this imaginary contradiction in Rumi's teachings may be found in his vision of the perfect man and the concept of "distinctive predestination" (*jabr khāṣṣib*) whereby man's choice is in total harmony with God's will.[179] From the Rumian perspective, while mankind is faced with the constant challenge (*balā*) of freely choosing how he spends his time on earth, nonetheless he is able to reach certain level of spiritual maturity to realize that in order to fulfill his responsibility as God's vicegerent, he must make sure his choices are in accordance with God's will. It is in this sense that Rumi engages in an intimate dialogue with God asking Him to remove the burden of free will: having to decide between the commands of his self (*nafs*) and what is pleasing to God. For, indeed, the battle between the various choices is valid when there is a separation between man and his Lord; however, in the state of union with God, man's wishes are dissolved in God's will. According to Zamāni, this level of spiritual purification is achievable by certain individuals; freely giving up freedom of choice and putting one's fate in the hands of predestination, is what Rumi calls "a unique version of predestination".[180] To this end, Rumi writes:

> I am like an emaciated camel, and my back is wounded by my free-will which resembles a pack-saddle.
> At one moment this pannier weighs heavily on this side, at another moment that pannier sags to that side.
> Let the ill-balanced load drop from me, that I may behold the meadow of the pious.[181]

Rumi on Trial and Tribulation and the Concept of Suffering

As stated in the general introduction, the central hypothesis of this study is that *ibtilā*, contrary to popular perception, is not synonymous with suffering. This notion was further discussed in the thematic typology of the Qur'anic narratives, and demonstrated that, in fact, *ibtilā* conveys a positive image, and that it is manifested in both adversity and prosperity. Therefore, in its all-inclusive connotation, *ibtilā* is the means by which mankind is granted the opportunity to actualize the potential of his inner nature. It is in accord with this understanding of *ibtilā* that the Qur'an explicitly affirms that man, as part of his human experience, will be put to the "test", *balā*, by various means of "good and bad"[182]. Consequently, the test encompasses the "negatives", illness, natural disasters, and loss of livelihood, and the "positives", wealth, and good health. What the Qur'an seems to emphasize, however, is man's behavior and how he perceives the particular circumstances of his life.[183] Needless to say that, by nature, while man strives for joy and happiness; he resists any undesirable situation which may cause him sadness and sorrow. In the words of Becker, the universal ambition of man is to strive for the highest level of prosperity and avoid anything that goes against this desire.[184] Contrary to this aspiration, however, from the Qur'anic perspective, adversity, misery, and human suffering, is central to man's spiritual development. Therefore, the concluding section of this Chapter is charged with examination of Rumi's teachings concerning the issue of adversity and suffering, as it relates to the notion of *ibtilā*.

The overall examination of the Qur'anic narratives regarding various types of adversities, as well as, suffering which may be associated with them is discussed explicitly and with clear examples. Nonetheless, as Bowker points out, these examples are indicative of the fact that the subject is not treated in the Qur'an as a "problem", or a theoretical issue, but rather as real occurrences to show that suffering is part of human experience.[185] Bowker further attests that a major portion of the Qur'anic narratives, whereby adversities and suffering is discussed, demonstrate that man's suffering is considered as a trial or test (*balā*). This notion, which frequently appears in explicit terms in the Qur'an, illustrates that suffering is an instrument in the fulfillment of purposes of God in creation of humankind. According to Bowker, it is in light of this perspective and the significance of omnipotence and compassion as characteristics of God that the Qur'an is able to uphold that, despite to what appears to be the contrary, God is in control of His creation, within which suffering is one of its components.[186] The theological aspects of Bowker's observation will be discussed in the following Chapter; for now, however, let's turn to Rumi and the mystical interpretation of suffering.

As highlighted in the preceding discussion, according to Rumi, man's ultimate mission is to realize his divine origins, and to strive on the path of spiritual development by means of self-purification. This mystical approach aims at severing attachments, which are viewed as anchoring human beings too deeply in the material world. Suffering is, therefore, a way of altering man to the need of detachment which is a notion explicitly stated in the Qur'an[187] and discussed in the teachings of the Muslim mystics. As Zamāni points out, in Rumi's view, man is in charge of his life; his priorities and main concerns in life are the result of his choices. Therefore, trials and tests "*balā*" are unique to humankind due to the fact that man is the only created being who enjoys the ability of free will. Thus, for Rumi, "*balā*" is a necessary component of man's creation.[188] Furthermore, Rumi frequently reminds his audience that because man is deeply attached to his selfhood, he is not able to understand the true situations of his life. He suffers through afflictions, yet these instances are wake up calls and beneficial to him; he occupies himself with transitory cheerfulness, even though many of them are harmful as they contribute to his state of negligence.[189] According to Chittick, in Rumi's view, "Trials and tribulations are all necessary stages of purification, through which man is delivered from attachment to himself and the world".[190] It may be noted that Rumi often refers to the trial of Prophet Joseph to demonstrate the positive consequence of *balā* and the lasting result of being set free of all attachments. According to Renard, in Rumi's view, "Joseph experienced his enslavement as a major trial, but it freed him from slavery to creatures so that he could be the slave of God alone."[191]

In his elucidation of *balā* in adversity, Rumi frequently references the primordial covenant, and points out that man is faced with afflictions and sorrow in order to be reminded of his covenant with God. For him, this is precisely the mission of the prophets:

> In order to pull us up and help us travel, messenger after messenger comes from
> that Source of existence:
> Every heartache and suffering that enters your body and heart pulls you by the
> ear to the promised Abode.
> He has afflicted you from every direction in order to pull you back to the
> Directionless.[192]

Rumi's reference to affliction of the body made in the above verse of the *Dīwān* is presented
fully in a number of his discourses in *Fīhi mā fīhi*. It can be seen from the following example
that, in Rumi's view, man has the tendency to forget God in two circumstances: in good health,
and prosperous life. Thus, health and wealth are two major objects in which *balā* is manifested:

> Between God and His servant are just two veils; and all other veils manifest out
> of thee: they are health, and wealth. The man who is well in body says, "Where
> is God? I do not know, and I do not see." As soon as pain afflicts him he begins
> to say, "O God! O God!" communing and conversing with God. So you see that
> health was his veil, and God was hidden under that pain. As much as man has
> wealth and resources, he procures the means to gratifying his desires, and is
> preoccupied night and day with that. The moment indigence appears, his ego is
> weakened and he goes round about God.[193]

Rumi's interpretation of the spiritual benefits of physical illness with regards to man's
spiritual growth is also illuminated in the teachings of Nursi and his paradoxical statement,
"For you, illness is good health". According to Michel, having experienced physical illness
first-hand, Nursi sheds light on a number of positive benefits and lessons when man is
afflicted with illness: it is a reminder of mortality without which people will continue in
their heedlessness; and that it is during the experience of sickness that people appreciate
the blessing of good health.[194] Michel further informs us that "For Nursi, sickness is a
human reality that, like all human realities, should lead the believer to God."[195] To this end,
Rumi emphasizes that if the believer's prayer in removing the hardship and suffering is not
answered by God, it is for his own benefit, to keep man in this state of nearness to God:

> God said, "It is not because he is despicable in My sight; the very deferment of
> the bounty is for the sake of helping him.
> Need caused him to turn towards Me from his forgetfulness: it dragged him by
> the hair into My presence.
> If I satisfy his need, he will go back and become absorbed in that idle play."
> Although he is now crying with all his soul, "O Thou whose protection is
> invoked", let him continue to moan with broken heart and wounded breast.
> It pleases Me to hear his voice saying, "O Lord" and his secret prayers.[196]

Furthermore, from the Qur'anic and, by extension, Rumian perspective, manifestation of *balā* in adversity has a profound impact on man's character. For if *balā* is the means by which man's inner potential becomes actualized, what is important here is man's response to a particular instance of *balā* such as in adversity and any suffering which may have been associated with it. According to Zarrinkub, in Rumi's view, when man undergoes a certain type of *balā*, his attitude, his reaction, and his action, are the testimony to his true characteristics.[197] A self-centered, egoistic person, whose purpose in life is to satisfy the desires of his animal soul, complains and questions God's justice. Conversely, a person with strong belief in the overall goodness of God's creation finds a meaning to this test, and strives to learn the spiritual lessons of the experience.[198] Moreover, according to Chittick, in Rumi's vision, "If a person tries to flee from suffering through various stratagems, he is in fact fleeing God. The only way to flee from suffering is to seek refuge from one's own ego with God."[199] Once again, it is in *Fīhi mā fīhi* that Rumi expounds upon that aspect of *balā* in which man's true character is exposed: while people may claim to hold certain qualities and traits, it is only through *balā* that the truth comes out:

> God tells us, "Just as I wanted to manifest My Treasure, so I wanted to manifest your ability to recognize that Treasure. Just as I wanted to display the Purity and Gentleness of this Ocean, so I wanted to display the high aspirations and growth through Gentleness of the fish and the creatures of the Sea". Hence they may behold their own fidelity and display their aspirations. "Do people think they will be let to say 'We believe' and that they will not be tried" (Q. 29:1-2)? Hundreds of thousands of snakes claim to be fish. Their forms are the form of fish, but their meanings are the meanings of snakes.[200]

Additionally, not only man's character is exposed through *balā*, the difficulty and the pain which accompanies *balā* is instrumental in building one's character. Rumi's view pertaining to the positive impact of *balā* in purifying the soul is evident from the following verse of the *Dīwān*:

> When someone beats a rug with a stick, he is not beating the rug– his aim is to get rid of the dust.
> Your inward is full of dust from the veil of I-ness, and that dust will not leave all at once.[201]

Furthermore, as established before, the concept of man's "separation" from his divine Source (*aṣl*) is fundamental to Rumi's thought and its importance becomes visible, once again, in his interpretation of suffering. As Chittick observes, in Rumi's view, man's major problem is his failure in realizing that adversities, pain, and suffering that he experiences in life, are meant to remind him of his separation from God, and to provide him with the opportunity to detach from his self and attain to the Self.[202] Zarrinkub also supports this notion, yet emphasizes the importance of man's submission to God's Will as a theme that is closely related to *balā* within the Rumian thought.[203] The following example illustrates Rumi's overall perspective with respect to man's worldly attachments, and the cause of his suffering:

> Consider that in spite of all of the world's bitternesses you are mortally enamoured of it and recklessly devoted to it.
> Deem bitter tribulation to be a Mercy...
> The cruelty of Time and every affliction that exists are lighter than farness from God and forgetfulness of Him,
> Because these afflictions will pass, but that forgetfulness, distance from Him, will not. Only he who brings his spirit to God awake and mindful of Him is possessed of felicity.[204]

It is worth mentioning here that the idea of ownership, which Nursi seems to emphasize, plays an instrumental role in how man responses to a particular hardship. According to Turner, in Nursi's view, while man may perceive himself as the "owner" of his own attributes such as power, wisdom, and knowledge; nonetheless, this apparently real ownership is, in fact, illusory.[205] In light of this understanding, the true owner of the manifestations of those attributes, i.e. their actual exhibitions, such as wealth and social status, belongs to the Creator as well. Therefore, the one who is being tested through the *balā* of loss of wealth is in the position to realize that, in reality, he /she were never the actual owner of the lost privilege. As a result of this adversity, then, man gains a level of spiritual refinement which he may not be able to attain otherwise. Furthermore, in the context of the given example, the whole notion of suffering becomes preventable. In other words, if man is able to understand *ibtilā* correctly, or in Rumi's words, if he can see beyond the form, the temporary effects of his adversity, and find the meaning of this *balā*, the realization that God is the true Owner of what appears to be "ours", there will not remain any ground for suffering. That suffering is a subjective matter is a notion that is supported by Aslan, where he draws attention to a number of elements in examination of the issue of suffering.[206]

This brings us to our final point of Rumi's exposition relating to adversity and its manifestation in the context of *balā*. The aim of this final inquiry is to highlight some of the practical guidelines of this mystical approach in man's encounters with suffering. In other words, what is expected of the one who is experiencing a *balā* in adversity? How can one overcome the difficulties of the adversity without going into despair, and at the same time, benefit from spiritual refinement? Confirming the significance of faith in God's Wisdom and Mercy, the very first advice of the Qur'an is for the believer to endure the hardship with patience "*ṣabr*".[207] It must be noted, however, that while *ṣabr* is a frequently mentioned virtue in the Qur'an, its significance in the context of *balā*, conveys a deeper meaning: patience as a result of faith, and not out of disparity.[208] The second major advice of the Qur'an is the virtue of truly trusting in God (*tawakkul*).[209] As Aslan points out, *tawakkul* protects man from suffering as it assures him that, there is goodness associated with the affliction, which reduces the anxiety.[210]

Correspondingly, the two notions of *ṣabr* and *tawakkul* are frequently visible in Rumi's teachings, and lend themselves to assist man in his encounters with the various difficulties and afflictions of his life. According to Zamāni, a well-known parable which addresses the overall issue of suffering while emphasizing the importance of *ṣabr* and *tawakkul* is the story of the chickpeas in Rumi's *Mathnawī*.[211] This parable appears in book three of *Mathnawī* and is based on an imaginary conversation between a housewife, who is preparing a food, and the chickpeas that are being cooked. As it is often the case with humankind, the chickpeas complain and question the housewife for positioning them in the pot with boiling water. Through the course of this dialogue, the chickpeas try to escape from this condition by continually jumping out of water; however, realizing their inability to end this misery, they frantically plead with their cook to take them out of the pot. Rumi then engages the housewife in this conversation to console the chickpeas in their suffering, so that they may learn that patiently enduring suffering is necessary for their spiritual growth.

> At the time of its being boiled, the chickpea comes up continually to the top of the pot and raises a hundred cries,
> Saying, "why are you setting the fire on me? Since you bought me, how are you turning me upside down?"
> The housewife goes on hitting it with the ladle. "No!" says she, "boil nicely and don't jump away from the one who makes the fire.
> I do not boil you because you are hateful to me: nay, 'tis that you may get taste and savour, this affliction of yours is not on account of your being despised.
> Continue, O chickpea, to boil in tribulation, that neither existence nor self may remain to thee."
> The chickpea said, "since it is so, O lady, I will gladly boil: give me help in verity!
> In this boiling thou art, as it were, my architect: smite me with the skimming-spoon, for thou smites very delightfully."[212]

As the final verse of this story reveals, for Rumi, the evidence of true submission to God's Will becomes visible when man reaches the station of inner contentment, *rizā*,. Therefore, as man journeys on the spiritual path and is faced with various types of *balā*, the two notions of *ṣabr* and *tawakkul* will be his wings to fly with, eventually leading him to the higher state of *rezā*. According to Zarrinkub, the love of the Beloved, which is central to Rumi's mysticism, plays a significant role in the process of man's spiritual refinement with all its hardships and steep hills.[213] In Rumi's view, reaching the station of *rezā*, therefore, is attainable through the gateway of God's love. Through various tribulations and suffering which are meant as *balā*, man's inner potential is realized, and he is able to transform his soul to its highest level of tranquillity which the Qur'an refers to as *"nafs muṭma'inna"*. As Zamāni observes, in Rumi's mysticism, it is in this state of the soul that man is pleased with his Lord regardless of the circumstances of his life, experiencing *balā* in adversity or in prosperity.[214]

Conclusion

Founded on the teachings of Perennial Philosophy, the primary concern of mysticism is to expound upon the most significant human potential, the divine element within man's inner nature, which enables him to see beyond the surface of things to understand the hidden reality beneath. Thus, a common theme for all religions, mysticism represents the esoteric dimension of a religion as compare to its exoteric teachings. Muslim mysticism, therefore, characterizes the esoteric and spiritual dimensions of Islam, which historically have been exemplified by Sufism.

The Muslim mystical literature in general and Rumi's teachings in particular encompass a comprehensive exploration of the notion of divine trial *"balā"*. While the mainstream Qur'anic exegesis, for the most part, seems to lack a comprehensive analysis of the concept of *balā*; Rumi's mystical approach, however, engages in an in-depth elucidation of this notion which appears to correspond more with the all-inclusive Qur'anic approach. Contribution of Rumi's perspective in underscoring the importance of the meaning of *balā* is illustrated in his overall worldview: his understanding of man's creation and position in the creational tree, man as the fruit of God's creation; and his interpretation of *balā* with its positive connotations in the overall spiritual development of mankind.

Several key Qur'anic themes such as Adam and the fall, the *alast* Covenant, man as God's vicegerent on earth, and the Trust, as well as their implications in the context of *balā*, were explored in light of Rumi's major works, particularly, *Mathnawī, Dīwān*, and *Fīhi mā fīhi*. As a result of the above examination, Rumi's mysticism and his practical guidelines relating to man's biggest challenges *"ibtilā"*, namely, self-knowledge and self-purification, received an exhaustive review. The result of this inquiry illustrates that Rumi's vision accords with the teachings of the Qur'an, where man as the fruit of the creation, is faced with many challenges during his life, i.e. trials and tests in good and bad. That man's affection to the attachments and desires of the lower self (*nafs*), are the main obstacles in his spiritual development, is clearly stated in the Qur'an, and discussed in various contexts in Rumi's teachings. Moreover, the underpinning cause of most human suffering is also related to his ego and the desires of the temporal world. Thus, both the Qur'an, and Rumi's mystical approach, aim at severing these attachments; manifestation of *balā* in adversity and suffering is therefore a way of alerting man to the need of detachment. Furthermore, man's ultimate *balā* is to realize that he has been separated from his divine essence, and to strive in the path of spiritual refinement to find the way back to his Source. Therefore, from the Rumian perspective, _balā_ is a necessary component of man's creation, and the means by which human potential is realized. This life long process of spiritual development assists man to become who he is, and become the polished mirror in which God's most beautiful names and attributes are manifested.

The concluding Chapter will examine the problem of evil and suffering, as it relates to the notion of _balā,_ from a theological perspective.

*When man suffers some affliction, he
cries out to Us, but when We favor
him with Our blessings, he says, "All
this has been given to me because of
my knowledge" – it is only a test,
though most of them do not know it.*
(Qur'an, 39:49)

5

Divine Trial and Muslim Theodicy

The notion of *ibtilā*, as discussed in the first chapter, is seen traditionally as being synonymous with adversity and suffering, and implies a negative connotation. However, as already established, from the Qur'anic perspective *ibtilā* is wholly positive in so far as it is an overarching notion which informs the creation of the universe, and is instrumental in actualization of the Divine purpose with respect to creation of the humankind. Furthermore, as the chapter on typology of the Qur'anic narratives highlighted, the fact that *ibtilā* is manifested both in prosperity and adversity further emphasizes its all-inclusive meaning, i.e. the actualization of human potential, and demonstrates the overall constructiveness of this concept. Nevertheless, because of the misconceptions surrounding it, *ibtilā* in its negative form, hardship and suffering, needs to be studied in the context of Muslim theodicy and the attendant concepts of "good" and "evil".

The wide-ranging "problem of evil" has been generally recognized as one of the most debated topics in the history of philosophy of religion. Although the theoretical dimension of the problem poses an intellectual challenge for many philosophers and theologians of various religious traditions, its existential dimension, evil encountered in real life, concerns every individual. It is claimed that the reality as well as the magnitude of many kinds of evil in the world shakes the very foundation of the traditional belief in God. As human beings we are faced with hardships, illnesses, pain, natural disasters that cause immense suffering, fear and anxiety, and injustice, all of which challenge faith. As Hick points out, by remembering the afflictions that invade many people of the world, "… we do indeed have to ask ourselves whether it is possible to think of this world as the work of an omnipotent creator who is motivated by limitless love…this is indeed the most serious challenge that there is to theistic faith."[1] Plantinga supports this notion and further attests that natural atheology which attempts to show that "God does not exist or that at any rate it is unreasonable or irrational to believe that He does, has to do with the so called problem of evil."[2] Therefore, the concept of evil has, for the most part, been discussed in terms of the core beliefs common to major theistic traditions. Moreover, scholarly works have paid attention to the issue of evil in the context of doctrinal concepts pertaining to specific religious traditions.

The overall examination of the problem of evil seems to suggest that the topic includes several forms and versions, and is composed of various interrelated issues and complex arguments. According to Peterson, the "technical" discussion regarding the very nature of the problem of evil, and differences of opinion amongst the philosophers regarding the exact structure of the problem and their approach, has resulted in many formulations of the issue.[3] Similarly, "in its 'existential' dimension, the problem of evil pertains not simply to the abstract analysis of propositions but to one's subjective experience, including a total sense of life or conscious attitude toward God."[4]

Furthermore, as discussed in the previous chapter, the underlying reason for most human suffering is "attachment" to the material world. People suffer because they see the world as imperfect, unjust, unfair, and full of adversity and suffering, and aspire to a perfect world, a utopia, a *madina al-fazila*. In the context of religion, the main criticism leveled at God concerns His apparent disregard for human "suffering", and the fact that suffering, adversity, and evil exist at all.

In this chapter, by adopting the method of deconstructionism, the notion of *ibtilā* in its negative manifestation, evil and human suffering, will be explored in the context of Muslim theodicy. An overview of the problem of evil and its various versions will be briefly discussed first, followed by a synopsis of some of the explanations offered from theistic perspectives and their theodicies. The final section of this chapter will examine the problem of evil and human suffering from the perspectives of Muslim theodicy in general, and the Ghazālian concept of the "*best of all possible worlds*" in particular. For, according to Ghazālī, this world is already the best possible world, including all of its apparent imperfections.

The Problem of Evil: An Overview

The overall "problem of evil", commonly referred to as the underlying cause of human suffering, makes itself known in the philosophical debates in Judeo-Christian thought as well as Muslim literature, and comprises an across-the-board scope.[5] Therefore, due to the extensive nature of the issue and its similar connotations within the monotheistic faiths, a general outline of the classical formulation of the problem of evil appears necessary. Scrutinizing the concept of evil according to the following framework not only will aid a more coherent understanding of the issue, it will also serve as a solid foundation for later discussions relating to Muslim theodicean thought.

The examination of the philosophical and theological literature seems to indicate that the problem of evil poses a major challenge to the belief that God exists, and an enormous amount of human suffering also exists. More precisely, the problem, in its comprehensive form, is generally identified in two broad categories: *theoretical* and *existential*. According to Peterson, the *theoretical* dimension which may further be divided into *logical* and *evidential* types, engages in theological discussions about the relationship of certain attributes of God and existence of evil.[6] A similar categorization is formulated by Inwagen who, in his Gifford lectures, classifies the problem of evil into the categories of *theoretical* and *practical*, where the former constitutes debates over "doctrinal" and "apologetic" problems.[7] Moreover, not finding the distinction between logical and evidential debates very useful, Inwagen proposes to differentiate between the "global" arguments from evil and various "local" arguments. Inwagen further argues that the intellectual challenges with respect to the belief in God, in the face of global evil and particular local evil, must be considered separately.[8]

With respect to the arguments about the problem of evil in its *logical* version, the purpose is to demonstrate that there is an inconsistency in the traditional theistic belief that an absolutely omnipotent and omniscient God exists, and the proposition that evil exists. An example of this attempt is seen from Mackie, who claims that it is impossible that an all-powerful God was unable to create a universe which contains moral good but no moral evil.[9] In an effort to refute Mackie's statement, Plantinga responses with a free will defense.[10] Plantinga's argument is grounded in the fact that God has created mankind with free will and that by virtue of having this freedom man may choose to do good or evil acts; moral evil is not in control of God. Plantinga concludes by affirming that there is no inconsistency in theistic belief; that it is indeed possible that an omnipotent God exists, and that the universe contains moral evil.[11]

The debate in the *evidential* version of the problem, on the other hand, takes an inductive approach to illustrate that, given the fact of evil in the world, theism is not reasonable or conceivable. An example of the philosophical argument and counter-argument in this debate may be seen from the works of Martin and Basinger.[12]

While the problem of evil has been largely discussed in its theoretical dimensions, nevertheless, the "*existential*" or "*practical*" dimension of this issue has also received the attention of various scholars. According to Peterson, "the existential problem involves how the experience of evil conditions one's attitude toward God and perhaps toward the world."[3] However, the scholarly works in the practical aspects of the problem do not, necessarily, illustrate how believers of religious traditions deal with the evil situation in their life, i.e. *balā* in the form of affliction and suffering. But rather, the attempt is to investigate how the adherents of religious traditions come to terms with their religious belief after they have encountered such an experience. In other words, does an encounter with evil, such as an earthquake which may be called a natural *balā*, change the perspectives of a theist insofar as complaining about God and the world that He has created? It is argued that the answer lies in the personal perspectives and world view of each individual. A generally happy individual who does not regret his own existence will not expressively question God and the creation of the world in which evil does exist. According to Hasker, "The judgment about the goodness or badness of existence as a whole is best made not from the standpoint of "a cosmic ideal observer", but from the standpoint of a human being – one who loves and struggles, who sorrows and rejoices, and who is glad for the opportunity to live out his life upon the earth."[14]

The aforementioned outline of the problem of evil, more or less, is applicable to Muslim philosophical thought as well. However, as Saeedimehr observes, for the majority of the Muslim philosophers, the problem of evil is presented under the umbrella of Divine Providence, which embodies three Divine attributes: God's knowledge of the best order of the universe, His being is the actual cause of the universe, and that He is pleased with the actual realization of the world.[15] Furthermore, there are two other versions of the problem of evil that have been discussed by Muslim scholars: the problem of creative dualism, which is the existence of two creators, one of whom creates evils, and the belief in God's wisdom which appears to be in contradiction with the existence of evil. In an attempt to reconcile these attributes of God and the proposition that evil is real, the philosophers engage in a discussion of Divine decree (*gadhā al-ilāhī*) and predestination (*taqdir al-ilāhī*).[16] To these topics we shall return later in the chapter. Moreover, Muslim scholars have generally been engaged in the theoretical version of the problem, although without emphasizing the distinction between the logical and evidential types, and seem to have not been concerned with the existential aspects. Aslan supports this notion, and affirms that the rational arguments developed by the philosophers relating to the problem of evil and suffering, are disconnected from the experience of real people who encounter the impact of suffering in their life. He further argues that the vital task is not to develop a theodicy in order to defend a specific theistic belief, but rather to show how a person who is going through adversity can overcome suffering; this is the task of the Qu'ran.[17] Nonetheless, it should be noted here that this undertaking seems to have been accomplished by the Muslim mystics. As Schimmel points out, by introducing the principle of love, the Mystics tried to solve the problem of evil and human suffering.[18] The perspectives of the Muslim philosophers as it relates to the problem of evil will be discussed in more detail in conjunction with the Muslim theodicean approach.

Perspectives in Theodicy: A Synopsis

The overall philosophical debates pertaining to the problem of evil, particularly in responding to the perennial question of human suffering, have resulted in various responses which are generally referred to as "*theodicy*". Gottfried Leibniz (1647-1716), the prominent German philosopher, is known for coining the term *theodicy* from the Greek words for God (*Theos*) and justice (*dike*).[19] The "problem of theodicy" arises when the problem of evil is placed alongside with the beliefs that are generally associated with ethical monotheism – divine attributes such as God is compassionate, all-powerful, and all-knowing – and seems to result in a formation of a logical contradiction. The attempt to provide specific explanations for many forms of human suffering in the world and defend God's aforementioned attributes, therefore, is the aim of the enterprise of theodicy. This effort, Green observes, "… aims to show that traditional claims about God's power and goodness are compatible with the fact of suffering."[20] Furthermore, in its narrower position, theodicy is concern with the special question of "optimism": is this world the best possible world that can be? In other words, does this world, with all of its apparent imperfections, represent the highest creative power of God, or is He able to create a more perfect world? It may be noted that certain themes in this perennial debate, in its overall treatment and with respect to the question of optimism, seem to appear in the works of Muslim theologians as well as Western thinkers.[21]

In solving the overall problem – the seeming inconsistency between certain attributes of God and the fact of evil – a number of theodicies have emerged in various historical periods. The Christian theodicean thought seems to have been greatly influenced by the teachings of St. Augustine (A.D. 354 – 430) who held that evil has no positive reality but it is rather *privatio boni*, the "privation of good"; and that evil is produced by human beings who misuse their freedom.[22] Moreover, as Green points out, St. Augustine fully elaborated on the doctrine of original sin and focused on merit punishment to explain the cause for human suffering.[23] Alternatively, the contemporary philosopher, John Hick (1922-2012), has developed the theodicy of "soul-making" which is based on the teachings of Bishop Irenaeus (c. 130-202) of the early Eastern Orthodox Church.[24] According to the Irenaean view, while the fact of evil and human suffering, as in the Augustinian view, is traced back to mankind's misuse of his freedom, its position in the divine plan is not the same. As observed by Peterson, this perspective does not view "evil in the world as the fall from a once perfect state, but rather as a necessary stage in the development of a relatively immature creation into a more mature state."[25] Thus, instead of looking to the past to solve the mystery of evil, this theodicy looks into the future. In Hicks' words: "Man is in the process of becoming the perfected being whom God is seeking to create…this is not taking place by a natural evolution, but through a hazardous adventure in individual freedom…we must find the meaning of evil in the part that it is made to play in the eventual outworking of that purpose."[26]

Likewise, the Muslim theological literature (*kalām*) reflects a variety of theodicean approaches which is largely an outcome of debates between two divergent theological factions: the Muʿtazilite and the Ashʿarite. As stated in *Muqaddimah* of *Ibn Khaldūn*, the theological differences of opinion emerged from diverse interpretations of the Qur'anic narratives concerning Divine attributes.[27] Thus, the roots of the early formulation of the Muslim theodicy appear to have arisen from a categorical emphasis on God's power.

The Muʿtazilite School of theology employed a rationalistic approach and sought to counterbalance the attribute of God's power with Divine justice. However, as Wolfson observes, the Muʿtazilite's emphasis on God's justice went too far which resulted in a reactionary response from some of its members, and ultimately the establishment of the Ashʿarite School of theology.[28]

From the Ashʿarite perspective, humans are obligated to act according to God's law of justice; God himself, however, is not subject to any rules; God is just in whatever He does.[29] Conversely, the Muʿtazilite held that God is subject to the same law of justice as the humans, that, indeed, He has a permanent obligation to act in just ways.[30] In opposition, Ibn Rushd (Averroës, d. 1198), the Andalusian Muslim philosopher, challenges both of these beliefs, and is of the opinion that the attribute of justice should not be used for man and God in one and the same fashion. In Averroës's philosophy, "man is just because he gains something good by being so, which he cannot gain otherwise. God is just, not that He may become more perfect by His justice, but because His perfection requires him to be just."[31] The insistence of the Ashʿarite view, which became the dominant "orthodox" strain of theology in Sunni Islam, on God's omnipotence, resulted in rejection of human free will and causality. Consequently, their approach had a profound impact on the understanding, or misunderstanding, of the problem of evil and, in turn, the concept of theodicy. As observed by the prominent Shiite philosopher, Morteza Muṭahharī (d. 1979), while the extreme tendency of the Ashʿarite approach – rejection of human free will and attribution of all acts to God – sought to vindicate God of any injustice, in reality, they exonerated human oppressors of any wrong doing. Muṭahharī further comments on this exaggerated theological view of the Ashʿarite and explains that the injustice of the oppressors was, in their opinion, the act of God and not the act of human beings.[32]

In order to determine whether the mainstream theological view of *ibtilā* is a negative one or not, we must first determine what constitutes the Muslim theological view of the issue of "good" and "evil". The main issue regarding the Muʿtazilite/Ashʿarite debate concerns whether the human intellect is able to discern that which is good and that which is evil without help from Divine revelation, or whether it is God alone Who determines what is good and what is evil, thus making human intellect dependent on revelation for guidance. According to the Ashʿarite school of thought, there is no intrinsic quality of good and bad in things; the revealed Law is the sole foundation of good and evil; that which God commands is good and obligatory and what He forbids is bad.[33] On the contrary, the Muʿtazilite held that human intellect is capable of making a distinction between good and evil independent of the revelation, and affirmed that it is through the faculty of reason that man comprehends the goodness of what God has revealed.[34] Likewise, the Shiʿite scholastic literature categorically emphasizes that the moral values of good and evil is indeed inherent in the acts themselves. An example of this statement is seen in the writings of Nasīr al-Dīn Tūsī (d. 1274), one of the most celebrated Shiʿite scholars of the Persian heritage. In his major book on theological concepts, *Kashf al-Morād – Tajrid al-iʿtiqad*, Tūsī strongly rejects the Ash'arite claim and makes elaborate comments relating to the rational deduction of good and bad (*ḥusn/qubḥ-e 'aqli*).[35] By drawing attention to examples of virtuous acts such as helping the poor and corrupt acts such as lying, Ṭūsī affirms that a non-believer is able to realize these qualities as well as a religious person; therefore, Divine law is not what makes these acts good or bad. Ṭūsī further claims that the authenticity and truthfulness of the prophetic message solely depends on whether man is able to validate that message through his own reasoning. In Ṭūsī's conclusion, without this rational deduction of good and bad, a firm religious belief is not attainable, as the foundation of such a conviction is based on weak and shaky ground.[36]

Additionally, the ontological nature of good and evil is rooted in the philosophical interpretation of existence (*wujūd*) and non-existence (*'adam*).[37] From the perspectives of Muslim philosophers, "good" is generally referred to a positive entity which stems from existence, whereas "evil" is viewed as a negative entity and is defined as non-existence.[38] Hence, the notion of evil as the "privation of good" appears to be at the core of the Muslim debate, and provides a strong explanation for the existence of evil and human suffering. Furthermore, this theory lends itself to a solid foundation for the Muslim optimistic worldview: the belief that this world is the best of all possible worlds. An example of the doctrine of evil as "privation of good" is presented in the writings of the prominent Muslim Philosopher, Ibn Sīnā (Avicenna, d. 428/1037). According to Inati, in Ibn Sīnā's view, who is influenced by Plato, Aristotle, and Plotinus, "being" is coextensive with "good" (*khayr*); and "non-being" or privation is "evil" (*sharr*).[39] Moreover, in his elucidation of the metaphysical nature of evil, Ibn Sīnā makes a distinction between two types of evil: "essential" evil (*sharr bidh-dhāt*) and "accidental" evil (*sharr bil-'araḍ*); where essential evil is privation but accidental evil is either being or privation.[40] It may be argued, therefore, that from Ibn Sīnā's perspective, *balā*, in the form of human suffering such as pain and grief, is "good" insofar as it is seen as existing positive realities.[41] In addition to metaphysical evil, moral evil which is the result of human freedom – caused by "ignorance" – is another type of evil discussed in Ibn Sīnā's philosophy.[42] It should further be noted that by making the distinction between the metaphysical (essential and accidental) and moral types of evil, Ibn Sīnā is in fact establishing the foundation for his theodicy. Various elements of Ibn Sīnā's theodicy will be highlighted during our discussion of al-Ghazālī's teachings. According to Inati seven theories may be identified from Ibn Sīnā's theodicy:

(1) God is good and providential, but precisely because of His goodness, God cannot intend any good or evil in the world; (2) there is more good than evil in the universe. Essential evil is rare; only non-essential evil is predominant; (3) evil is a necessary consequence of the good, and to wish the removal of evil is to wish the removal of the good; (4) evil is a necessary means for the good; (5) God is not omnipotent; that is, God cannot free the world from evil; (6) essential evil is privation of being, and therefore cannot be caused by God, who

is the cause of being only; (7) human evil is due to human free will, resulting from knowledge.[43]

Furthermore, Sadr al-Din Shirāzī (1571–1636) known as Mullā Sadrā, has had a significant influence in shaping Muslim philosophical thought. As Rizvi points out, "Mullā Sadrā was given the title of Sadr al-Muta'allihin (Master of the theosists) for his approach to philosophy that combined an interest in theology and drew upon insights from mystical intuition…he became famous as the thinker who revolutionized the doctrine of existence in Islamic metaphysics."[44] In his *Mafātih Al-ghayb*, Mullā Sadrā asserts that absolute existence is absolute good; that God is the sole Necessary Being, and, therefore, He is the absolute good; all other beings lack a certain degree of perfect good.[45] Thus, Rahman, in examining Mullā Sadrā's philosophy stated in his *magnum opus*, *Asfār*, informs us that from Mullā Sadrā's perspective, "absolute existence has no opposite, nor peer…evil, therefore, is never absolute, but only relative, partial, and negative….and is infected with absolute contingency and, as such, suffers from the darkness of negation".[46] It should further be mentioned that in Mullā Sadrā's view, this world has been created in a perfect manner, and that the amount of evil that is present is in fact insignificant to the good that is inherent in our world.[47] Therefore, one may argue that *ibtilā* for Mullā Sadrā is positive insofar as it is part of the perfect world created by God who is the absolute Good.

To recapitulate, the non-existence theory of evil proposed by Muslim philosophers indicates that evil is nothing but privation of good. Additionally, the Muslim theologians' interpretation of Divine attributes of Providence, as well as ascription of moral evil to the faculty of human free will, constitutes the Muslim theodicean approach relating to "good" and "evil". This overall positive approach, then, forms the foundation for the doctrine of the optimum (*al-aṣlaḥ*), i.e., that this world is the most excellent creation. In what follows, we will examine the notion of *balā* in its manifestation as affliction and suffering, in the context of al-Ghazālī's statement, "there is not in possibility anything more wonderful than what is" (*laysa fi'l-imkān abdaʿ mimmā kān*).

Ghazālian Theodicy: Concept of the "Best of All Possible Worlds"

From the perspective of Muslim theologians this world represents the excellent creative power of God – the most Perfect One who is the ultimate source of existence. However, the problem of evil, *balā*, in the form of affliction and human suffering, calls the perfectness of the world – the doctrine of the optimum – into question. In the face of many imperfections, and various degrees of negative *balā*, is this world the best world that it can possibly be? In other words, is it possible for God to create a world without *balā* where human beings would not be subjected to a high degree of misfortune and suffering? Perhaps the most decisive answer is exemplified in the teachings of Abū ḥāmid al-Ghazālī (AH 450-505/1058-1111), the prominent Muslim intellectual of fifth century Islam. For al-Ghazālī, not only this world is indeed the best that it can be, "there is not in possibility anything more wonderful than what is" (*laysa fi'l-imkān abda' mimmā kān*).[48]

Al-Ghazālī was a renowned Muslim jurist, theologian, and mystic: a prominent thinker who is well known for his comprehensive influence in the formation of various disciplines of Muslim scholarly thought. His contributions have earned him the honorific title *ḥujjat al-Islām* "the proof of Islam".[49] Al-Ghazālī was born in Ṭūs, a town located in eastern Iran, and while he lost his father at a young age, under the guidance of his caretaker he received a great education. Following several years of studying under the greatest theologian of the time, al-Juwaynī, at the age of thirty-three, al-Ghazālī was appointed to the main professorship at the Niẓāmīyah College in Baghdad, one of the most distinguished positions in the academic world of his time. However, after four years and following a mystical religious experience, al-Ghazālī abandoned his position and adopted the life of a mystic.[50] He settled in Damascus for two years, where he devoted his life to prayer and contemplation, and subsequently performed the pilgrimage to Mecca. Al-Ghazālī returned to his homeland where he spent the next ten years in seclusion, and composed his encyclopedic work titled *Iḥyā' 'ulūm al-dīn*, "The Revivification of the Religious Sciences". He eventually returned to teaching, and spent the last few years of his life writing summaries of *Iḥyā'*, the composition of his celebrated autobiography, and books on *kalām* and jurisprudence – the subjects that had occupied him before his mystical experience. According to Watt, "When he became a mystic he did not cease to be a good Muslim any more than he ceased to be an Ash'arite theologian."[51] Al-Ghazālī died in Ṭūs at the age of 55 in 505/1111.

As mentioned previously, the task of this part of the study is to examine the notion of *balā* in the context of al-Ghazālī's overall theological view with special interest in his statement of "the best of all possible worlds" – Ghazālian theodicy. However, in order to understand al-Ghazālī's thought and the framework in which the statement was articulated, a concise discussion of his mystical experience seems necessary. Much of what is known about al-Ghazālī's condition leading up to the mystical experience and his motivations for leaving Baghdad is through his spiritual autobiography, *al-Munqidh min al-ḍalāl*, "Deliverance from Error". In spite of his extraordinary achievements, al-Ghazālī had become skeptical of the truth of religious knowledge and sought instead for a kind of knowledge that could provide "certitude" in the authenticity of faith. In Burrell's words, al-Ghazālī "resolved to go in search of an answer to the question deep in most human hearts: how do I *know* religion is *true?*"[52] According to Bowker's observation, al-Ghazālī' felt that the great volume of knowledge and the skilful demonstration of it through vigorous argumentation "amounted to nothing – nothing, if it did not bring him into a direct experience of that which he could describe externally with such fluency, the nature of God and of man's relatedness to Him[53]. After making a thorough study of the various categories of truth seekers, namely philosophers, theologians, and Gnostics, he declared that the true knowledge of religion is attainable if what he knows is connected to and is grounded in direct mystical experience. Thus, he writes: "I knew with certainty that I had learned all I could by way of theory.

There remained, then, only what was attainable, not by hearing and study, but by fruitional experience and actually engaging in the way."[54]

Al-Ghazālī acknowledged that attainment of this higher knowledge which would ultimately lead him from the dark alleys of "doubtfulness" to the light of "certainty" is achievable by shunning fame and fortune. However, after months of inner struggle, he realized that the path was not easy; as severing from worldly attachments did not come without serious affliction and suffering, *balā*. It is in facing a serious physical and spiritual illness that al-Ghazālī experiences an inner transformation which results in leaving his professorial position, family, and wealth, to search for the authentic knowledge of religion and a personal experience of God. Thus, we are told:

> I therefore reflected unceasingly on this for some time, while I still had freedom of choice. One day I would firmly resolve to leave Baghdad and disengage myself from those circumstances, and another day I would revoke my resolution. I would put one foot forward, and the other backward.....mundane desires began tugging me with their chains to remain as I was, while the herald of faith was crying out: "Away! Up and away"...As such thoughts the call would reassert itself and I would make an irrevocable decision to run off and escape. Then Satan would return to the attack and say: "This is a passing state"....thus I incessantly vacillated between the contending pull of worldly desires and the appeals of the afterlife for about six months, starting with Rajab of the year 488 (July 1095 A.D.). In this month the matter passed from choice to compulsion. For, God put a lock upon my tongue so that I was impeded from public teaching. I struggled with myself to teach for a single day, to gratify the hearts of the students who were frequenting my lectures, but my tongue would not utter a single word: I was completely unable to say anything. As a result that impediment of my speech caused sadness in my heart accompanied by an inability to digest; food and drink became unpalatable to me so that I could neither swallow broth easily nor digest a mouthful of solid food. That led to such a weakening of my powers that the physicians lost hope of treating me and said: "This is something which has settled in his heart and crept from it into his humors; there is no way to treat it unless his heart is eased of the anxiety which has visited it."...Then, when I perceived my powerlessness, and when my capacity to make a choice had completely collapsed, I had recourse to God Most High as does a hard pressed man who has no way out of his difficulty. And I was answered by Him Who "answers the needy man when he calls on Him" (Q. 27: 62-63), and He made it easy for my heart to turn away from fame and fortune, family, children, and associates.[55]

It should be noted here that al-Ghazālī's exposition of this experience seems to accord with the wholly positive nature and all-inclusive meaning of *balā* emphasized in the Qur'an, which was discussed in Chapter One of the study. For it is through undergoing this multidimensional trial, *balā* in the form of physical and mental illness, that al-Ghazālī's intellectual and spiritual potential is fully realized. Consequently, this devastating *balā* which appeared as entirely negative encompassing many tribulations and hardships, proved to be the most constructive experience of his life. As Humā'ī observes, the new and transformed al-Ghazālī' became one of the most influential thinkers who revolutionized the intellectual prospects of humanity.[56] Watt supports this notion and points out that the reflections of what al-Ghazālī' learnt in the years of solitude is vividly communicated in his greatest work *Iḥyā' 'ulūm al-dīn*. This *magnum opus* provides both a theoretical justification of al-Ghazālī's position and a highly detailed elucidation of it which emphasized the deeper meaning of the external acts; it shows how a profound inner life may be integrated with sound theological doctrine.[57] Additionally, in Horten's opinion, "Al-Ghazālī drew attention to conscience in religion, the spiritual-intellectual element, in the light of which the store of positive and external Islamic elements could be understood and reverentially conserved."[58]

It may be inferred from the above brief discussion that al-Ghazālī's personal experience with *balā*, as manifested in a crisis affecting both his physical and mental health, becomes visible at the heart of his theodicy – and by extension – the affirmation that "there is not in possibility anything more wonderful than what is" (*laysa fi'l-imkān abda' mimmā kān*). Prior to the scrutiny of this statement, al-Ghazālī's theological thought, as it relates to the overall concept of Creation, needs to be discussed briefly. In other words, the inquiry for the next section is to examine the conditions of a Creation that, in Ghazālī's view, establishes the premise for the doctrine of "the best of all possible worlds", and in turn, affirmation of the wholly positive nature of *balā*.

Ghazālī on God and Creation-in-Time

The concept of God and creation, and the relationship between the two, in so far as existence is concerned, presents itself as one of the most fundamental discourses in Muslim theological thought. The origin of the debate appears to address the following question: has the universe always coexisted with God, or has it been created by God at a specific time? The discussion, which is reflected in the works of *falasifa* and *mutakallimun*, attempts to shed light on the distinction between "eternity" or *qidam* and that which is eternal or *qadīm*, and "creation-in-time" or *ḥudūth*, and that which is created-in-time or *ḥadith*.[59] As defined by philosopher and theologian Nasīr al-Din al- Tūsī, *qadīm* is applied to that which is not preceded by anything else and therefore is eternal. On the other hand, *ḥadith* is referred to that which has not existed before its existence, i.e., its existence is contingent, and therefore is created-in-time.[60] Accordingly, since God is the only "necessary" being, Tūsī affirms, He is the only "eternal"; everything else – the world, the non-God (*mā siwā Allah*) – is contingent, temporal, and alterable; indeed, the world may not exist at all.[61]

Furthermore, while the existence of the world is contingent and subject to possibilities of existence and nonexistence, from the Muslim philosophical perspective, its creation is "necessary" due to the preceding will and knowledge of its Creator. However, as Burrell observes, the philosophers "enamoured with eternal emanation were bound to be seen as compromising the majesty of Allah as well as obscuring a cardinal feature of Divine revelation: that the universe itself is God's gracious gift."[62]

The doctrine of creation-in-time, which was the position of the orthodoxy, was first challenged by Ibn Sīnā and led to his formulation of the doctrine of "contingency" or *imkān zāti*. As Rahman points out, while the notion of temporal creation did not agree with Ibn Sīnā's philosophical worldview, he nevertheless took the demands of traditional Islam seriously and sought to synthesize between the two.[63] Ibn Sīnā demonstrated that there is a radical distinction between God and the world, in that " although there can be no temporal gap between God and the world, there is surely a gap in the nature of being between the two, a sort of ontological hiatus or rupture which is expressed in the doctrine of necessity and contingency."[64] In Ibn Sīnā's view, the universe is the creative work of God Who creates according to His knowledge and due to His generosity; since God is "eternal" and it is in His nature to create, therefore, the object of His creation must also be "eternal". According to Rahman, the theory of contingency, as well as the doctrine of distinction between "essence" and "existence" is the hallmark of Ibn Sīnā's philosophy – its profound impact is evident in later Muslim philosophy and Medieval Latin thought.[65]

However, the contingency doctrine and eternity of the world which emphasized that creation is innately contingent but extrinsically necessary, met with strong objections from orthodox Muslim theologians. This conclusion, Goodman observes, seemed too strong for the *mutakallimun* for it "appeared to tie God's hands and to ignore the radical contingency of finite being, which was the linchpin of Kalām creationism."[66] The highlights of this opposition are particularly reflected in the teachings of al-Ghazālī. In al-Ghazālī's view, the creation of the universe is the work of an omnipotent, omniscient Creator; His creation is not out of caprice and due to necessity, but indeed, out of His will and wisdom, and for the benefit of the world.[67] According to Marmura, in Ash'arite theology and by extension for al-Ghazālī, "whatever the divine eternal will chooses and decrees must come about. In this sense the existence of what it decrees is necessary".[68] Nevertheless, opposing Ibn Sīnā's doctrine, al-Ghazālī affirms that "God's will does not have to decree the creation of the world; it does so "freely" by an eternal voluntary act...by this act it decrees the world's creation out of nothing (*ex nihilo*) at a finite time."[69]

Furthermore, the implication of the creation in time theory, Ormsby points out, is the presupposition that God chose one moment rather than another to bring the world into existence.[70] In his *al-Iqtiṣād fi'l-iʿtiqād*, written prior to his experience of *balā* and at the peak of his career in Baghdad, al-Ghazālī engages in a theological discussion about the creation-in-time theory and attempts to establish his argument. In al-Ghazālī's theology, "the world comes to be at that time when the eternal will stands in nexus with its coming-to-be...the world is specified in a specific measure and a specific position. To ask why it distinguishes or specifies one time or one thing rather than another is to ask, why is it a will, or, why is will will?"[71] As Ormsby observes, from the Ghazālian perspective:

> The world is a realization of one possibility among many possibilities, all of them utterly equal in response to God. With respect to itself, the world could as easily not exist as exist; and this inescapable fact applied to very object and every event in the world... The corollary of this is that whatever does exist is a product of divine will: "every contingent is willed". So, too, whatever does not exist, does not exist because its nonexistence God has knowingly foreordained and willed. Nothing is random; nothing is happenstance; whatever exists, whatever occurs, is intended.[72]

It may be noted here that al-Ghazālī's theological viewpoints, such as the creation of the world discussed briefly above, are, for the most part, outlined in his works composed during the period of his professorship in Baghdad. However, the profound practical implications of much of his teachings, and the extent of his influence in shaping the Muslim theological and mystical thought, is explicitly communicated in his writing following his experience of *balā*. It is, therefore, in Book 35 of the *Iḥyā' 'ulūm al-dīn*, where al-Ghazālī's famous statement makes itself known: "there is not in possibility anything more wonderful than what is" (*laysa fi'l-imkān abda' mimmā kān*). In the following section al-Ghazālī's dictum will be examined and its association to the notion of *balā* will be emphasized. Furthermore, al-Ghazālī's experience of *balā* and its impact on his intellectual and spiritual development will be highlighted.

The Best of All Possible Worlds: Context for Trust in God

As mentioned previously, during the year 1095, al-Ghazālī experienced a major physical and mental crisis, *balā* in its negative form, which had a profound consequence on his intellectual and spiritual life. According to his autobiography, *al-Munqidh min al-ḍalāl*, in addition to his physical suffering – inability to speak, eat, or drink – he also suffered mentally from a strong sense of sadness. After six months of this struggle, he renounced his professorship position, donated all his wealth, and left Baghdad to pursue a life of seclusion and poverty.[73] According to Zarrinkūb, the authenticity of religious knowledge and the level of "certitude" which al-Ghazālī pursued for much of his life through rational deductions bore fruit after his illness and significant mystical experience.[74]

Al-Ghazālī's *Iḥyā' 'ulūm al-dīn*, which contains the statement of "the best of all possible worlds", is considered his *magnum opus* and was composed during the next decade of his life following the experience of *balā*. It may be argued, therefore, that al-Ghazālī's experience of *balā* demonstrates the constructiveness of *balā* emphasized in the Qur'an and discussed in Chapter One of this study. This notion is supported by Bowker who, in his study of the problem of suffering in world's religions, points out that "suffering is treated in the Qur'an as it occurs, in direct and simple terms, not as a theoretical problem....there is a sense in which it is almost dissolved as a problem"[75]. Did not the Qur'an pronounce: "...You may dislike something although it is good for you, or like something although it is bad for you: God knows and you do not"?[76]

According to Ormsby, during his ten years of seclusion al-Ghazālī seems to have reached an inner state of conviction and insight which enabled him to view the world perfect as is: "the perfect rightness of the actual".[77] For al-Ghazālī, this world, with all of its "good" and "evil", and apparent imperfections, is indeed the best world and there is nothing in possibility better than what is.[78] As already established, in al-Ghazālī's theology, discussed in *al-Iqtiṣād fī'l-iʿtiqād*, the world is contingent, i.e., can equally be and not be; its creation was actualized through God's will and at a specific time. The fact that the world came to being, and that its creation occurred in time, illustrates that what came to be is the creative work of an omniscient Creator. Thus, while it is logical to assert that our world could be "other" than what is, theologically, it is not permissible to affirm that our world could be "better" than what is.[79] In al-Ghazālī's view, our present world with all of its circumstances is most excellent and just. From this perspective, it may be argued that the assumption that a world without *balā* – not currently in existence – will be superior to the presently created world, where *balā* is part of its structure, is not conceivable.

Al-Ghazālī's memorable dictum of "the best of all possible worlds", appears in Book 35 of the *Iḥyāʾ ʿulūm al-dīn: Kitāb al-tawḥīd waʾ l-tawakkul*, Divine Unity and Trust in God. Following an in-depth presentation on the doctrine of *tawḥīd* and its practical implications, the practice of seeing God as the only true agent in the world and the One whom man must continuously find hope in and depend on, al-Ghazālī states:

> Everything that God distributes among men such as sustenance, life-span "*ajal*", happiness and sadness, weakness and power, faith and unbelief, obedience and apostasy – all of it is unqualifiedly just with no injustice in it, true with no wrong infecting it. Indeed, all this happens according to a necessary and true order, according to what is appropriate as it is appropriate and in the measure that is proper to it; nor is anything more fitting, more perfect, and more attractive within the realm of possibility. For if something was to exist and remind one of the sheer omnipotence of God and not of the good things accomplished by His action, it would be miserliness which utterly contradicted God's generosity, and injustice contrary to divine justice. And if God were not omnipotent, He would be impotent, thereby contradicting the nature of divinity.[80]

The statement gave rise to much controversy in al-Ghazālī's lifetime, and continued for several centuries. According to his critics, the fact that this proclamation strictly compromised divine power – it is not possible for God to create a more excellent world – is contrary to the belief of the orthodoxy and must be rejected at once. According to Ormsby, in addition to al-Ghazālī's apparent disregard for certain Ashʿarite theological thought pertaining to divine attributes, two other major objections were also raised: resemblances of the passage to the Muʿtazilite doctrine of *al-aṣlaḥ*, and the possibility that al-Ghazālī had been influenced by the teachings of the philosophers.[81] Humāʾī is of the same opinion, and sheds light on various arguments and counter arguments that preoccupied the minds of many of al-Ghazālī's critics and defenders.[82] Despite the fact that al-Ghazālī responded to his critics on several occasions and attempted to clarify his position, the controversy and the heated discussions surrounding it went too far. According to Humāʾī's observation, the core of these discussions concerns matters which are above and beyond human understanding, that man with his limited "reasoning" is incapable of making a judgment on God and whether or not His creation could be better than what is.[83]

In scrutinizing al-Ghazālī's dictum, it is important to note that this statement makes itself known in the context of the notion of *tawakkul*, "trust in God". In his book, *The Ninety-Nine Beautiful Names of God*, "al-*Maqṣad al-asnā fī sharḥ maʿānī asmāʾ Allāh al-ḥusnā*", al-Ghazālī engages in an in-depth discussion of the divine attribute of *Al-Wakīl*, the Trustee, and illustrates how God, in His essence, deserves to have matters entrusted to him.[84] Moreover, according to Soroush, *tawakkul*, based on the teachings of the Qur'an, may be considered the fruit of *tawḥīd*; it entails the affirmation that there is only One true agent in the world, as well as the sincere belief that the effectiveness of all other "causes" (*asbāb*) actualizes through Him.[85] As Griffel points out, al-Ghazālī's famous passage marks the end of his comments on the importance of the belief in *tawḥīd*, at which point the notion of *tawakkul* is linked to it.[86] While the statement contains various elements of classical formulation of theodicy, such as justification of God's attributes in face of evil, it nevertheless, aims to prescribe practical ways by which trust in God is achievable. For al-Ghazālī, one's belief in divine unity is manifested in the level of one's trust in God. In Burrell's observation, al-Ghazālī's purpose is to illustrate that "the test of our understanding of divine unity will not come by way of clever philosophical schemes but through a life of trust, *tawakkul*, in which concerted practice will bring each of us personally to the threshold of the only understanding possible here, that of unveiling".[87] To this end, in the passage preceding "the best of all possible worlds" statement, al-Ghazālī explicitly expounds on his purpose:

> The faith in divine unity which brings about the state of trust in God is only perfected by faith in God's mercy "*raḥma*", and in His wisdom, "*ḥikma*". And if faith in divine unity brings about insight into the cause of the causes "*musab-bib al-asbāb*", the state of trust in God will only be perfected by confidence in the trustee ʿ*wakīl* and tranquility of heart towards the benevolent sponsor....it would take too long to explain the path of those experiencing the unveiling to show how they develop their strong trust in God....we can only briefly show their way so that whoever aims to develop a firm trust in God believes in it...a belief without any doubt.[88]

The practical implication of such an elevated level of trust in God, one may infer, is the cornerstone of al-Ghazālī's dictum of "the best of all possible worlds". In other words, *tawakkul,* which is considered one of the most significant stations in man's spiritual development – its manifestation truly visible when faced with a negative *balā* – is not attainable without a true conviction that this world is indeed the best and most excellent of all possible worlds. Moreover, in leading up to his famous dictum, al-Ghazālī makes it perfectly clear that the divine attributes of "wisdom" and "will" are instrumental in observing the world as the most excellent world, and are regarded as the foundation for the total trust in its Creator. As Ormsby points out, al-Ghazālī's emphasis on divine wisdom which is a central theme in his theodicy was objected to by his fellow Ashʿarite; as for them, any attempt to rationalize God's actions was against orthodoxy. Therefore, his stress on divine wisdom may be viewed as an effort to modify the strict Ashʿarite assertion of God's autonomous unaccountability, and affirm that God's creation is, in fact, based on divine wisdom.[89] Consequently, in al-Ghazālī's vision, this world – including all of its apparent deficiencies – insofar as it is designed and planned according to God's will and wisdom, is the most excellent world. One may infer that, in the Ghazālian scheme, it is only through this indispensable worldview that man is able to trust in God and, by extension, realize the wholly positive nature of the notion of *balā.* In other words, a true confirmation that this world is the most excellent created work of God is to affirm that divine wisdom is implanted in all experiences of life: *balā* in prosperity and in adversity.

From the Ghazālian perspective, the signs and verifications of divine wisdom are abundantly visible throughout this universe; indeed, its impact permeates each and every creature. In the *Iḥyāʾ,* al-Ghazālī makes references to what may seem to be the most insignificant creatures such as an ant, a bee, or a spider, and elucidates the amazing ways in which these tiny animals are sustained in this world.[90] Additionally, to substantiate his argument for divine wisdom, al-Ghazālī frequently refers to the human body and the perfect appropriateness of its anatomy. For him, the design, the position, and the functionality of each and every part of the human body provide the most convincing example of divine wisdom.[91] To this end, he describes the perfectness of various body parts, such as the structure of the human eye and the functionality of numerous veins and muscles, to remind man of the marvels of his own body and to illustrate the instrumentality of divine wisdom in His flawless creation. As Ormsby points out, al-Ghazālī's portrayal of the creation of the human body is very precise, "for he wishes to emphasize the meticulous rightness of things as they are."[92] Once again, al-Ghazālī makes a serious effort to persuade his readers that this world, which is the created work of God according to His will and wisdom, is perfect in each and every aspect. This sincere belief is a necessary prerequisite for those who, in the path of spiritual development, are seeking to reach the apex of the station of *tawakkul;* the extent and the genuineness of this conviction is tested in face of *balā.*

Trial and Tribulation in the Context of the "Best of All Possible Worlds"

The implicit reference to the notion of *balā* becomes visible when al-Ghazālī's doctrine of the perfect appropriateness of things as they are is extended to the social order. In his view, divine will remains at the core of all human affairs; undoubtedly, the events of this world unfold not randomly but according to God's will. In his book, *The Forty Foundations of Religion*, "*Kitāb al-arbaʿīn fī uṣūl al-dīn*", al-Ghazālī writes:

> He wills all existent things, directing all that occurs. Nothing transpires in the physical or spiritual world, whether it be little or much, small or large, good or bad, beneficial or harmful, belief or disbelief, knowledge or ignorance, victory or loss, increase or decrease, obedience or disobedience, except by His decree, destining, wisdom, and willing. For whatever He wills is, and whatever He does not will is not.[93]

Moreover, the aforementioned two principles, that God is the only true agent in the world and that His will directly influences all situations in human life, further signify that there is complete justice in this world. While al-Ghazālī does not deny the actuality and presence of negative *balā* – hardship and adversity – in human life, he asserts that their existence is necessary and instrumental in demonstrating the perfect rightness of the world. Thus, the *Iḥyāʾ* text continues:

> Indeed, all kinds of poverty, loss, and adversity in this world represent a deficiency in this world, but an increase and enhancement in the next world. And everything which amounts to a deficiency in the next world for one person spells a benefit for another. For if there was no night one would never realize the value of daylight; were it not for illness, the healthy person would never enjoy good health; and if there were no hell, the inhabitant of paradise would not know the extent of their blessing. If the imperfect is not created, the perfect will not be known. If beasts had not been created, the dignity of human beings would not be evident, for the perfect and the imperfect are manifested in relation to one another. Therefore, Divine generosity and wisdom require that Creation includes both perfect and imperfect.[94]

It may be argued that the all-encompassing meaning of *balā* which the Qur'an emphasizes – divine trial in adversity and prosperity – discussed in Chapter One of the study, is highlighted in various sections of al-Ghazālī's writings, and that his doctrine of the best of all possible worlds presupposes the notion of *balā* . It is in viewing the creation from a cosmic perspective and trust in God, not from an individual's limited knowledge, that man can truly affirm the perfectness of the world. As Watt observes, the overall attitude of the Qur'an is that *balā* in its form of suffering is caused or permitted by God, and that humankind's attempt to understand in detail the purposes of God is not always fruitful.[95] Therefore, al-Ghazālī does not make any attempt to absolve God from responsibility for the evils of this world. According to Ormsby, "the question of the ultimate authorship of evil does not arise, or at least does not occupy the central position, in his version of theodicy, that it occupies in Western versions".[96]

The doctrine of "the best of all possible worlds" also appears in the writings of Leibniz, as mentioned earlier, who is recognized for coining the term "theodicy". While there appear to be affinities between al-Ghazālī's statement and what Leibniz attempted to establish almost six centuries later in Europe, there are also distinctive differences between the two scholars. As mentioned previously, from the Ghazālian perspective, the principle of creation–in-time is essential in affirmation that this world is the best created work of its Creator.[97] For al-Ghazālī the fact that this world was created at a specific time and according to God's will and wisdom, makes it the best and most excellent creation. Conversely, in his discussion of God as the "*first reason of things*", and the contingency of the existence of the world, Leibniz engages in a discussion of other possible worlds that God could have created. For Leibniz, the divine choice to create this world out of infinite possibilities makes it the most perfect world:

> One must seek the reason for the existence of the world, which is the whole assemblage of *contingent* things, and see it in the substance which carries with it the reason for its existence, and which in consequence is *necessary* and eternal. Moreover, this cause must be intelligent: for this existing world being contingent and an infinity of other worlds being equally possible,…the cause of the world must needs have had regard or reference to all these possible worlds in order to fix upon one of them…that if there were not the best (optimum) among all possible worlds, God would not have produced any…and that God must have chosen the best, since he does nothing without acting in accordance with supreme reason.[98]

Furthermore, it may be argued that, while both al-Ghazālī and Leibniz utilize rational deductions in their writings, nonetheless, their worldview and perspective differ greatly from one another. Al-Ghazālī's goal was to demonstrate the perfection of the world and the actual rightness of everything existent by underscoring the importance of divine wisdom without limiting God's power and His freedom. The overarching purpose for al-Ghazālī, however, was to construct a solid foundation for *tawakkul* and convince his readers how to attain this conviction. Leibniz, on the other hand, while underlining the divine wisdom in the design of His creation, nonetheless emphasizes the instrumentality of human reason and its ability to comprehend God's harmonic creation "without being aided by the light of faith".[99] According to Kermani, "Leibniz's apologetic interest is directed at God on the surface, but actually at human reason, which must be capable of explaining God – so as to behave in God-like fashion".[100]

In addition to the aforementioned differences between al-Ghazālī and Leibniz, as they relate to the notion of "the best of all possible worlds", Aslan argues that the two thinkers belong to different traditions of scholarship; therefore, their discourses and their intended audiences, as well as what they attempted to achieve is quite different.[101] In his opinion, al-Ghazālī's passage appears in the *Iḥyāʾ* to educate the general Muslim public in their spiritual development; hence, the goal is not to justify the existence of suffering. Leibniz's idea, on the other hand, appears in one of his philosophical essays articulated in a rationalistic approach in order to convince other philosophers, as well as to develop a consistent theodicy.[102]

In our analysis of the Qur'anic concept of *balā* in the context of al-Ghazālī's doctrine of "the best of all possible worlds", attention should also be paid to his elucidation of the concept of "patience" (*ṣabr*), which is a closely related theme to *balā* not only in face of hardship and adversity but equally in prosperity. Book 32 of the *Iḥyāʾ ʿulūm al-dīn*, titled: *Kitāb al-ṣabr waʾ l-shukr', Patience and Thankfulness*, includes al-Ghazālī's deep engagement with the all-inclusive meaning of *balā*, where he outlines various circumstances of man's life – good and bad – and provides guidance on proper behavior in each condition.

In this section of the *Iḥyāʾ*, al-Ghazālī explains that the human experience in this world involves two diverse conditions of life, desirable and undesirable, and in both circumstances man is in need of patience.[103] The first kind is when he is enjoying good health, experiencing prosperity, happiness, prestige, and views the circumstances of his life as being in harmony with his desires; yet, he needs to exercise patience. Here al-Ghazālī engages in a thought-provoking discussion pertaining to the notion of *balā* and its manifestation in "good"; his explication appears to accord with the all-encompassing meaning of *balā* that is emphasized in the Qur'an and has already been illustrated in previous chapters of this study. Shedding light on the importance of *ṣabr*, and its practical application during the time that man is enjoying life's delightful conditions, "trial of good fortune", al-Ghazālī explains:

> If man does not restrain himself from irresponsible living and a propensity for this, he will lose himself in legitimate pleasures that lead to transgression. As stated in Qur'an: *"Surely man transgresses; for he believes himself to be self-sufficient"* (Q. 96:6-7). As some of the Gnostics say patience in well-being is more difficult than patience in tribulation. The true believer is he who patiently endures well-being; this means that he does not rely on it. He knows that well-being is entrusted to him, and it may be that it shall soon be taken back, and so he should not yield himself wholly to its enjoyments. He does not persist obstinately in a life of luxury, physical pleasure, frivolity and amusement. He must care about God's claims regarding the expenditure of his wealth, regarding the way he dispenses succor for creation,... regarding all else that God has favoured him with. This patience is linked to thankfulness. Patience in good fortune is more difficult, because it is related to the capacity for endurance... A hungry man is better able to endure his hunger when food is not available

than when delicious, good foods are set before him, and he could eat. In this situation the trial of good fortune is great.[104]

The second kind of condition in man's life, according to al-Ghazālī, includes those uninvited circumstances that are contrary to man's desires and causes him stress and unhappiness, and yet he has no choice but to go through this experience – *balā* in adversity. From his perspective, the actualization of the virtue of *ṣabr*, in its elevated degree, is demonstrated when man encounters misfortunes and calamities, such as loss of wealth, major illnesses, death of a loved one, and various other kinds of tribulations.[105]

Al-Ghazālī further distinguishes between absolute and relative *balā* in the context of this world and the Hereafter. Absolute *balā* in this world applies to disbelief and disobedience; it is man's obligation not to be patient in this *balā*; he must change this status and become a believer; otherwise this will turn to absolute tribulation in the Hereafter: he will be placed at a distance from God. On the other hand, relative *balā* in this world applies to tribulations and adversities which, while considered hardships, do not affect one's religion; these kinds of *balā* require man to exercise patience.[106]

The link between the concept of *balā* and al-Ghazālī's dictum of "the best possible worlds" becomes particularly evident as he begins to elucidate on the wholly positive nature of *balā*, and sheds light on means by which man can benefit from these adversities. This kind of *balā* is, in reality, a blessing:

> Thus, patience in this world refers to what is not an absolute tribulation, but to what can also be considered a blessing. This is why it is possible for the functions of patience and thankfulness to be combined in it. For example, wealth may be the cause of man's destruction, he can be a target because of his money; he and his children even be killed. Health too can be considered in the same way. Every worldly blessing …can also become a tribulation; while every worldly tribulation can also become a blessing. It may be that poverty and illness are what is best for a servant; if his body was healthy, and his wealth manifold, he may behave with pride and insolence. God has said, *were God to expand His provision to all his servants, they would act insolently on earth* (Q.42:27).[107]

It should be noted here that ʿAbd al-Jabbār, the Muʿtazilite theologian, who has written extensively on the issue of illness and pain inflicted by God, supports the above notion. In ʿAbd al-Jabbār's opinion, although man may go through a period of suffering and pain as a result of an illness, however, there is larger good hidden in this experience – this illness is, in fact, a *lutf* from God.[108]

As already established, the notion of divine wisdom is central to al-Ghazālī's famous statement and his assertion that this world is the most perfect world. This emphasis makes itself known, once again, as he demonstrates that God creates nothing unless it encompasses a blessing for His creatures.[109] In al-Ghazālī's view, divine wisdom is evident in His creation of tribulations, for there is hidden blessing in every kind of *balā* that is created by God. It should also be pointed out that a similar view is held by the contemporary Muslim theologian and thinker, Bediuzzaman Said Nursi (d. 1960).[110] From the Nursian perspective, "Beneath the veil of events like storms, an earthquake, and plague, is the unfolding of numerous hidden immaterial flowers. The seeds of many potentialities which have not developed sprout and grow beautiful because of events which are apparently ugly."[111]

Moreover, al-Ghazālī reminds his readers that, in addition to being patient, in encountering *balā* in adversities, man should also be thankful to God, for his *balā* could have been much greater with higher level of hardship and suffering. Moreover, for al-Ghazālī, thankfulness during *balā* is the sign of a true monotheist who loves only the One and is content with whatever his situation is. To this end, al-Ghazālī emphasis a particular aspect of patience: the "pleasing patience" "*ṣabr jamiīl*", where the person who is going through a difficult *balā* is not identifiable from others around him, for as much as he feels the pain in his heart, he upholds his calmness and sustains his usual outwardly behavior.[112]

In recapitulating the all-encompassing meaning of *balā*: means by which human potential is realized, as emphasized in the Qur'an and discussed previously, the character-building element of the notion of *balā* which is emphasized in al-Ghazālī's teachings deserves some attention here. As Zarrinkub points out, from the Ghazalian perspective, the underlying reason for much of man's wrongdoings and transgressions is due to his adoration and attachment to the material world.[113] The preoccupation with worldly affections and desires forms a veil between man and God leading him away from the straight path.[114] The remedy for severing the love of the material world, al-Ghazālī asserts, lies in the experience of *balā* in trial and tribulation:

> Another way in which misfortunes of this world are roads to the Hereafter is that all sins leading to perdition are to be found in the love of this world, while all of the means of deliverance are to be found in turning the heart away from the abode of vanities. Were blessings to be granted according to desires, without mixing them with tribulation and misfortune, the heart would find itself at home in this world and in its means, until it becomes as a Paradise for it...there are, therefore, blessings in tribulation in this respect, and one must rejoice in them, even when the pain is, necessarily, there.[115]

It may be argued that the above passage sheds light on another aspect of al-Ghazālī's teachings: that *balā*, in its perceived negative version, plays an instrumental role in man's spiritual development and his relationship to God. In his later work *Kimyā' al-Saʿāda, The Alchemy of Happiness*, he offers an extensive commentary on human's soul (*nafs*)' and the importance of its purification. For al-Ghazālī, *balā* in adversity and illness is, indeed, a blessing and a sign of divine's grace (*lutf*); through the experience of *balā* man is able to sever the excessive desire for worldly attachments, and preoccupy his heart with that which is of vital significance – the divine love.[116] As Elkaisy-Friemuth points out, in al-Ghazālī's view, the essence of human soul is divine insofar as it has been created in the image of God; the purpose of its creation in the material world is to provide the platform for the *nafs* to attain the necessary knowledge and experience.[117] Consequently, *nafs* is hindered from following its *fitra* due to the many desires of the physical body, detaching from the unnecessary desires is the key to the spiritual development of *nafs*.[118]

It should also be pointed out that John Hick's "soul-making theodicy", briefly mentioned at the beginning of this chapter, seems to resemble al-Ghazālī's view as it pertains to the process and ways by which human soul reaches its full potential. From Hick's perspective, there are two stages to man's creation: the first stage was brought forward by an omnipotent creator; the second stage, however, cannot be accomplished by the all-powerful God, but rather, its completion is contingent upon man's cooperation.[119] The first stage is when the divine creative power initiated the existence of the physical universe, and in the course of various stages, organic life was brought forward; ultimately this led to the emergence of man as the creature with various potentials and the ability to experience a personal life. The second stage, Hick informs us, is of a different kind due to the fact that personal life is free and self-directing. Hence, divine command cannot make man perfect, but rather, man's perfection is only attainable through his own free choices as he experiences various conditions of life – good and bad – and willingly actualizes his potential, *balā* in adversity and prosperity. In criticizing the antitheistic writers such as Hume who question the existence of a loving and powerful God in face of evil in this world, Hick argues:

> The question that we have to ask is not, is the architecture of the world the most pleasant and convenient possible? The question that we have to ask is rather, is this the kind of world that God might make as an environment in which moral beings may be fashioned, through their own insights and responses..., to live a personal life of eternal worth? We have to recognize that the presence of pleasure and the absence of pain cannot be the supreme and overriding end for which the world exists. Rather, this world must be a place of soul-making. And its value is to be judged, not primarily by the quantity of pleasure and pain occurring in it at any particular moment, but by its fitness for its primary purpose, the purpose of soul-making... The good that outshines all ill is not a paradise long since lost but a kingdom which is yet to come in its full glory and permanence.[120]

It is worth pointing out that while there are certain similarities between al-Ghazālī's "the best of all possible world" statement and Hick's "soul-making" theodicy, nevertheless, there appears to be a distinctive feature in their overall approach which gives each a unique perspective. Al-Ghazālī seems to view the structure of the world from a divine perspective and through the lens of divine attributes. For him, if man does not have a firm belief that this world is the most excellent world, then he is questioning the divine attributes of goodness and power which, in al-Ghazālī's view, is inconceivable even in the face of much evil in the world. Hence, his emphasis is different than the classical formulation of the problem of evil which casts doubts on God's attributes. As previously discussed, al-Ghazālī makes a serious effort to demonstrate the perfectness of the world as is to lead the way in attaining a total trust in God.[121] On the other hand, Hick seems to view the structure of the world from a human perspective. In his view, this world is the best and most perfect environment for man to actualize his full potential and earn the "personal life of eternal worth". For Hick, a world without problems and hardships is a morally static environment which does not provide the necessary condition for man, to freely and willingly find God, and attain goodness as he overcomes the various temptations of his life.[122].

Likewise, Nursi is of the opinion that the realization of man's inner-most potential is doable through various circumstances of life. As Stowasser informs us, in Nursi's view, "Adam's expulsion from paradise, served but as a means to unfold his potentialities; human striving occurs only through the challenges that are posed to the human by the existence of evil spirits and harmful things".[123] Furthermore, this notion is also supported by Muslim philosopher, Sir Muhammad Iqbal (1877-1938). In discussing the Qur'anic view of the dynamic conception of the universe and the purposefulness of its creation, Iqbal argues that it is in facing the many challenges and the exercise of faculty of his volition that man plays a critical role in realizing the divine purpose for the creation of the universe.[124] According to Ward, in Iqbal's view, "…the production of finite egos is a production of true creative centers, with their own potentiality and capacity for evil as well as good."[125]

From the Muslim perspective, therefore, the notion of *balā* and its manifestation in adversity and hardship is part and parcel of the world which is, indeed, the best possible and most excellent world. It is through facing countless challenges of life – *balā* in good and bad – that humans are able to actualize their potential and earn the eternal life of happiness and tranquility that is emphasized in the Qur'an.

Conclusion

The all-inclusive meaning of *balā* in the Qur'an and its positive connotation has been discussed in various parts of this study. Nevertheless, due to the fact that *balā* is traditionally seen as synonymous with suffering, it should also be examined in the context of Muslim theodicy and the attendant concepts of "good" and "evil".

The widespread "problem of evil", generally referred to as the principal cause of human suffering, is recognized as a primary concern in the history of philosophy of religion – in Judeo-Christian thought as well as Muslim literature. These theological and philosophical discussions seem to be concerned mainly with the "theoretical" aspects of the problem – logical and evidential – and less with the "existential / practical" versions. Moreover, this extensive debate, comprised of many elements and versions, seems to include several interrelated problems which contribute to the complexity of the topic. In general, these discussions revolve around the idea that the problem of evil poses a major challenge to the belief that, in face of much human suffering, an omnipotent and loving God exists.

The attempt to provide specific explanations for the existence of evil, i.e. *balā* in its negative version, and to demonstrate that there is no inconsistency between the conviction that God is compassionate, all-knowing and all-powerful, and that the world does contain various forms of human suffering, resulted in the emergence of a number of theodicies. Christian theodicean thought has been greatly influenced by St. Augustine, who asserted that evil has no positive reality and advocated for the doctrine of *privatio boni* "privation of good". However, in more recent years, John Hick constructed the theodicy of "soul-making", and affirmed that the world including its various forms of evil and human suffering, is the most excellent environment for man to become the perfect creature that God intended to create.

The Muslim philosophical (*falsifa*) and theological literature (*kalām*) also reflects a variety of discussions relating to the problem of evil. Although the root of an early formulation of Muslim theodicy goes back to the uncompromising emphasis on God's power, themes such as divine justice and human free will contributed to the rise of conflicting views. The debate further intensified as the two theological schools, the Muʿtazilite and the Ashʿarite, sought to establish, based on the teachings of the Qurʾan, the superiority of their thought. The Ashʿarite school of thought, which maintained God's omnipotence and rejected human free will, prevailed and became the orthodox school of Sunnite Islam. The Muʿtazilite, on the other hand, employing rational deductions in their teachings, influenced Shiite Islam.

Furthermore, optimism – referred to as the special problem of theodicy – also received attention in the theological discussions: is this world the best that it can be in face of human suffering, negative *balā*? In al-Ghazālī's opinion, not only this world is the most perfect and excellent world, there is not in possibility anything more wonderful than what is. Having experienced a major negative version of *balā* in his life – physical and mental illness which had a profound impact on his character – al-Ghazālī's "best of all possible worlds" dictum affirmed that, even with its apparent imperfections, this world is the most excellent creation of a wise and omnipotent God. Al-Ghazālī's exposition of this experience, fully explained in *al-Munqidh min al-ḍalāl*, seems to accord with the overall positive connotation of *balā* emphasized in the Qurʾan. Additionally, the instrumentality of *balā* and its positive impact on man's spiritual development, which the Qurʾan seems to impart, is clearly manifested in al-Ghazālī's trial. For it is by going through this experience, of what seemed to be a devastating *balā* – adversity and suffering – that al-Ghazālī transformed to become one of the most influential thinkers of the Muslim world.

Al-Ghazālī's "the best of all possible worlds" statement contains several elements of classical formulation of theodicy; nevertheless, this famous dictum appears in the book of *tawakkul*, Trust in God, of the *Iḥyāʾ ʿulūm al-dīn*. Therefore, due to the fact that the statement makes itself known in the context of *tawakkul,* al-Ghazālī seems to have been more concerned with man's spiritual development and sought to demonstrate how to attain the highest level of trust in God. Moreover, the notion of *ṣabr,* patience, and *shukr,* thankfulness, the two topics which are closely related to *balā,* are highlighted in the *Iḥyāʾ 'ulūm al-dīn.* In his elucidation of these concepts, al-Ghazālī expounds upon the benefits of a negative form of *balā,* i.e., adversity, illness, and misfortune, and points out the character-building element of *balā;* as well as, *balā* as means by which man is able to detach from the material attachments.

It may be concluded that in al-Ghazālī's vision, *balā,* even in its negative form, is entirely positive; and contrary to misperceptions surrounding it, is beneficial to man's spiritual development. The highlight of al-Ghazālī's teachings accords with the aim of the Qur'an and sheds light on how man's psychological and spiritual state may be developed, if he is to face trials and tribulations, and the inevitable difficulties of life without despair and anxiety, but rather with a positive attitude. As Iqbal points out, "the main purpose of the Qur'an is to awaken in man the higher consciousness of his manifold relations with God and the universe."[126] A critical time when this relationship is strengthened is when man is faced with difficult times, misfortune and misery, and yet remains a sincere believer. To use the language of the Qur'an, those who, when faced with *balā,* patiently persevere and assert: "*We are from Allah and to Him we shall return*". We may conclude, therefore, that the Qur'an does not develop a systematic theodicy, but rather aims to educate, to build character, and to prepare and empower man to overcome occasions of suffering.[127]

*It is He who made you successors
on the earth and raises some of
you above others in rank, to test
you through what He gives you.*
(Qur'an, 6:165)

Conclusion

The main objective of this book is to shed light on the all-encompassing meaning of the notion of trial and tribulation, *balā*, within the context of the Qur'anic teachings which had thus far been overlooked. By using the method of textual analysis, fifty verses of the Qur'an whereby the concept of *balā* is emphasized were scrutinized exhaustively; the result of which formed a distinctive typology. The foundation of this study, therefore, is grounded in the revelation itself and the framework which the typology of the Qur'anic narratives seems to suggest. According to the findings of this typology, the overall Qur'anic portrayal of the notion of Divine trial – presented mostly by utilizing the two major terms of *balā* and *fitna* – demonstrates that *balā* is the *raison d'etre* of the creation and, as such, is wholly positive and purposeful; and that it is instrumental in man's spiritual development and actualization of his inner-nature potential. Moreover, the statistical survey of *balā* / *fitna* narratives indicates that Divine trial remained at the core of the Qur'anic teachings during both phases of the revelation, the Meccan and Medinan periods, which underscores the importance of this concept and its all-inclusive meaning.

In order to expound upon the multi-dimensional aspects of *balā* emphasized in the Qur'an, the two most important sources of Islamic sciences, namely the *hadith* collections and Muslim exegetical literature were examined thoroughly. The study of the Sunnite *hadith* collections illustrates that there are a limited number of prophetic traditions about *balā*, and even then, the traditions mainly point out the negative aspects of *balā* as it is manifested in adversities and calamities. A more comprehensive discussion of *balā*, however, is found in the teachings of Imam Ali as represented in the book of *Nahjol-Balāgha*. Furthermore, to answer one of the key research questions, namely to discover whether or not the Qur'anic exegetes engage in an in-depth exposition of *balā*, twelve narratives discussed in the typology were studied in light of six Sunnite and Shiite Qur'anic commentaries of the classical period to contemporary time. The result of this critical analysis demonstrates that the mainstream

Qur'anic exegetical literature, for the most part, fails to engage in an in-depth discussion of *balā*, and therefore, does not contribute to a comprehensive comprehension of this topic. Therefore, the lack of engagement on the part of exegetes and their limited understanding of this highly emphasized Qur'anic theme may have contributed to the misconceptions that currently surround this topic, namely that it is equated with suffering, and that it has a negative connotation.

As illustrated in the typology of the Qur'anic narratives, a large number of *balā* / *fitna* narratives, in which Divine trial is treated in its most comprehensive meaning, pertain to the notion of prophethood. Due to the fact that prophethood is treated in the Islamic scripture as a universal phenomenon, and the fact that the stories of the prophets and their addressee communities occupy a major portion of the Islamic revelation, a specific chapter was dedicated to investigate how *balā* is manifested in the lives of the prophets. The critical examination of these narratives demonstrates that the prophets experienced many trials and tribulations in the course of their life which proved to be instrumental in their spiritual development. Additionally, as the ideal prototype and the best role model to be followed, prophets' conduct and behavior during these times provided the inspiration and guidance for their communities. The result of this examination, discussed in full detail in Chapter three, clarifies some of the main misconceptions about *balā* and illustrates that the sole purpose of trial and tribulation is not for God to punish sinful individuals, and that *balā* is manifested not just in adversity but also in prosperity, as in the case of Solomon and David. Moreover, the scrutiny of Divine trial in the lives of the ten Qur'anic prophets presented in the exegetical literature further confirmed that the majority of the exegetes seem to have missed the constructive and positive aspects of *balā* which the prophets encountered throughout their lives, both prior to becoming a prophet and after they were charged with the prophetic mission. The study also shows that the mainstream Qur'anic exegetes seem to be more concerned with the non-factual details of the prophetic tales, rather than the purposefulness of a particular *balā*. An example of this is seen in their exposition of *balā* of Ibrahim – when God commands him to sacrifice his son – and the serious attempt made by most of the Qur'anic commentaries to prove the identity of Ibrahim's son – a point which the Qur'an itself is silent on. Therefore, the exegetes' emphasis on some of the most insignificant aspects of the prophetic trials may explain their lack of engagement with the positive nature and the all-encompassing meaning of *balā*.

Although the mainstream Qur'anic exegetical literature, which mostly throws light on the exoteric teachings of the Qur'an, seems to lack a thorough and widespread analysis of the notion of *balā*, the mystical literature which is concerned with the esoteric interpretation of the revelation, on the other hand, appears to reveal its full and multi-dimensional meanings. Muslim mysticism, historically represented by Sufism, is primarily concerned with man's inner nature and the divine element ingrained in its roots. From the perspective of Muslim mystics in general, and Rumi's teachings in particular, the concept of *balā* is viewed in conjunction with key Qur'anic themes such as Adam and the fall, the *alast* covenant, man's viceregal role, and the Divine Trust bestowed on to him. In Rumi's mysticism, themes such as self-knowledge and self-purification, which lead to God's awareness, are closely related to *balā*; and man's trials and tribulations, as well as times of prosperity and well-being, are viewed as the context and means by which man travels on the spiritual journey and gains higher status. Rumi's contribution in expounding upon the significance of the creational tree, and man's position as the fruit of God's creation, further enhances the in-depth meaning of *balā* and its instrumental role in man's spiritual development.

The findings of this study also illustrate that *balā* manifested in adversity and hardship, which may lead to human suffering, from the Rumian perspective is purposeful as it assists man in severing worldly attachments. This understanding is grounded in the fact that most human suffering is due to man's desire for the temporal world and the continuous demands of his ego; by going through hardship in form of *balā*, man has the opportunity to realize the divine essence of his nature and detach from the material world. Rumi emphasizes that mankind's most important *balā* is that he has been separated from his divine essence, and that every situation in life, good and bad, is the means by which man is able to actualize his potential and ultimately find his way back to the Divine. From this mystical understanding, therefore, *balā* is a necessary element in man's creation: it provides him with the opportunity to purify his soul in order to become the perfect reflection of God's most beautiful names and His attributes.

As the findings of this study indicate, the positive nature and the all-encompassing meaning of *balā* is highlighted throughout the Qur'an; however, since *balā* is sometimes manifested in adversity and hardship, which in turn may result in human suffering, it was also examined in view of Muslim theodicean thought and the attendant concepts of "good" and "evil". The "problem of evil", which is at the core of philosophical and theological discussions within the Judeo-Christian thought as well as Muslim literature, generally is referred to as the main cause for human suffering. While the overall "problem of evil" includes different versions – comprehensively discussed in the history of philosophy of religion – the main debate revolves around the seeming inconsistency between the existence of evil, and the belief in the existence of God who is all-powerful, all-wise, and omnipotent. The effort to explain, and to reconcile certain theistic belief with the existence of evil and human suffering in the world, has resulted in the creation of various theodicies.

From the perspective of the Christian theodicean thought, greatly influenced by the teachings of St. Augustine, the question of evil is explained best through the doctrine of *privatio boni*, "privation of good", and the notion that evil has no positive reality. More recently, however, John Hick's "soul-making" theodicy, and the assertion that this world, with all of its evil and human suffering, is the best environment for man to become the creature that God planned to create, has attracted the attention of many. Likewise, the "problem of evil" has been discussed in Muslim philosophy and theology. While its earliest debate emphasized the categorical belief in God's power, the dispute eventually extended to include conflicting views about divine justice, human free will, and reward and punishment.

The two theological schools, the Ash'arite and the Mu'tazilite, attempted to establish their views on the teachings of the Qur'an: Sunnite Islam accepted the views of the Ash'arite and their assertion of God's power and the rejection of human free will, while Shiite Islam was largely influenced by the Mu'tazilite.

At the core of Muslim theodicean thought lies the question of optimism: in face of calamities and human suffering – *balā* manifested in its negative version – is this world the most excellent world that it can be? This special problem of theodicy has been addressed by al-Ghazālī, who experienced the impact of a serious physical and mental illness, and affirmed that not only is this world the best that it can be, there is no possibility of anything more wonderful than what is. Al-Ghazālī's famous dictum of "the best of all possible worlds", which was raised by Leibniz in Europe several centuries later, includes various components of theodicy; nonetheless, the statement reveals itself in the book of *tawakkul*, Trust in God, of the *Iḥyā' 'ulūm al-dīn*. By introducing "the best of all possible worlds" statement in the context of Trust in God, al-Ghazālī appears to engage in an expressive discussion about the practical aspects of *balā* to remind his readers that this world, including its imperfections, is in fact the most excellent world, and that by going through trials and tribulations of life, man is able to grow spiritually and attain the highest levels of trust in God. Moreover, al-Ghazālī provides an extensive discussion on two important Qur'anic terms that are used in conjunction with *balā*, namely *ṣabr*, patience, and *shukr*, thankfulness, to emphasize that *balā* in good and bad, is instrumental in man's spiritual development.

Al-Ghazālī's theodicean thought, which is highly influenced by his personal experience of a negative *balā* – adversity, physical and mental illness, and suffering – throws light on the all-inclusive meaning and the positive connation of *balā* which the Qur'an emphasizes. For it is through this difficult experience, what seemed to be a destructive form of evil, that al-Ghazālī's potential is realized, and he is transformed into one the most influential thinkers of the Muslim world.

The material presented in this book demonstrates that the Qur'anic notion of trial and tribulation, *balā*, is multi-dimensional and wholly positive; it is not equated with suffering as its manifestation becomes known both in adversity and prosperity; that it is not meant to punish the sinful, as all human beings, including the prophets, are tested in good and bad. Furthermore, trials and tribulations are instrumental in man's spiritual development as they provide him with the opportunities to "become" who he "is". A further conclusion is that the Qur'anic exegetical materials do not, for the most part, engage in an in-depth elucidation of *balā*; and that the all-comprehensive nature, and the entirely positive meaning of trial and tribulation emphasized in the Qur'an, is largely discussed in the Muslim mystical and theodicean literature.

Appendix

Balā Narratives in the Qur'an

	Sura / Verse K/M	Translation	Context / Comments
1	2:49, M	Children of Israel: Remember when We delivered you from the folk of Pharaoh who were visiting you with evil chastisement, slaughtering your sons, and sparing your women; and in that was a grievous <u>trial</u> from your Lord.	Example of other nations Linking trial to Allah
2	2:124, M	And when his Lord tested Abraham with certain words, and he fulfilled them. He said "Behold, I make you a leader for the people." Said he, "And of my seed?" He said "My covenant shall not reach the evildoers".	Example of Abraham's test The result becoming the Imam
3	2:155, M	Surely We will try you with something of fear and hunger, and diminution of goods and lives and fruits; yet give thou good tidings unto the patient	Refers to time of warfare for Muslims Tangible items of test
4	2:249, M	And when Salūt went forth with the hosts he said, "God will try you with a river; whosoever drinks of it is not of me, and whose tasted it not, he is of me,…"	Example of other nations Drinking from the River : Test
5	3:152, M	…God has been true in His promise towards you…Then He turned you from them, that He might try you; and He has pardoned you..	Battle of Uhud – when some Muslims left the stage to look for war gifts
6	3:154, M	Then He sent down upon you, after grief, security…Say: "Even if you had been in your houses, those for whom slaying was appointed would have sallied forth unto their last couches"; and that God might try what was in your breasts, and that He might prove what was in your hearts; God knows the thoughts in the breasts.	Battle of Uhud-

7	3:186, M	You shall surely be tried in your possessions and your selves, and you shall hear from those who were given the Book before you, and from those who are idolaters, much hurt; but if you are patient and god-fearing – surely that is true constancy	Hardships of Muslims at the time and in general: Afflictions / suffering; also grief from those outside of their faith, Patience is prescribed
8	5:48, M	For every community We decreed a law and a way of life. Had God willed, He could have made you a single community – but in order to test you in what He revealed to you. So vie with one another in virtue. To God is your homecoming, all of you, and He will then acquaint you with that over which you differed.	The Book / Law are the subject in which communities are tested by. Diversity in Scripture is in Divine Plan and is due to natural differences between people of different times; the aim of all Revelations is for man to grow and actualize his potential; ultimate goal is for man to be virtuous and strive to grow spiritually
9	5:94, M	O Believers, God will surely put you to the test in some of the game that your hands and lances shall garner, in order that God may know who truly fears Him in the realm of the Unseen. Thereafter, whoso transgresses, a painful torment awaits him.	Killing game is forbidden in the state of Ihram Purpose: for God to know (kalam aspects)
10	6:165, K	It is He Who made you inheritors of the earth, and elevated some of you above others in degree in order to test you in what He bestowed upon you.	Diverse status of people on earth is part of the Divine plan to test some with others; differences are purposeful and are the mechanism for tests
11	7:141, K	Exactly as in 2:49 (#1)	Example of other nations Linking trial to Allah
12	7:163, K Tarif Khalidi	Ask them about a town by the sea, when they broke the Sabbath. Their fish would swim to them from every side on the day of the Sabbath. When they did not keep the Sabbath, the fish would not come to them. This is how We put them to the test because of their iniquity.	Example of other nations Linking trial to Allah
13	8:17, M	You did not slay them; it was God who slew them. It was not you who threw when you threw, but God it was Who threw, in order to bestow upon the believers, from His grace, a fine achievement. God is All-Hearing...; Yusuf Ali: "in order that He might test the believers by a gracious trial"	Refers to the battle Badr; how Muslims won with God's help even though they had much less arm forces

14	11:7, K	He is Who created the heavens and the earth in six days, and His throne was upon the waters, so as to test you: who among you is the best in works…; Yusuf Ali: That He might try you, which of you is best in conduct,….	Key verse: pointing to the fact that (1) Test / Trials are part of Creation; (2) Creation as we see around us is not a sport; our life is our opportunity to develop our potentials ;(3) Is the test the goal of creation or what comes as the result of the test? (4) Mutazila's thought on how God's acts are based on purposes, (5) No one is exempt from this Divine Plan
15	14:6, K	Same context as in 2:49 & 7:141 (# 1 & 5)	Example of other nations Linking trial to Allah
16	16:92, K	And do not be like the woman who unravels her weaving, once made fast, into shreds. You consider the oaths you swear among yourselves as trickery, whenever one party is more numerous than another. But God will assuredly put you to the **test** because of this, and on the Day of Resurrection He will make fully clear to you what you once disputed about.	Oaths are the means of tests
17	18:7, K	We fashioned what lies upon the earth as an ornament for it, to test them as to who shall be the best in works. And We shall turn all that lies upon it into a desolate plain.	Key verse: (1)Everything on this earth is a test; wealth, position, glory, (all that we strive for), they test a man's true quality: some who become their slave, some who use them but don't fall into despair if don't get them,(2) our potentials actualize based on how we choose to live (3) No one is exempt
18	21:35, K Yusuf Ali	Every soul shall have a taste of death: and We test you by evil and by good by way of trial. To Us you must ye return.	Key verse: Use of both terms bala / fitna Evil & Good: Adversity & Prosperity
19	33:11, M	It was there that the believers were tested, and convulsed a mighty convulsion	Battle
20	37:106, K	That was indeed a conspicuous ordeal; Yusuf A.: For this was obviously a trial	Example of Prophet's test Ibrahim's test to sacrifice his son; the end result was the goal not the actual sacrifice; trial was just a test; reward for those who do right

21	44:33, K	And We brought them wonders, in which was a clear ordeal; Yusuf A.: And granted them Signs in which there was a manifest trial	Example of other nations - Linking trial to Allah; People of Israel (freedom from Pharaoh; the chosen nation; but all was a test)
22	47:4, M	..Yet, had God willed, He could Himself have vanquished them, but it was so in order that He might test some of you through others…	Refers to time of battle; unbelievers and believers are being tested
23	47:31, M	We shall put you to the test , to know who are truly exerting themselves for God and are standing firm, and We shall put to the test your secret thoughts	Refers to time of battle
24	76:2-3, M	We created man from a sperm drop of fluids commingled, that We may test him; and formed him to hear and see; We guided him upon the way, be he grateful or ungrateful.	Key verse: Man is being reminded of how he was created and then given certain faculties and was guided; the test.
25	89:15, K	And as for man, if his Lord <u>tries</u> him, honors him, and prospers him, he will say: "My Lord has honoured me"	God tries us both by prosperity and adversity; instead of showing humility and kindness man puffs
26	89:16, K	But if He tries him, and constricts his livelihood, he will say: "My Lord has demeaned me"; Yusuf Ali: But when He tried him, restricting his subsistence for him, then said he (in despair), "My Lord hath humiliated me!"	up as he sees permanency in this status; in adversity instead of patience man gets depressed; Points: (1) Repeating the word bala in two verses indicates that both His giving and restricting is His test (similar to 21:35 tests in good & evil) (2) gifts from God is an honor but when man does not use it on the right path it becomes the reason for his punishment (3) wealth or lack of it is not a sign of being closer to God, rather good conduct is
27	67:2, K	He Who created death and life to test you as to which of you is most righteous in deed; He is Almighty, All-Forgiving	Key verse: (1) death is before life and it is created – death is not a negative state (2) when Life as we know is ceased existence continues in a another state (3) Test is the mean where man can grow and built his life to go into eternity; this verse relates to the other key verses about creation

28	68:17, M	We are testing them, as We once tested the owners of the garden	Meccans who called the Prophet a mad man were tested comparing them to the owners of the garden at a different time in history!
29	86:9, K	The Day when the secrets of hearts are put on trial.	Day of judgment is when the Truth of the hearts comes to surface. Are not all the tests for this reason? What is hidden will be evident on that day! See 2:284

K = Revealed in Mecca (15 verses)
M = Revealed in Medina (14 verses)

Fitna Narratives in the Qur'an

	Sura / **Verse** **K/M**	**Translation**	**Context / Comments**
1	5:41, M	O Messenger! Let not those grieve thee, who race each other into Unbelief: (Whether it be) among those who say "We believe with their lips but whose hearts have no faith; or it be among the Jews-Men who will listen to any lie....If anyone's trial is intended by Allah, thou hast no authority in that least for him against Allah.	
2	6:53, K	Thus did We try some of them by comparison with others that they should say; "Is it these then that Allah hath favoured from amongst us?" Doth not Allah know best those who are grateful?	The influential / wealthy people felt they are better than those who Allah had selected to Send his teachings to!
3	7:155, K	And Moses chose seventy of his people for Our place of meeting: when they were seized with violent quaking, he prayed: "O My Lord! If it had been Thy Will thou couldst have destroyed, long before, both them and me: Wouldst Thou destroy us for the deeds of the foolish ones among us? This is no more than Thy trial: by it Thou causes whom Thou wilt to stray, and Thou leadest whom though will into the right path..	Other nations / Moses
4	8:28, M	And know ye that your possessions and your progeny are but a trial, and that it is Allah with whom lies your highest reward.	Some people in Medina shared Prophet's decisions with the Meccans to protect their wealth and kids in Mecca
5	9:126, M	See they not that they are tried every year once or twice? Yet turn not in repentance, and they take no heed.	The purpose of trial is for people to repent and come back. The means of trial not mentioned
6	17:60, K	Behold! We told thee that thy Lord doth encompass mankind round about: We granted the Vision which We showed thee but as a trial for me- as also the Cursed Tree (mentioned) in the Qur'an: We put terror (and warning) into them, but it only increases their inordinate transgression!	Some commentators take this as referring to the Miraj, others to other spiritual visions. Prophet's vision / Tree;

7	20:40, K	Behold! Thy sister went forth and said, "Shall I show you one who will nurse and rear the (child)? So we brought thee back to thy mother...then thou didst slay a man, but We saved thee from trouble, and We tried thee in various ways...	Other prophet :Life of Moses / many trials
8	21:35, K	Every soul shall have a taste of death: and We <u>test</u> you by evil and by good by way of <u>trial</u>. To Us you must ye return.	Key verse: Use of both terms *bala / fitna* Evil & Good: Adversity & Prosperity
9	21:111, K	"I know not but that it may be a trial for you and a grant of (worldly) livelihood (to you) for a time.	It may be that the enjoyment of this world's goods is but a trial.
10	22:11, M	There are among men some who worship Allah, as it were, on the verge: if good befalls them, they are, therewith, well content; but if a trial comes to them, they turn on their faces: they lose both this world and the Hereafter: that is loss for all to see!	Firm mind in faith is the key in passing the tests in life
11	22:53, M	That He may make the suggestions thrown in by Satan, but a trial for those in whose hearts is a disease and who are hardened of heart: verily the wrongdoers are in a schism far (from the Truth)	22:52 Satan's suggestions in revelation
12	25:20, K	And the messengers whom We sent before thee were all (Men) who ate food and walked through the streets. We have made some of you as a trial for others: will ye have patience? For Allah is One Who sees (all things).	Prophet is rejected due to being an ordinary man; in Allah's plan people serve as a test for each other (rich for the poor and vice versa)
13	29:2, K	Do men think that they will be left alone on saying, "we believe", and that they will not be tested?	Profession of Faith is not enough- it must be tested during life's circumstances. This is in Allah's Plan as everyone goes through the tests. Pay attention to Allah will know
14	29:3, K	We did test those before them, and Allah will certainly know those who are true from those who are false.	
15	39:49, K	Now, when trouble touches man he cries to Us: but when We bestow a favour upon him as from Ourselves, he says, "This has been given to me because of a certain knowledge (I have)! Nay, but this is but a trial, but most of them understand not!	Prosperity is a test as much as adversity See 30:33, 39:8, 28:78

16	44:17, K	We did, before them, try the people of Pharaoh: There came to them a messenger most honourable.	The test of Egyptians / Moses
17	54:27, K	For We will send the she-camel by way of trial for them. So watch them, (O Salih), and possess thyself in patience!	Other nations / prophet: Salih
18	60:5, M	"Our Lord! Make us not a (test and) trial for the Unbelievers, but forgive us, our Lord! For Thou are the Exalted in Might, the Wise."	
19	64:15, M	Your riches and your children may be but a trial: but in the Presence of Allah is the highest Reward.	Children / wealth: how we perceive them in life, our affections for them, etc.
20	72:17, K	Verse 16: (And Allah's message is): "if they (the Pagans) had only remained on the (right) Way, We should certainly have bestowed on them Rain in abundance – 17: "that We might try them by that (means). But if any turns away from the remembrance of his Lord, He will cause him to undergo a severe Penalty.	Rain as a mean for test: in prosperity
21	74:31, K	And We have set none but angels as guardians of the Fire; and We have fixed their number only as a trial for Unbelievers- in order that the People of the Book may arrive at certainty, and Believers may increase in Faith..	Number 19 (angels guarding hell)

K = Revealed in Mecca (14 verses)
M = Revealed in Medina (7 verses)

Notes

Introduction

1 The Qur'an, 11:7.
2 The attempt to explain that there is no contradiction between God's attributes of power and goodness with the fact that evil exists is generally referred to as Theodicy. See Ronald M. Green, 'Theodicy', in Lindsay Jones (ed.), *Encyclopedia of Religion* (2 edn., 13; Detroit, USA: Macmillan Reference, 2005).
3 See Morteza Mutahhari, `Adl-E Elahi* (Tehran, IR: Sadra, 1385).
4 For various connotations of *balā* see Hamed Naji, '*Ibtila*', in B. Khorramshahi (ed.), *The Encyclopedia of the Holy Qur'an* (1; Tehran, IR: Dustan & Nahid, 1999), pp. 113-14.
5 The Qur'an, 89:15-16.
6 See Abdol Ali Bazargan, 'Man's Tests and Trials', <http://bazargan.com/abdolali/>, accessed 12/10/2010.
7 The Qur'an, 38:27.
8 Naji, 'Ibtila'.
9 The typology of the Qur'anic narratives is presented in Chapter One of the study.
10 The Qur'an, 11:7.
11 Abu Jafar Muhammad B. Jarir Al-Tabari, *Jami Al-Bayan an Tawil Ay Al-Quran* (Beirut: Dar al-Marefa, 1412) Vol. 6, pp. 173.
12 Abul Qasim Mahmud Zamakhshari, *Al-Kashaf an Haga`Ig Ghawamid Al-Tanzil Wa-Uyun Al-Aqawil Fi Wujuh Al-Tawi*, trans. Masud Ansari (Tehran, IR: Dar al-Kitab al- Arabi, Beirut / Qoqnoos, Tehran, 1389 Solar), Vol. 2, pp. 493-94.
13 For example see Nasīr Al-Dīn Tūsī, *Kashf Al-Morād, Sharh Tajrid Al-I`Tiqad*, ed. `Allameh Helli, trans. Abol Hassan Sha`Rani (Tehran, IR: Islami, 1370).
14 For example see Jalal Al-Din Rumi, *The Mathnawi of Jalaluddin Rumi*, trans. Reynold A. Nicholson (Cambridge, ENG: E.J.W. Gibb Memorial, 2001, 1926).
15 For full discussion on the linguistic aspects of *balā* and *fitna* see Chapter One.
16 Toshibiko Izutsu, *Ethico - Religious Concepts in the Qur'an* (Montreal, CA: McGill-Queen's University Press, 2002), pp. 24-41.

Chapter 1

1 *Insān* "man" occurs sixty-five times in the Qur'an. It applies to both men and women, as of course does the generic "man" in English. See M.A.S. Abdel Haleem, *The Qur'an, English Translation* (Oxford University Press, US, 2004), p. 594
2 Fazlur Rahman, *Major Themes of the Qur'an* (Second edn.; Minneapolis, USA: Bibliotheca Islamica, 1994), p. 8.
3 Abdullah Yusuf Ali, *The Meaning of the Holy Qur'an* (11 edn.: Amana).P.1673
4 For a discussion on chronology of the Qur'an see W. Montgomery Watt and Richard Bell, *Introduction to the Qur'an* (Edinburgh, UK: Edinburgh University Press, 1970), p. 108.
5 Rahman, *Major Themes of the Qur'an*, p. 9.
6 As cited in Kabir Helminski, *The Vision of the Qur'an* (California: The Book Foundation, 2004), p. 68.
7 John Bowker, *Problems of Suffering in Religions of the World* (Cambridge Univ. Press, 1970), p. 109.
8 Margaretha T. Heemskerk, 'Suffering', in Jane Dammen Mcauliffe (ed.), *Encyclopedia of the Qur'an* (Leiden-Boston: Brill, 2006) Vol. 5, pp. 132-36.

9   The test of nations and prophets will be discussed further in Chapter Three.

10 Yusuf Ali, *The Meaning of the Holy Qur'an*, p. 1646.

11 Edward William Lane, 'Arabic - English Lexicon', (London: Williams and Norgate 1968) Vol. 1, p. 255.

12 Abbolnabi Ghayyem, 'Farhang-Moaser Arabic - Persian', (Tehran, Iran: Farhang Moaser, 1381 H.S.).

13 John Nawas, 'Trial', in Jane Dammen Mcauliffe (ed.), *Encyclopedia of the Qur'an* (Leiden-Boston: Brill, 2006) Vol. 5, p. 362.

14 Abdulkader Tayob, 'An Analytical Survey of Al-Tabari's Exegesis of the Cultural Symbolic Contstruct of Fitna', in G.R. Hawting and Abdul-Kader A. Shareef (eds.), *Approaches to the Qur'an* (New York: Routledge, 2002).

15 Lane, 'Arabic - English Lexicon', Vol. 6, p. 2335.

16 As cited in Tayob, 'An Analytical Survey of Al-Tabari's Exegesis of the Cultural Symbolic Contstruct of Fitna', p. 158.

17 Ghayyem, 'Farhang-Moaser Arabic - Persian', p. 776.

18 L. Gardet, 'Fitna', in P. Bearman, Bianquis (ed.), *Encyclopedia of Islam* (Second edn., II: Brill), p. 930.

19 Izutsu, *Ethico - Religious Concepts in the Qur'an*.

20 Ibid., pp. 37-41.

21 Neal Robinson, *Discovering the Qur'an: A Contemporary Approach to a Veiled Text* (Washington D.C.: Georgetown University Press, 2003a), p. 71. Also, see Watt and Bell, *Introduction to the Qur'an*, p. 180.

22 Maulana Abul Kalam Azad, *Tarjuman Al- Qur'an*, trans. Syed Abdul Latif (3; New Delhi: Kitab Bhavan, 1978), p. 148.

23 Yusuf Ali, *The Meaning of the Holy Qur'an*, p. 1497.

24 Ibid., p. 1571.

25 This category does not include any *bala* narrative from Medinan period.

26 This category does not include any *fitna* narrative in Medinan period.

27 Mahmoud Ayoub, *Islam, Faith and History* (Oxford: Oneworld, 2004), p. 22.

28 One of the verses in this category (21:35) was discussed in the *bala* section as it utilizes both the terms *bala* and *fitna*.

29 See Ayoub, *Islam, Faith and History*, pp. 30-50.

30 The "Parable of the People of the Garden" is elucidated in verses 17-32 of the same *Sura*.

31 Yusuf Ali's translation: "to test you".

32 Yusuf Ali, *The Meaning of the Holy Qur'an*, p. 166.

33 Ayoub, *Islam, Faith and History*, p. 25.

34 *Bala* is translated by Haleem to mean Divine favor, however, according to Yusuf Ali it means "to test the believers by a gracious trial", see Yusuf Ali, *The Meaning of the Holy Qur'an*, p. 418.

35 Frederick Mathewson Denny, *An Introudution to Islam* (USA: Prentice Hall, 2011), p. 66.

36 Abdel Haleem, *The Qur'an, English Translation*, p. 180.

37 The Night Journey, which gives the *Sura* its title, is mentioned in verse 1 and 60. Towards the end of the Meccan period, God caused Muhammad, in the space of a single night, to journey from Mecca to Jerusalem and from there to heaven and back again. See ibid., p. 283.

38 Ibid., p. 289.

39 For a discussion on doctrines of faith see Denny, *An Introudution to Islam*, p. 99.

40 For a full discussion on *bala* in the lives of the prophets see Chapter Three.

41 For a full discussion on the story of Moses and *bala* see Q. 7:148-155.

42 See Yusuf Ali, *The Meaning of the Holy Qur'an*, p. 604, note 1878.

43 Ibid., p. 1288, note 4713.

44 Ibid., pp. 36-365, notes 1043 & 44.

45 Ibid., p. 103, note 284.

Chapter 2

1 Wilfred Cantwell Smith, *What Is Scripture?* (Minneapolis, USA: Fortress Press 1993), p. 70.

2 Mahmoud Ayoub, 'Qur'an: Its Role in Muslim Practice and Life', in Lindsay Jones (ed.), *Encyclopedia of Religion* (Detroit: McMillian Reference USA, 2005) Vol.11, pp. 7570-74.

3 Carl W. Ernst, *Folowing Muhammad, Rethinking Islam in the Contemporary World* (North Carolina, USA: The University of North Carolina Press, 2003), p. 80.

4 Denny, *An Introudution to Islam*, p. 151.

5 Ibid.

6 Jonathan A.C. Brown, *Hadith, Muhammad's Legacy in the Medieval and Modern World* (One World, UK, 2009), p. 31.

7 Muhammad Isma`Il Al-Bukhārī, 'Hadith Collections of Al-Bukhari', <http://www.hadithcollection.com/sahihbukhari.html>, accessed May 25, 2010.

8 Ibid.

9 Muslim Al-Hajjaj, 'Sahih Muslim', <http://www.hadithcollection.com/sahihmuslim.html>, accessed May 30, 2010.

10 Abu-Dawūd, 'Sunan Abu- Dawud', <http://www.searchtruth.com/>, accessed May 30, 2010.

11 Tirmidhi, 'Sunan Tirmidhi', <http://www.hadithcollection.com/shama-iltirmidhi.html>, accessed May 30, 2010.

12 Ibid.

13 Ibid.

14 Abu Jafar Kulini, *Usul Al-Kafi, English Translation by Muhammad Sarwar*, trans. Muhammad Sarwar (Islamic Seminary, New York, 2005), Vol. 2, p. 210.

15 Ibid. 2:211.

16 Ali Bn Abi-Taalib Imam Amir Al-Muminin, *Nahjol-Balagha: Peak of Eloquence, English Translation by Sayyid Ali Reza* (Ansariyan, Qum-Iran, 1999), pp. 408-25.

17 Ibid.

18 Ibid., pp. 411-12.

19 Ibid., pp. 413-14.

20 Ibid., p. 252.

21 Ibid., p. 587.

22 Ibid., p. 321.

23 Ibid., p. 323.

24 Mahmoud Ayoub, *The Qur'an and Its Interpreters* (Albany: State University of New York Press, 1984), p. 1.

25 Ibid.

26 Jane Dammen Mcauliffe, *Qur'anic Christians, an Analysis of Classical and Modern Exegesis* (New York, USA: Cambridge University Press, 1991), pp. 38-43.

27 Ayoub, *The Qur'an and Its Interpreters*, Vol. 1, p. 4.

28 Ibid., p. 5.

29 Mcauliffe, *Qur'anic Christians, an Analysis of Classical and Modern Exegesis*, p. 51.

30 Al-Dāwūdi, *Tabagāt*, 2:136, as quoted by McAuliffe in *Qur'anic Christians*, p. 52

31 Zafar Ishag Ansari, *Towards Understanding the Qur'an: English Version of Tafhim Al-Qur'an* (London, UK: The Islamic Foundation, 1988), p. xiii.

32 Aboulghasem Radford, 'Tafhim Al-Qur'an', in B. Khorramshahi (ed.), *The Encyclopedia of the Holy Qur'an* (Tehran, Iran: Dustan & Nahid Publishers, 1999).

33 Ansari, *Towards Understanding the Qur'an: English Version of Tafhim Al-Qur'an*, p. xii.

34 See Meir M. Bar-Asher, *Scripture and Exegesis in Early Imami Shiism* (London, UK: Brill, 1999).

35 Mahmoud Ayoub, 'The Speaking Qur'an and the Silent Qur'an: A Study of the Principles and Development of Imami Shi'i *Tafsir*', in Andrew Rippin (ed.), *Approaches to the History of the Interpretation of the Qur'an* (Oxford, UK: Clarendon Press, 1988).

36 Jouya Jahanbaksh, '*Tafsir* Abul Futuh Razi', in B. Khorramshahi (ed.), *The Encyclopedia of the Holy Qur'an* (Tehran, IRan: Doustan & Nahid Publishers, 1991b), pp. 661-62.

37 See Abu Al-Hassan Sh'rani, *Muhaddimah, Abu Al-Futuh Razi's Rawh Al-Jinan Wa Ruh Al-Janan* (Tehran, Iran: Ketabfurushi-yi Islamiyah, 1962).

38 Shafi'I, M., *Mufassirān*, as quoted by McAuliffe in *Qur'anic Christians*, p. 55

39 McAuliffe, *Qur'anic Christians*, p. 76

40 Jouya Jahanbaksh, 'Tafisr Mulla Fath Allah Kashani', in B. Khorramshahi (ed.), *The Encyclopedia of the Holy Qur'an* (Tehran, Iran: Dustan & Nahid Publishers, 1991a), p. 766.

41 Ayoub, *The Qur'an and Its Interpreters*, p. 7.

42 Nasr, S. Hussein, Foreword, English translation of Muhammad Hussain Tabatabai, *The Qur'an in Islam*, trans. Seyyed Hossein Nasr (London, UK: Zahra, 1987).

43 Al-Tabari, *Jami Al-Bayan an Tawil Ay Al-Quran*, Vol. 6, pp. 173-76.

44 Ibid.

45 Ibid., Vol. 3, p. 10.

46 Ibid., Vol. 29, p. 2.

47 Zamakhshari, *Al-Kashaf an Haga`Ig Ghawamid Al-Tanzil Wa-Uyun Al-Aqawil Fi Wujuh Al-Tawi*, Vol. 2, pp. 493-94.

48 Ibid.

49 Ibid.

50 Ibid., Vol. 3, pp. 10-11.

51 Ibid.

52 Ibid., Vol. 4, pp. 704 -05.

53 Sayyid Abul a`La Mawdudi, 'Tafhim Al-Qur'an', <http://www.searchtruth.com/tafsir/tafsir.php?chapter=37>, <http://www.searchtruth.com/tafsir/tafsir.php?chapter=11> accessed August 15, 2011.

54 Ibid. <http://www.searchtruth.com/tafsir/tafsir.php?chapter=18>

55 Ibid. <http://www.searchtruth.com/tafsir/tafsir.php?chapter=67>

56 Abu Al-Futuh Razi, *Rawh Al-Jinan Wa-Ruh Al-Janan* (Tehran: Kitabfurush-yi Islamiyah 1384/1964) Vol. 6, pp. 245-46.

57 Ibid.

58 Ibid.

59 Ibid., Vol. 7, p. 300.

60 Ibid., Vol. 11, pp. 210-11.

61 Ibid.

62 Mulla Fath Allah Kashani, *Minhaj Al-Sadigin Fi Ilzam Al-Mukhalifin* (Tehran, IR: Kitabfurushi-yi Islamiyah, 1347 {solar} / 1969). 4:402

63 Ibid. 9:350.

64 Ibid., Vol. 5, p. 328.

65 Muhammad Hussain Tabatabai, *Al-Mizan*, trans. Seyed M. Bagher Musavi-Hamedani (Qum, Iran: Daftar Intisharat Islami, 1367 Solar) Vol. 10, pp. 225-29.

66 Ibid., Vol. 13, p. 232.

67 Ibid., Vol. 19, p. 585.

68 Al-Tabari, *Jami Al-Bayan an Tawil Ay Al-Quran*. Vol. 30, p. 116

69 Ibid., Vol. 21, pp. 303-04.

70 Ibid.

71 Zamakhshari, *Al-Kashaf an Haga`Ig Ghawamid Al-Tanzil Wa-Uyun Al-Aqawil Fi Wujuh Al-Tawi* Vol. 4, p. 934.

72 Ibid.

73 Mawdudi, 'Tafhim Al-Qur'an', Chapter 89.

74 Ibid. Chapter 39.

75 Razi, *Rawh Al-Jinan Wa-Ruh Al-Janan*. Vol. 12, p. 83-84.

76 Ibid., Vol. 9, p. 411.
77 Kashani, *Minhaj Al-Sadigin Fi Ilzam Al-Mukhalifin*. Vol. 10, p. 240.
78 Ibid., Vol. 8, p. 105.
79 Tabatabai, *Al-Mizan*. Vol. 30, p. 472.
80 Ibid., Vol. 17, pp. 413-15.
81 Ibid.
82 Al-Tabari, *Jami Al-Bayan an Tawil Ay Al-Quran*. Vol. 2, pp. 26-27.
83 Ibid., Vol. 6, pp. 173-76.
84 Ibid., Vol. 21, p. 303.
85 Zamakhshari, *Al-Kashaf an Haga`Ig Ghawamid Al-Tanzil Wa-Uyun Al-Aqawil Fi Wujuh Al-Tawi*. Vol. 1, pp. 257-58.
86 Ibid., Vol. 2, pp. 272-73.
87 Ibid.
88 Ibid., Vol. 4, p. 673.
89 Mawdudi, 'Tafhim Al-Qur'an', <http://www.searchtruth.com/tafsir/tafsir.php?chapter=67>.
90 J.H Kramers, 'Abd Allah Al-Abbas', *Encyclopedia of Islam* (UK: Brill, 1960) Vol. 1, p. 40.
91 Razi, *Rawh Al-Jinan Wa-Ruh Al-Janan*, Vol. 2, p. 226.
92 Ibid.
93 Ibid., Vol. 5, pp. 386-89.
94 Ibid., Vol. 11, p. 174.
95 Kashani, *Minhaj Al-Sadigin Fi Ilzam Al-Mukhalifin*. Vol. 1, p. 365.
96 Ibid., Vol. 4, p. 173.
97 Ibid., Vol. 9, p. 308.
98 Tabatabai, *Al-Mizan*. Vol. 1, pp. 530-31.
99 Ibid., Vol. 9, pp. 47-48.
100 Ibid., Vol. 19, p. 517.
101 Al-Tabari, *Jami Al-Bayan an Tawil Ay Al-Quran*. Vol. 21, p. 78.
102 Ibid., Vol. 1, pp. 213-17.
103 Ibid., Vol. 18, p. 145.
104 Zamakhshari, *Al-Kashaf an Haga`Ig Ghawamid Al-Tanzil Wa-Uyun Al-Aqawil Fi Wujuh Al-Tawi*. Vol. 4, p. 74.
105 Ibid., Vol. 1, p. 172.
106 Ibid., Vol. 3, pp. 393-94.
107 Ibid.
108 Mawdudi, 'Tafhim Al-Qur'an', Chapter37.
109 Ibid. Chapter 2.
110 Ibid. Chapter 25.
111 Razi, *Rawh Al-Jinan Wa-Ruh Al-Janan*, Vol. 9, p. 325.
112 Ibid., Vol. 1, p. 262.
113 Ibid., Vol. 8, p. 259.
114 Kashani, *Minhaj Al-Sadigin Fi Ilzam Al-Mukhalifin*, Vol. 8, p. 8.
115 Ibid., Vol. 1, p. 199.
116 Ibid., Vol. 6, p. 363.
117 Tabatabai, *Al-Mizan*, Vol. 17, p. 232.
118 Ibid., Vol. 1, p. 286.
119 Ibid., Vol. 15, pp. 266-68.
120 Ibid.

Chapter 3

1   John Renard, *All the King's Falcons, Rumi on Prophets and Revelation* (State University of New York Press, Albany, 1994), p. 2.

2   Abraham J. Heschel, *The Prophets* (Perennial classics edn.; New York, USA: HarperCollins, 2001), p. 27.

3   Rahman, *Major Themes of the Qur'an*, p. 9.

4   Heschel, *The Prophets*, pp. 25-27.

5   Uri Rubin, 'Prophets and Prophethood', in Jane Dammen Mcauliffe (ed.), *Encyclopaedia of the Qur'an* (4; Washington D.C.: Brill, 2001), pp. 289-306.

6   Brannon M. Wheeler, *Prophets in the Qur'an, an Introduction to the Qur'an and Muslim Exegesis* (New York: Continuum, 2002), p. 8.

7   Ayoub, *Islam, Faith and History*, p. 33.

8   Wheeler, *Prophets in the Qur'an, an Introduction to the Qur'an and Muslim Exegesis*, p. 8.

9   Abdel Haleem, *The Qur'an, English Translation*, p. 507.

10 Ayoub, *Islam, Faith and History*, p. 34.

11 Rubin, 'Prophets and Prophethood', p. 292.

12 Uri Rubin, 'Prophets and Prophethood', in Andrew Rippin (ed.), *The Blackwell Companiion to the Qur'an* (West Sussex, UK: John Wiley & Sons Ltd., 2009), pp. 234-47.

13 Rahman, *Major Themes of the Qur'an*, p. 24.

14 Farid Esack, *The Qur'an: A User's Guide* (Oxford, England: Oneworld, 2005), p. 152.

15 Heschel, *The Prophets*, p. 19.

16 Rubin, 'Prophets and Prophethood', p. 45.

17 William M. Brinner, 'Noah', in Jane Dammen Mcauliffe (ed.), *Encyclopedia of the Qur'an* (3; Washington, DC: Brill, 2001), pp. 544-47.

18 Tabatabai, *Al-Mizan*, Vol. 10, pp. 370-403.

19 Tabātabā`i is of the opinion that the entire population on earth vanished, *Al-Mizan*, Vol. 10, p. 396.

20 Zamakhshari, *Al-Kashaf an Haga`Ig Ghawamid Al-Tanzil Wa-Uyun Al-Aqawil Fi Wujuh Al-Tawi*, Vol. 2, p. 517.

21 Reuven Firestone, 'Abraham', in Jane Dammen Mcauliffe (ed.), *Encyclopedia of the Qur'an* (1; Washington, D.C.: Brill, 2001), pp. 5-10.

22 Ibid.

23 Tabatabai, *Al-Mizan*, Vol. 1 & 5.

24 Quoted by Helmut Gatje, *The Qur'an and Its Exegesis: Selected Texts with Classical and Modern Muslim Interpretations*, trans. Alford T. Welch (Translated from German edn.; Oxford, England: Oneworld, 1996), p. 90.

25 Rubin, 'Prophets and Prophethood', p. 235.

26 Tabatabai, *Al-Mizan*, Vol. 17, pp. 230-33.

27 Mawdudi, 'Tafhim Al-Qur'an'.

28 For example: Zamakhshari, *Al-Kashaf an Haga`Ig Ghawamid Al-Tanzil Wa-Uyun Al-Aqawil Fi Wujuh Al-Tawi*, Vol. 4, pp. 76-77.

29 Heribert Busse, 'Lot', in Jane Dammen Mcauliffe (ed.), *Encyclopedia of the Qur'an* (3; Washington, D.C: Brill, 2001), pp. 231-32.

30 The exact number of 'messengers' is not mentioned in the Qur'an; however, the exegetes refer to them as two or three.

31 Zamakhshari, *Al-Kashaf an Haga`Ig Ghawamid Al-Tanzil Wa-Uyun Al-Aqawil Fi Wujuh Al-Tawi*, Vol. 2, pp. 167-69.

32 Quoted in Wheeler, *Prophets in the Qur'an, an Introduction to the Qur'an and Muslim Exegesis*, p. 122.

33 Tabatabai, *Al-Mizan*, Vol. 10, pp. 531.

34 Qur'anic exegetes have commented that Lot offered marriage to his daughters and did not encourage adultery; that as the prophet, Lot is considered the father to all girls of the community.

35 Tabatabai, *Al-Mizan*, Vol. 10, pp. 503-38.

36 Seyed Hashim Rasouli Mahallati, *Tales of the Prophets; from Adam to Muhamamd* (Tehran: Daftar Nashr Farhang Islami, 1374 Solar), p. 194.

37 Tabatabai, *Al-Mizan*, Vol. 10, p. 527.

38 Ibid., p. 528.

39 Cornelia Schock, 'Moses', in Jane Dammen Mcauliffe (ed.), *Encyclopedia of the Qur'an* (3; Washington D.C.: Brill, 2001), pp. 419-26.

40 Ibid.

41 Brannon M. Wheeler, 'Moses', in Andrew Rippin (ed.), *The Blackwell Companion to the Qur'an* (West Sussex, UK: John Wiley & Sons Ltd, 2009), pp. 248-65.

42 Zamakhshari, *Al-Kashaf an Haga`Ig Ghawamid Al-Tanzil Wa-Uyun Al-Aqawil Fi Wujuh Al-Tawi*, Vol. 2, p. 255.

43 Tabatabai, *Al-Mizan*, Vol. 16, p. 16.

44 Schock, 'Moses', p. 421.

45 According to Tabātabā'i this refers to the disease of leprosy; ensuring Moses that white color does not mean he has the leprosy, but rather this is a sign from God. *Al-Mizan*, Vol. 16, p. 46

46 Wheeler, 'Moses', p. 250-53.

47 Tabatabai, *Al-Mizan*, Vol. 16, pp. 57-63.

48 According to Qur'anic exegete,Ibn Kathir, the forty nights took place during the month of Dhu al-Qa`dah and the first ten days of Dhu al-Hijjah which is the time Muslim Hajj takes place; quoted by Wheeler, *Prophets in the Qur'an, an Introduction to the Qur'an and Muslim Exegesis*, p. 201.

49 Zamakhshari, *Al-Kashaf an Haga`Ig Ghawamid Al-Tanzil Wa-Uyun Al-Aqawil Fi Wujuh Al-Tawi*, Vol. 3, pp. 556.

50 Razi, *Rawh Al-Jinan Wa-Ruh Al-Janan*, Vol. 5, pp. 274-76.

51 Zamakhshari, *Al-Kashaf an Haga`Ig Ghawamid Al-Tanzil Wa-Uyun Al-Aqawil Fi Wujuh Al-Tawi*, Vol. 2, pp. 204-05.

52 Ibid., Vol. 2, pp. 204-205.

53 Wheeler, 'Moses', p. 253.

54 Ibid.

55 Wheeler, 'Moses', p. 255.

56 Razi, *Rawh Al-Jinan Wa-Ruh Al-Janan*, Vol. 7, pp. 355.

57 Schock, 'Moses', p. 426.

58 Heribert Busse, 'Jonah', in Jane Dammen Mcauliffe (ed.), *Encyclopedia of the Qur'an* (Washington, D.C., 2003), pp. 52-55.

59 Sadreddin Balaghi, *Qisa Al-Anbiya (Stories of the Prophets)* (Tehran: Amir kabir Publishing 1387 Solar), p. 214.

60 Ibid., p. 215-17.

61 Heribert Busse, 'Jonah', in Jane Dammen Mcauliffe (ed.), *Encyclopedia of the Qur'an* (3; Washington, D.C.: Brill, 2003), pp. 52-55.

62 Zamakhshari, *Al-Kashaf an Haga`Ig Ghawamid Al-Tanzil Wa-Uyun Al-Aqawil Fi Wujuh Al-Tawi*, Vol. 3, pp. 223-24.

63 Tabatabai, *Al-Mizan*, Vol. 17, pp. 251-57.

64 Ibid.

65 Ibid.,, Vol. 14, pp. 445-50.

66 A.H. Johns, 'Job', in Jane Dammen Mcauliffe (ed.), *Encyclopedia of the Qur'an* (3; Washington, D.C.: Brill, 2003), pp. 50-51.

67 Wheeler, *Prophets in the Qur'an, an Introduction to the Qur'an and Muslim Exegesis*, p. 149.

68 Ibid., p. 158.

69 Balaghi, *Qisa Al-Anbiya (Stories of the Prophets)*, p. 212.

70 Abubakr `Tigh Neishabur Surabadi, *Tafsir Surabadi*, ed. Sa`Idi Sirjani (3; Tehran: Farhamg Nashr-Nu 1381 Solar), Vol. 3, p. 2140.

71 Johns, 'Job'. P. 51; for a more in-depth discussion see A.H. Johns, 'Narrative, Intertext an Allusion in the Qur'anic Presentation of Job', *Journal of Qur'anic Studies*, 1/1 (1999), pp. 1-25.

72 S. Goldman, 'Joseph', in Jane Dammen Mcauliffe (ed.), *Encyclopedia of the Qur'an* (3; Washington, D.C.: Brill, 2003), pp. 55-57.

73 Balaghi, *Qisa Al-Anbiya (Stories of the Prophets)*, p. 87.

74 Tabatabai, *Al-Mizan*, Vol. 11, pp. 349-60.

75 Ibid., Vol. 11, pp. 365-72.

76 Esack, *The Qur'an: A User's Guide*, p. 156.

77 Shaikh Muhammad Al Ghazali, *A Thematic Commentary on the Qur'an*, trans. `Ashur A. Shamis (Issues in Contemporary Islamic Thought, 14; Virginia, USA: International Institute of Islamic Thought 1999), p. 43.

78 Isaac Hasson, 'David', in Jane Dammen Mcauliffe (ed.), *Encyclopedia of the Qur'an* (1; Washington D.C.: Brill, 2001), pp. 495-97.

79 This is said to be an allusion to David's acquisition of another man's wife to add to his own numerous wives. Abdel Haleem, *The Qur'an, English Translation*, p. 455.

80 Hasson, 'David', p. 496.

81 Ibid.

82 Tabatabai, *Al-Mizan*, Vol. 17, pp. 288-305.

83 Wheeler, *Prophets in the Qur'an, an Introduction to the Qur'an and Muslim Exegesis*, p. 263.

84 Priscilla Soucek, 'Solomon', in Jane Dammen Mcauliffe (ed.), *Encyclopedia of the Qur'an* (5; Washinton D.C.: Brill, 2006), pp. 76-78.

85 Ibid.

86 Rasouli Mahallati, *Tales of the Prophets; from Adam to Muhamamd*, p. 549.

87 Zamakhshari, *Al-Kashaf an Haga`Ig Ghawamid Al-Tanzil Wa-Uyun Al-Aqawil Fi Wujuh Al-Tawi*, Vol. 4, pp. 118-19.

88 Tabatabai, *Al-Mizan*, Vol. 17, pp. 308-9.

89 Wheeler, *Prophets in the Qur'an, an Introduction to the Qur'an and Muslim Exegesis*, p. 271.

90 Neal Robinson, 'Jesus', in Jane Dammen Mcauliffe (ed.), *Encyclopedia of the Qur'an* (3; Washington, D.C.: Brill, 2003b), pp. 11-24.

91 David Marshall, 'Zechariah', ibid.(6, 2006), pp. 574-5.

92 Andrew Rippin, 'John the Baptist', ibid.(3, 2003), pp. 51-52.

93 Barbara Freyer Stowasser, 'Mary', ibid., pp. 288-95.

94 Tabatabai, *Al-Mizan*, Vol. 3, p. 274.

95 Stowasser, 'Mary', p. 289.

96 Zamakhshari, *Al-Kashaf an Haga`Ig Ghawamid Al-Tanzil Wa-Uyun Al-Aqawil Fi Wujuh Al-Tawi*, Vol. 1, p. 442.

97 Stowasser, 'Mary', p. 293.

98 Neal Robinson, 'Jesus', ibid., pp. 11-24.

99 Tabatabai, *Al-Mizan*, Vol. 3, p. 303.

100 Zamakhshari, *Al-Kashaf an Haga`Ig Ghawamid Al-Tanzil Wa-Uyun Al-Aqawil Fi Wujuh Al-Tawi*, Vol. 1, p. 734.

101 Robinson, 'Jesus', p. 15.

102 Ibn Kathir calls him the "seal of the Israelite prophets" as quoted in Wheeler, *Prophets in the Qur'an, an Introduction to the Qur'an and Muslim Exegesis*, p. 134.

103 Tabatabai, *Al-Mizan*, Vol. 3, p. 312.

104 Esack, *The Qur'an: A User's Guide*, p. 155.

105 Rasouli Mahallati, *Tales of the Prophets; from Adam to Muhamamd*, p. 622-24.

106 Zamakhshari, *Al-Kashaf an Haga`Ig Ghawamid Al-Tanzil Wa-Uyun Al-Aqawil Fi Wujuh Al-Tawi*, Vol. 1, p. 726.

107 Tabatabai, *Al-Mizan*. 5:217; for an extended discussion on Jesus in the Qur'an see *Al-Mizan*, Vol. 3, pp. 441-509.

108 Mawdudi, 'Tafhim Al-Qur'an', <http://www.searchtruth.com/tafsir/tafsir.php?chapter=4>, accessed November 1, 2011.

109 Todd Lawson, *The Crucifixion and the Qur'an; a Study in the History of Muslim Thought* (Oxford, England: Oneworld, 2009), p. 12.

110 Zamakhshari in Gatje, *The Qur'an and Its Exegesis: Selected Texts with Classical and Modern Muslim Interpretations*, p. 121.

111 Rasouli Mahallati, *Tales of the Prophets; from Adam to Muhamamd*, p. 628.

112 *Qur'an*, Muhammad is not the father of any of you men; he is God's Messenger and the seal of the prophets: God knows everything (33:40)

113 Muhammad Ibn Ishag, *Ibn Hisham's Life of Prophet Muhammad*, trans. Seyed Hashim Rasouli Mahallati, 2 vols. (Tehran, IR: Ketabkhane Islamieh, 1955 edition).

114 Seyyed Hossein Nasr, *Muhammad Man of God* (Chicago, IL: Kazi, 1995), p. 15.

115 Ernst, *Folowing Muhammad, Rethinking Islam in the Contemporary World*, p. 85.

116 Karen Armstrong, *Muhammad: A Biography of the Prophet* (New York, NY: HarperCollins, 1992), p. 81.

117 Ibid.

118 Uri Rubin, 'Muhammad', in Jane Dammen Mcauliffe (ed.), *Encyclopedia of the Qur'an* (3; Washington, D.C.: Brill, 2003), pp. 440-57.

119 Ibid.

120 Tamara Sonn, 'Introducing', in Andrew Rippin (ed.), *The Blackwell Companion to the Qur'an* (West Sussex, UK: John Wiley & Sons, 2009), p. 7.

121 Martin Lings, *Muhammad: His Life Based on the Earliest Sources* (Rochester, NY: Inner Traditions International, 1983).

122 Rubin, 'Muhammad', p. 449-50.

123 See Armstrong, *Muhammad: A Biography of the Prophet*.

124 Rubin, 'Muhammad', p. 452.

125 Ibn Ishag, *Ibn Hisham's Life of Prophet Muhammad*. V. 1 & 2.

126 Abdel Haleem, *The Qur'an, English Translation*. The introductory remarks, p. 586.

127 Abu 'Ali Al-Fadl Ibn Al-Hassan Tabarsi, *Majma' Al-Bayan Fi Tafsir Al-Qur'an*, trans. Ahmad Beheshti (Tehran, IR: Farahani, 1350 Solar), Vol. 10, p. 437.

128 Zamakhshari, *Al-Kashaf an Haga'Ig Ghawamid Al-Tanzil Wa-Uyun Al-Aqawil Fi Wujuh Al-Tawi*, Vol. 4, p. 866.

129 Tabatabai, *Al-Mizan*, Vol. 20, pp. 324-33.

130 For an excellent book on sciences of the Qur'an; see Nasr Hamed Abuzeid, *Mafhum al-Nass*, trans. Morteza Karimi Nia (Tehran, IR: Tarh-e Nuu, 1990).

Chapter 4

1   Walter T. Stace, *Mysticism and Philosophy* (Los Angeles, CA: Jeremy P. Tarcher, Inc., 1960), pp. 15-16.

2   Louis Dupre, 'Mysticism ', *Enciclopedia of Religion* (1987).

3   Ibid.

4   Evelyn Underhill, *Mysticism the Nature and Development of Spiritual Consciousness* (Oxford, England: Oneworld, 1993), pp. xiv-xv.

5   Dupre, 'Mysticism ', p. 6341.

6   William James, *The Varieties of Religious Experience* (Centenary edn.; London, England: Routeldge, 2002), pp. 294-95.

7   Ibid.

8   Ibid.

9   Ibid.

10 Ibid., p. 324.

11 Roger Gaetani, in Jean-Louis Michon and Roger Gaetani (ed.), *Sufism: Love & Wisdom* (Indiana: World Wisdom, 2006), p. xv.

12 Frithjof Schuon, *Understanding Islam* (Bloomington, Indiana: World Wisdon, 1998), p. 127.

13 Ibid., p. 128.

14 See Aldous Huxley, *The Perennial Philosophy* (Harper Perennial Modern Classics edn.; New York: HarperCollins, 2009).

15 See Frithjof Schuon, *The Transcendent Unity of Religions* (Wheaton, IL: Quest Books, 2005).

16 See Rudolph Otto, *Mysticism East and West: A Comparative Analysis of the Nature of Mysticism* (New York: Meridian Books, 1957).

17 Huxley, *The Perennial Philosophy* p. viii.

18 Underhill, *Mysticism the Nature and Development of Spiritual Consciousness*, p. 4.

19 William Stoddart, 'Aspects of Islamic Esoterism', in Jean-Louis Michon and Roger Gaetani (ed.), *Sufism: Love & Wisdom* (Indiana: World Wisdom, 2006), p. 239.

20 For a discussion on nonreligious mysticism see Dupre, 'Mysticism ', p. 6342.

21 Eric Geoffroy, *Introduction to Sufism: The Inner Path of Islam*, trans. Roger Gaetani (Indiana: World Wisdom, 2010), pp. 4-5.

22 For more on development of Sufism see Victor Danner, *The Early Development of Sufism*, ed. Seyyed Hossein Nasr (Islamic Spirituality: Foundations; New York: Crossroad, 1987), pp. 239-64.

23 Smith Huston, *The World Religions* (New York: HarperCollins, 1991), p. 258.

24 Reynold A. Nicholson, *The Mystics of Islam* (London, England: Penguin, 1989), p. 29.

25 Ibid.

26 Danner, *The Early Development of Sufism*, Vol. 1, pp. 239-40.

27 Geoffroy, *Introduction to Sufism: The Inner Path of Islam*, p. 22.

28 Seyyed Hossein Nasr, *The Heart of Islam: Enduring Values for Humanity* (New York: HarperCollins, 2004), p. 67.

29 Ibid.

30 For more on mysticism and Sufism see Titus Burckhardt, 'Sufi Doctrine and Method', in Jean-Louis Michon and Roger Gaetani (ed.), *Sufism: Love & Wisdom* (Indiana: World Wisdom, 2006), 1-20.

31 For a detailed biography on Rumi, see Shams Al-Din Ahmad Aflaki, *Manageb Al-Arefin* (Tehran, IR: Donya-ye Ketab, 1983).

32 Muhammad Este` Alami, *The Mathnawi of Jalaloddin Rumi* (Tehran, IR: Zavvar, 1371), pp. 17-18.

33 Badi` Ozzaman Furuzanfar, *Risalah Dar Tahqiq-I Ahwal Wa Zendegi-Ye Mowlana Jalaloddin* (Tehran, IR: Taban, 1333), as quoted by Este`alami, pp. 18-20.

34 Ibid.

35 Jalal Al-Din Huma`I, *Mulawi Nameh: What Is Rumi Saying?* (Tehran, IR: Nashr-e Huma, 1358), p. 21.

36 Ibid., pp. 22-23.

37 Abdolhusin Zarrinkob, *Step by Step Towards Meting God: Life and Spiritual Practices of Rumi* (Tehran, IR: Elmi, 1373), pp. 112-15.

38 Abdolkarim Soroush, *Ghomar-E `Asheghaneh: Rumi and Shams* (Tehran, IR: Serat, 1379), pp. 20-23.

39 Muhammad Reza Shafiei Kadkani, *Mowlana Rumi's Ghazaliat Shams Tabrizi* (Tehran, IR: Sokhan, 1388), p. 2.

40 Ali Asghar Halabi, *The Essentials of Mysticism and the Lives of the Muslim Mystics* (Tehran, IR: Asatir, 1385), p. 575.

41 Karim Zamani, *Sharh Jame` Mathnavi Ma`Navi (a Comprehensive Commentary of Mathnavi)* (Tehran, IR: Etela`at, 1381 Solar), Vol.1, p. 39.

42 Abd Al-Husayn Zarrinkub, *Sirr Nay: A Critical Analysis and Commentary of Masnavi* (Tehran, IR: Ettellat 1388), Vol. 1, p. 340.

43 Afzal Iqbal, *The Life and Work of Jalaluddin Rumi* (London: Oxford University Press, 1999), p. 175.

44 Zarrinkub, *Sirr Nay: A Critical Analysis and Commentary of Masnavi*, p. 342-43.

45 Ibid.

46 Baha-Aldin Khorramshahi, *Qur'an and Mathnawi: The Influence of Qur'anic Narratives in Mathnawi* (Tehran, IR: Nashr Ghatreh, 1386), pp. 16-17.

47 For more information on this topic see: John Renard, *Knowledge of God in Classical Sufism* (Mahwah, NJ: Paulist Press, 2004).

48 See Rahman, *Major Themes of the Qur'an*, pp. 1-16; 65-79.

49 For a detailed discussion on the topic see: Tilman Nagel, *The History of Islamic Theology from Muhammad to the Present*, trans. Thomas Thornton (Princeton, NJ: Markus Wiener, 2006).

50 Annemarie Schimmel, *The Triumphal Sun: A Study of the Works of Jalalodin Rumi* (Albany, NY: State University of New York Press, 1993), p. 237.

51 Rumi, *The Mathnawi of Jalaluddin Rumi*, IV:3700.

52 Ibid., VI:3172, 83.

53 Badi` Ozzaman Furuzanfar, *Ahadith-E Mathnavi* (Tehran, IR: Tehran Univ. Press, 1361 Solar), p. 29.

54 William C. Chittick, *The Sufi Path of Love: The Spiritual Teachings of Rumi* (Albany, NY: State University of New York Press, 1983), p. 47.

55 Rumi, *The Mathnawi of Jalaluddin Rumi*, IV:3028.

56 Ibid., IV:1166-68.

57 Jalal Al-Din Rumi, *Masnawi-Ye Ma`Navi* (Tehran, Iran: Amir Kabir,1957), III:1128-29.

58 The Qur'an, 11:7

59 For an analysis of this notion see Annemarie Schimmel, *Mystical Dimentions of Islam* (Chapel Hill, NC: The University of North Carolina Press, 1975), p. 188.

60 See Chittick, *The Sufi Path of Love: The Spiritual Teachings of Rumi*, p. 82-83.

61 See, Zamakhshari, *Al-Kashaf an Haga`Ig Ghawamid Al-Tanzil Wa-Uyun Al-Aqawil Fi Wujuh Al-Tawi*, Vol 1, pp. 157-58.

62 Zamani, *Sharh Jame` Mathnavi Ma`Navi (a Comprehensive Commentary of Mathnavi)* IV:2970, p. 835.

63 Rumi, *The Mathnawi of Jalaluddin Rumi*, III:2759; 3198; 2300.

64 See Zarrinkub, *Sirr Nay: A Critical Analysis and Commentary of Masnavi*, Vol. 1, p. 545.

65 Rumi, *The Mathnawi of Jalaluddin Rumi* IV:521.

66 For example see, Razi, *Rawh Al-Jinan Wa-Ruh Al-Janan*, Vol. 6, p. 246.

67 Zarrinkub, *Sirr Nay: A Critical Analysis and Commentary of Masnavi*, Vol. 1, pp. 548-54.

68 See Tabatabai, *Al-Mizan*, Vol:8, pp. 400-21.

69 Ibid., Vol:16, pp. 524-31.

70 Zarrinkub, *Sirr Nay: A Critical Analysis and Commentary of Masnavi*, Vol.1, p. 548.

71 Huma`I, *Mulawi Nameh: What Is Rumi Saying?*, Vol. 1, p. 77.

72 Schimmel, *The Triumphal Sun: A Study of the Works of Jalalodin Rumi*, p. 257.

73 Rahman, *Major Themes of the Qur'an*, p. 14.

74 Zarrinkub, *Sirr Nay: A Critical Analysis and Commentary of Masnavi*, p. 549.

75 Ibid., Vol.1, pp.374-75.

76 Ibid.

77 Ibid.

78 Badi` Ozzaman Furuzanfar, *Sharh Mathnavi Sharif* (Tehran, IR: Zawwar, 1367 Solar), p. 269.

79 Rumi, *The Mathnawi of Jalaluddin Rumi* V:174-76; 246.

80 Chittick, *The Sufi Path of Love: The Spiritual Teachings of Rumi*, pp. 68-69.

81 Ibid., p. 69.

82 Schimmel, *The Triumphal Sun: A Study of the Works of Jalalodin Rumi*, p. 250.

83 Rumi, *The Mathnawi of Jalaluddin Rumi* I:110.

84 Ibid., V:2735-36.

85 Jalal Al-Din Rumi, *Diwan Shams Tabrizi* (Tehran, IR: Peyman, 1379), II:2951. Translation is from Schimmel's The Triumphal Sun, p. 247.

86 Rumi, *The Mathnawi of Jalaluddin Rumi*, IV:3759-60.

87 Ibid., IV:3765-67.

88 Huma'I, *Mulawi Nameh: What Is Rumi Saying?*, Vol.2, pp. 762-79.

89 Schimmel, *The Triumphal Sun: A Study of the Works of Jalalodin Rumi*, pp. 251-53.

90 Furuzanfar, *Ahadith-E Mathnavi*, p. 365.

91 Rumi, *The Mathnawi of Jalaluddin Rumi*, IV:1194.

92 Ibid.,,, VI:3138-9.

93 See for example Zamakhshari, *Al-Kashaf an Haga'Ig Ghawamid Al-Tanzil Wa-Uyun Al-Aqawil Fi Wujuh Al-Tawi*, Vol.3, pp. 766-67.

94 Jalal Al-Din Rumi, *Fihi Ma Fihi (Discourses of Rumi)*, trans. Arthur John Arberry (London & New York: Routledge, 2004), pp. 26-28.

95 Rumi, *The Mathnawi of Jalaluddin Rumi*, I:1254.

96 See Franklin D. Lewis, *Rumi: Past and Present, East and West; the Life, Teachings and Poetry of Jalal Al-Din Rumi* (Oxford, ENG: Oneworld, 2008), pp. 411-14. Also, Huma'I, *Mulawi Nameh: What Is Rumi Saying?* Vol.1, pp. 86-95.

97 Rumi, *The Mathnawi of Jalaluddin Rumi*, I:618-19.

98 Zarrinkub, *Sirr Nay: A Critical Analysis and Commentary of Masnavi*, Vol. 1, pp. 548-49.

99 Schimmel, *Mystical Dimentions of Islam*, p. 188.

100 Rumi, *Fihi Ma Fihi (Discourses of Rumi)*, p. 118.

101 See Geoffroy, *Introduction to Sufism: The Inner Path of Islam*, pp.11-12.

102 Abolfazl Rashid Al-Din Maybudi, *Kashf Al-Asrar (Unveiling of Mysteries)* (Tehran, IR: Amir Kabir, 1371 solar),Vol:10, pp. 545-47.

103 Seyed Yahya Yasrebi, *Practical Mysticism* (Tehran, IR: Bustan-e Ketab, 1389/2010), pp. 20-24.

104 Seyed Yahya Yasrebi, *Erfan-E Nazari: Theoretical Mysticism, a Research into the Evolutionary Trend and the Principles and Issues of Tasawwuf* (Tehran, IR: Bustan-e Ketab, 1386/2007), p. 90.

105 Jean-Louis Michon, 'The Spiritual Practices of Sufism', in Seyyed Hossein Nasr (ed.), *Islamic Spirituality* (1; New York, US: Crossroad, 1987), p. 285.

106 Ibid.

107 Zarrinkub, *Sirr Nay: A Critical Analysis and Commentary of Masnavi*, Vol.1, p. 17.

108 Rumi, *The Mathnawi of Jalaluddin Rumi*, I:1-2; 3; and 11

109 Muhammad Jafar Musafa, *Ba Pir-E Balkh: Application of Masnavi in Self-Knowlege* (Tehran, IR: Parishan, 1380), p. 13.

110 Jalal Al-Din Rumi, *Majalis-I Sab'ah (the Seven Sessions)*, ed. Tofigh Sobhani (Tehran, IR: Keyhan, 2011/1390), p. 39.

111 Rumi, *The Mathnawi of Jalaluddin Rumi*, V:3340-41.

112 Karim Zamani, *Minagar-E Eshgh: A Thematical Commentary of the Mathnawi Ma'Nawi* (Tehran, IR: Nashr-e Nay, 1384 solar), pp. 231-32.

113 Rumi, *Fihi Ma Fihi (Discourses of Rumi)*, p. 30.

114 Rumi, *The Mathnawi of Jalaluddin Rumi*, III: 2648-53.

115 Jurisprudence (*figh*) and scholastic theology (*kalām*)

116 Rumi, *The Mathnawi of Jalaluddin Rumi*, III: 2654-56.

117 Khalifa Abdul Hakim, *The Metaphysics of Rumi: A Critical and Historical Sketch* (New Delhi: Adam, 1959), p. 19.

118 Chittick, *The Sufi Path of Love: The Spiritual Teachings of Rumi*, pp. 19-24.

119 Rumi, *The Mathnawi of Jalaluddin Rumi*, I:1735; and IV:3218.

120 Seyyed Hossein Nasr, *The Ideals and Realities of Islam* (Chicago, IL: ABC International, 2000), p. 10.

121 Rumi, *The Mathnawi of Jalaluddin Rumi*, III:998-1001.

122 The Qur'an, 33:21

123 Seyyed Hossein Nasr, *Sufi Essays* (Chicago, IL: ABC International, 1999), pp.32-34.

124 For example see, Bahrol 'Ulum, *Resaleh Sir Wa Soluk*, ed. Hassan Mostafawi (Tehran, IR: Amir Kabir, 1367), Javad Maleki Tabrizi, *Leqa'Llah* (Qum: 'Al Ali, 1385), Muhammad Shoja'I, *Maqalat Dar Tazkie Nafs* (3; Tehran, IR: Sorush, 1375).

125 Nasr, *Sufi Essays*.

126 See Bediuzzaman Said Nursi, *Risale-i Nūr*, <http://www.erisale.com>.

127 Gavin Picken, 'Tazkiat Al-Nafs: The Qur'anic Paradigm', *Journal of Qur'anic Studies*, 7/2 (2005), p. 102.

128 For example see: Tabatabai, *Al-Mizan*, Vol. 20, pp. 495-505. Also, Seyed Mahmoud Taleghani, *Partuvi Az Qur'an (a Ray of the Qur'an)* (Tehran, IR: Sherkat Sahami Enteshar, 1347) Vol.3, pp. 103-21.

129 Abdol Ali Bazargan, *Nazm-E Qur'an* (Tehran, IR: Ghalam, 1381), Vol. 4, p. 132.

130 Taleghani, *Partuvi Az Qur'an (a Ray of the Qur'an)*, Vol.3, p. 120.

131 Picken, 'Tazkiat Al-Nafs: The Qur'anic Paradigm', (p. 103).

132 Ibid., p. 104.

133 Bazargan, *Nazm-E Qur'an*, Vol. 4, p. 134.

134 Picken, 'Tazkiat Al-Nafs: The Qur'anic Paradigm', (pp.107-10).

135 Bazargan, *Nazm-E Qur'an*, Vol. 4, p. 132.

136 The Qur'anic references regarding the three levels of human soul are, respectively: 12:53, 75:2, and 89:27-30.

137 Geoffroy, *Introduction to Sufism: The Inner Path of Islam*, p. 149. Also, see Schimmel, *Mystical Dimentions of Islam*, pp. 109-18.

138 Huma`I, *Mulawi Nameh: What Is Rumi Saying?*, Vol.1, pp. 185-86.

139 Zarrinkub, *Sirr Nay: A Critical Analysis and Commentary of Masnavi*, Vol. 1, pp. 15-24.

140 Schimmel, *The Triumphal Sun: A Study of the Works of Jalalodin Rumi*, p. 289.

141 Nasr, *The Ideals and Realities of Islam*, p. 118.

142 Syed Ali Ashraf, 'The Inner Meaning of the Islamic Rites: Prayer, Pilgrimage, Fasting, Jihad', in Seyyed Hossein Nasr (ed.), *Islamic Spirituality - Foundations* (1; New York: Crossroad, 1987), p. 111.

143 Frithjof Schuon, 'The Spiritual Significance of the Substance of the Prophet', in Seyyed Hossein Nasr (ed.), *Islamic Spirituality: Foundations* (New York: Crossroad, 1987), pp. 49-50.

144 Zamani, *Minagar-E Eshgh: A Thematical Commentary of the Mathnawi Ma`Nawi*, p. 632; 63-70.

145 Huma`I, *Mulawi Nameh: What Is Rumi Saying?*, Vol. 2, pp. 616-19.

146 Chittick, *The Sufi Path of Love: The Spiritual Teachings of Rumi*, p. 120.

147 Ibid., pp. 150-51.

148 Rumi, *Fihi Ma Fihi (Discourses of Rumi)*, p. 24.

149 Ibid., pp. 182-83.

150 Reza Shah-Kazemi, *Spiritual Quest: Reflections on Qur'anic Prayer According to the Teachings of Imam Ali* (London: I.B. Tauris, 2011), p. 12.

151 Michon, 'The Spiritual Practices of Sufism', p. 275.

152 Ibid.

153 Rumi, *Fihi Ma Fihi (Discourses of Rumi)*, p. 183.

154 Rumi, *The Mathnawi of Jalaluddin Rumi*, II:748-54.

155 Ibid., VI:4040-41.

156 Chittick, *The Sufi Path of Love: The Spiritual Teachings of Rumi*, p. 150.

157 Furuzanfar, *Ahadith-E Mathnavi*, p. 63.

158 Rumi, *Diwan Shams Tabrizi*, I:1602.

159 Schimmel, *The Triumphal Sun: A Study of the Works of Jalalodin Rumi*, pp. 291 & 303.

160 Rumi, *Fihi Ma Fihi (Discourses of Rumi)*, pp. 71-72.

161 Huma`I, *Mulawi Nameh: What Is Rumi Saying?*, Vol. 2, pp. 803-06.

162 Rumi, *Fihi Ma Fihi (Discourses of Rumi)* p. 20.

163 Rumi, *The Mathnawi of Jalaluddin Rumi*, II:2163-66.

164 Yasrebi, *Practical Mysticism*, pp. 191-245.

165 Zamani, *Sharh Jame` Mathnavi Ma`Navi (a Comprehensive Commentary of Mathnavi)*, Vol. 6, p. 1250.

166 Schimmel, *The Triumphal Sun: A Study of the Works of Jalalodin Rumi*, pp. 304-05.

167 Zamani, *Minagar-E Eshgh: A Thematical Commentary of the Mathnawi Ma`Nawi*, pp. 538-44.

168 Rumi, *The Mathnawi of Jalaluddin Rumi*, VI:1829.

169 Ibid., III:286-89.

170 Yasrebi, *Practical Mysticism*, pp. 310-19.

171 Schimmel, *Mystical Dimentions of Islam*, pp. 118-19.

172 Ibid.

173 Zamani, *Minagar-E Eshgh: A Thematical Commentary of the Mathnawi Ma'Nawi*, pp. 532-36.

174 Rumi, *The Mathnawi of Jalaluddin Rumi*, I:908-37. Also, see a similar story in V:2419-2427.

175 Chittick, *The Sufi Path of Love: The Spiritual Teachings of Rumi*, pp. 160-61.

176 For a discussion on naughting the self, see Chittick, *The sūfī Path of Love*, pp. 173-5.

177 Rumi, *The Mathnawi of Jalaluddin Rumi*, VI:202-14.

178 Zamani, *Sharh Jame' Mathnavi Ma'Navi (a Comprehensive Commentary of Mathnavi)*, pp. 78-81.

179 Ibid.

180 Zamani, *Minagar-E Eshgh: A Thematical Commentary of the Mathnawi Ma'Nawi*, pp. 282-84.

181 Rumi, *The Mathnawi of Jalaluddin Rumi*, VI:214-16.

182 For example see Q. 21:35.

183 An example of this is evident in the following Qur'anic verses: 18:7; 39:49, and 89:15-16.

184 Ernest Becker, *Escape from Evil* (New York, USA: The Free Press, 1975), p. 2.

185 Bowker, *Problems of Suffering in Religions of the World*, p. 101.

186 Ibid., pp. 109-13.

187 See for example: Q. 6:42-44; Q. 7:94-95

188 Zamani, *Minagar-E Eshgh: A Thematical Commentary of the Mathnawi Ma'Nawi*, p. 518.

189 Karim Zamani, *Comprehensive Commentary of Rumi's Fihi Ma Fihi* (Tehran, IR: Moin, 1390), p. 531.

190 Chittick, *The Sufi Path of Love: The Spiritual Teachings of Rumi*, p. 238.

191 Renard, *All the King's Falcons, Rumi on Prophets and Revelation*, p. 61.

192 Rumi, *Diwan Shams Tabrizi* 35486-87; 3952. Translation by Chittick in Sufi Path of Love, p. 238.

193 Rumi, *Fihi Ma Fihi (Discourses of Rumi)*, p. 240.

194 Thomas Michel, 'For You, Illness Is Good Health: Said Nursi's Spirituality in His Approach to Physical Illness', in Ibrahim M. Abu-Rabi' (ed.), *Spiritual Dimensions of Bediuzzaman Said Nursi's Risale-I Nur* (State University of New York Press, 2008), p. 181.

195 Ibid., p. 187.

196 Rumi, *The Mathnawi of Jalaluddin Rumi*, VI:4222-26.

197 Zarrinkub, *Sirr Nay: A Critical Analysis and Commentary of Masnavi*, p. 55.

198 Rumi, *The Mathnawi of Jalaluddin Rumi* III:682-86.

199 Chittick, *The Sufi Path of Love: The Spiritual Teachings of Rumi*, p. 238.

200 Rumi, *Majalis-I Sab'ah (the Seven Sessions)*, p. 161. Translation is from Chittick in *Sufi path of love*, p. 49.

201 Rumi, *Diwan Shams Tabrizi*. Translation is from Chittick in *Sufi Path of Love*, p. 239.

202 Chittick, *The Sufi Path of Love: The Spiritual Teachings of Rumi*, p. 237.

203 Zarrinkub, *Sirr Nay: A Critical Analysis and Commentary of Masnavi*, Vol. 1, p. 61.

204 Rumi, *The Mathnawi of Jalaluddin Rumi*, VI:1735-36; 56-57.

205 Colin Turner (ed.), *The Six-Sided Vision of Said Nursi: Toward a Spiritual Architecture of the Risale-I Nur*, ed. Ibrahim M. Abu-Rabi' (Spiritual Dimensions of Bediuzzaman Said Nursi's Risale-I Nur, Albany, NY: State University of New York Press, 2008), p. 34.

206 Adnan Aslan, 'The Fall, Evil, and Suffering in Islam ', in Peter Koslowski (ed.), *The Origin and the Overcoming of Evil and Suffering in the World Religions* (Netherlands: Kluwer Academic Publishers, 2001), p. 45.

207 For example see Qur'an 2:177.

208 For a discussion on *ṣabr* see for example: Tabatabai, *Al-Mizan* Vol. 11, p. 141; and Vol. 13, p. 417.

209 See for example: Qur'an 9:129; 33:48; 58:10.

210 Aslan, 'The Fall, Evil, and Suffering in Islam ', pp.44-45.

211 Zamani, *Minagar-E Eshgh: A Thematical Commentary of the Mathnawi Ma'Nawi*, p. 518.

212 Rumi, *The Mathnawi of Jalaluddin Rumi*, III:4160-64; 78; 97-98.

213 Zarrinkub, *Sirr Nay: A Critical Analysis and Commentary of Masnavi*, Vol. 1, p. 492.

214 Zamani, *Minagar-E Eshgh: A Thematical Commentary of the Mathnawi Ma'Nawi*, p. 543.

Chapter 5

1   John Hick, *An Interpretation of Religion* (New Haven and London: Yale University Press, 2004), p. 118.
2   Alvin Plantinga, *God, Freedom, and Evil* (Cambridge, UK: WM. B. Berdmans, 1974), p. 7.
3   Michael L. Peterson, *The Problem of Evil, Selected Readings* (Indiana, USA: Univ. of Notre Dame, 2011), pp. 2-3.
4   Ibid.
5   According to G. E. Von Grunebaum, while in Christianity evil is both structural and accidental, in Islam evil is only accidental. See G. E. Von Grunebaum, 'Observations on the Muslim Concept of Evil', *Studia Islamica* (http://www.jstor.org/stable/1595068: Maisonneuve & Larose, 1970), p. 119.
6   Peterson, *The Problem of Evil, Selected Readings*, pp. 3-4.
7   Peter Van Inwagen, *The Problem of Evil* (New York, USA: Oxford University Press, 2006), pp. 7-9.
8   Ibid.
9   J. L. Mackie, 'Evil and Omnipotence', in Marilyn Mccord and Adams Adams, Robert Merrihew (ed.), *The Problem of Evil* (New York, USA: Oxford Univ. Press, 1994), 25-37.
10 Plantinga, *God, Freedom, and Evil*, p. 29.
11 Ibid., pp. 12-40.
12 Michael Martin, 'Is Evil Evidence against the Existence of God?', in Michael L. Peterson (ed.), *The Problem of Evil: Selected Readings* (Indiana, US: University of Notre Dame, 2011), 135-39. And, David Basinger, 'Evil as Evidence against God's Existence', ibid.(Univ. of Notre Dame), 141-52.
13 Peterson, *The Problem of Evil, Selected Readings*, p. 7.
14 William Hasker, 'On Regretting the Evils of This World', in Michael L. Peterson (ed.), *The Problem of Evil, Selected Readings* (Indiana, USA: University of Notre Dame, 2011), p. 165.
15 Mohammad Saeedimehr, 'Islamic Philosophy and the Problem of Evil: A Philosophical Theodicy', *Intl. J. Humanities*, 17 (2010), 127-48.
16 Ibid.
17 Aslan, 'The Fall, Evil, and Suffering in Islam ', pp. 24-25.
18 Schimmel, *Mystical Dimentions of Islam*, pp. 196-200.
19 Green, 'Theodicy', p. 9112.
20 Ibid.
21 See, Eric L. Ormsby, *Theodicy in Islamic Thought: Dispute over Al-Ghazali's "Best of All Possible Worlds"* (Princeton, NJ: Princeton Univ. Press, 1984).
22 See St. Augustine, 'A Good Creation's Capacity for Evil (from City of God)', in Michael L. Peterson (ed.), *The Problem of Evil: Selected Readings* (Indiana, US: Univ. of Notre Dame, 2011), 191-96.
23 Green, 'Theodicy', p. 9117.
24 John Hick, *Evil and the God of Love* (New York, NY: Palgrave Macmillan, 2007), pp. 211-15.
25 Peterson, *The Problem of Evil, Selected Readings*.
26 Hick, *Evil and the God of Love*, pp. 253- 61.
27 Abdol Rahman Ibn Khaldūn, *Muqaddimah of Ibn Khaldūn*, trans. Mohammad P. Ghonabadi, 2 vols. (Tehran, IR: Sherkat Elmi Farhangi, 1375), Vol. 2, pp. 942-50.
28 Harry Austryn Wolfson, *The Philosopy of Kalam* (Cambridge, MA: Harvard University Press, 1976), pp. 35-37.
29 See, W. Mongomery Watt, 'Ash`Ariyya', in H.A.R. Gibb, Kramers, J.H. (ed.), *Encyclopedia of Islam* (I; Leiden: Brill, 1986), p. 696.
30 D. Gimaret, 'Mu`Tazila', in E. Van Donzel C.E. Bosworth and W.P. Heinrichs and Ch. Pellat (eds.), *The Encyclopedia of Islam* (New edn., VII; Leiden: Brill, 1993), p. 789.
31 Ibn Rushd (Averroes), *The Philosophy and Theology of Averroes*, trans. Mohammad Jamil Rehman (Lexington, KY: ForgottenBooks, 1921), p. 287.
32 Mutahhari, `Adl-E Elahi, pp. 50-51.
33 Watt, 'Ash`Ariyya'.

34 Richard C. And Woodward Martin, Mark R., *Defenders of Reason in Islam: Mu`Tazilism from Medieval School to Modern Symbol* (Oxford, ENG: Oneworld, 1997), pp. 16-17.

35 Tūsī, *Kashf Al-Morād, Sharh Tajrid Al-I`Tiqad*, pp. 421-26.

36 Ibid.

37 For a discussion on Muslim philosophers' interpretation of wujūd and *`adam* See, Seyyed Hossein Nasr, *Islamic Philosophy from Its Origin to the Present* (Albany, NY: State University of New York Press, 2006), pp. 65-68.

38 Saeedimehr, 'Islamic Philosophy and the Problem of Evil: A Philosophical Theodicy', (p.132-3)

39 Shams C. Inati, *The Problem of Evil: Ibn Sina's Theodicy* (Albany, NY: State Univ. of New York Press, 2000), p. 66.

40 Ibid.

41 For Ibn Sīnā's view on 'Existence' see: Michael E. Marmura, *Avicenna: The Metaphysics of the Healing* (Provo, Utah: Brigham Young University Press, 2005a), pp. 22-38.

42 Inati, *The Problem of Evil: Ibn Sina's Theodicy*, pp. 103-25.

43 Ibid., pp. 169-72.

44 Sajjad Rizvi, 'Mulla Sadra', *Stanford Encyclopedia of Philosophy* (http://plato.stanford.edu/entries/mulla-sadra/: Stanford University, 2009). Accessed January 13, 2013.

45 Sadr Al-Din Mulla Sadra Shirazi, *Mafatih Al-Ghayb*, trans. Mohammad Khajawii (Tehran, IR: Mola, 1387), p. 388.

46 Fazlur Rahman, *The Philosophy of Mulla Sadra* (Albany, NY: State Univ. of NY Press, 1975), p. 36.

47 Mulla Sadra Shirazi, *Mafatih Al-Ghayb*, pp. 389-91.

48 Abū ḥāmid Al-Ghazālī, *Iḥyā' `ulūm Al-Dīn*, trans. Mohammad Khajawii (4; Tehran, IR: Shirkat Intisharat Elmi va Farhangi, 1377) Vol. 4, p. 445.

49 W. Mongomery Watt, 'Ghazali, Abu Hamid', in Lindsay Jones (ed.), *Encyclopedia of Religion* (Second edn., 5; USA: Macmillan Reference, 2004), 3469-72.

50 Ibid.

51 W. Mongomery Watt, *The Faith and Practice of Al-Ghazali* (Oxford: Oneworld, 2007), p. 12.

52 David Burrell, preface to Abū ḥāmid Al-Ghazālī, *Al-Munqidh Min Al-Dalal, Deliverance from Error*, trans. R.J. Mccarthy (Louisville, KY: Fons Vitae, 2006), p. 10.

53 John Bowker, *The Religious Imagination and the Sense of God* (Oxford, ENG: Oxford University Press, 1978), p. 195.

54 Al-Ghazālī, *Al-Munqidh Min Al-Dalal, Deliverance from Error*, p. 52.

55 Ibid., pp. 53-55.

56 Jalal Al-Din Huma`I, *Ghazālī-Nāmah, Sharh-I Hāl Va Āsār Va `aqā`id* (Tehran, IR: Huma, 1368), p. 9.

57 Watt, *The Faith and Practice of Al-Ghazali*, pp. 12-13. Also, Watt, 'Ghazali, Abu Hamid', p. 3472.

58 Max Horten, 'Moral Philosophers in Islam', *Islamic Studies* (http://www.jstor.org/stable/20846901, 13; Islamabad: Islamic Research Institute, Int. Islamic University, 1974), p. 15.

59 See Muhammad Hussain Tabatabai, *Nihayah Al-Hikmah (the Utmost of Philosophy)*, ed. Hadi Khosroshahi, trans. Mahdi Tadayyon (Ghom, IR: Bustan-e Ketab, 1387/2008), pp.92-136.

60 Tūsī, *Kashf Al-Morād, Sharh Tajrid Al-I`Tiqad*, pp. 47-48.

61 Ibid., pp. 83; 220.

62 David Burrell, 'Creation or Emanation', in David Burrell and Bernard Mcginn (ed.), *God and Creation: An Ecumenical Symposium* (Notre Dame, IN: University of Notre Dame Press 1990), p. 29.

63 Fazlur Rahman, 'Ibn Sina's Theory of the God-World Relationship', in David Burrell and Bernard Mcginn (ed.), *God and Creation: An Ecumenical Symposium* (Notre Dame, IN: University of Notre Dame Press, 1990), pp. 38-44.

64 Ibid., p. 45.

65 Ibid., pp. 50-51.

66 L. E. Goodman, 'Time in Islam', in Ian Richard Netton (ed.), *Islamic Philosophy and Theology* (3; London, ENG: Routledge, 2007), p. 13.

67 Al-Ghazālī, *Iḥyā' 'ulūm Al-Dīn*, Vol. 1, pp. 208-09.

68 Michael E. Marmura, 'Al-Ghazālī', in Peter Adamson and Richard Taylor (ed.), *The Cambridge Companion to Arabic Philosophy* (Cambridge, UK: Cambridge University Press, 2005b), pp. 141-42.

69 Ibid.

70 Eric L. Ormsby, 'Creation in Time in Islamic Thought with Special Reference to Al-Ghazali', in David Burrell and Bernard Mcginn (ed.), *God and Creation: An Ecumenical Symposium* (Notre Dame, IN: University of Notre Dame Press, 1990), p. 252.

71 Abū Ḥāmid Al-Ghazālī, *Al-Iqtisād Fi'l-I'tiqād* (Ankara, 1962), pp. 104-07. Cited in Ormsby, 'Creation in Time in Islamic Thought', pp. 254-55.

72 Ormsby, 'Creation in Time in Islamic Thought with Special Reference to Al-Ghazali', p. 255.

73 See Al-Ghazālī, *Al-Munqidh Min Al-Dalal, Deliverance from Error*.

74 Abdolhusin Zarrinkub, *Farar Az Madrasah - Life and Teachings of Al-Ghazali* (Tehran, IR: Amir Kabir, 1387), p. 124.

75 Bowker, *Problems of Suffering in Religions of the World*, p. 101.

76 Qur'an, 2:216.

77 Ormsby, 'Creation in Time in Islamic Thought with Special Reference to Al-Ghazali', p. 256.

78 Al-Ghazālī, *Iḥyā' 'ulūm Al-Dīn*, Vol. 4, p. 445.

79 Ormsby, 'Creation in Time in Islamic Thought with Special Reference to Al-Ghazali', p. 257.

80 Abū Ḥāmid Al-Ghazālī, *Kitāb Al-Tawḥīd Wa' L-Tawakkul, Faith in Divine Unity & Trust in Divine Providence*, trans. David Burrell (Louisville, KY: Fons Vitae, 2001), pp. 45-46.

81 Ormsby, *Theodicy in Islamic Thought: Dispute over Al-Ghazali's "Best of All Possible Worlds"*, pp. 32-33.

82 Huma'I, *Ghazālī-Nāmah, Sharh-I Hāl Va Āsār Va 'aqā'id*, pp. 428-29.

83 Ibid., p. 430.

84 Abū Ḥāmid Al-Ghazālī, *The Ninety-Nine Beautiful Names of God, Al-Maqsad Al-Asnā Fī Sharḥ Ma'ānī Asmā' Allāh Al-Ḥusnā* trans. David B. Burrell (Cambridge, UK: The Islamic Text Society, 1992), p. 126.

85 Abdolkarim Soroush, *Hekmat Wa Ma'Ishat* (Tehran, IR: Serat, 1373), pp. 375-76.

86 Frank Griffel, *Al-Ghazālī's Philosophical Theology* (New York, NY: Oxford University Press, 2009), p. 227.

87 David Burrell, in introduction to Al-Ghazālī, *Kitab Al-Tawḥīd Wa' L-Tawakkul, Faith in Divine Unity & Trust in Divine Providence*, p. xv.

88 Ibid., p. 44; with modification in the English translation.

89 Ormsby, *Theodicy in Islamic Thought: Dispute over Al-Ghazali's "Best of All Possible Worlds"*, p. 47.

90 Al-Ghazālī, *Iḥyā' 'ulūm Al-Dīn*, Vol. 4, p. 550.

91 Ibid., p. 555.

92 Ormsby, *Theodicy in Islamic Thought: Dispute over Al-Ghazali's "Best of All Possible Worlds"*, p. 50.

93 Abū Ḥāmid Al-Ghazālī, *Kitāb Al-Arba'īn Fī Uṣūl Al-Dīn'*, trans. Aaron Spevack (Ghazālī on the Principles of Islamic Spirituality - Selections from the Forty Foundations of Religion Woodstock, VT: Sky Light Paths, 2012), p. 21.

94 Al-Ghazālī, *Kitāb Al-Tawḥīd Wa' L-Tawakkul, Faith in Divine Unity & Trust in Divine Providence*, p. 46. With modifications in the English translation.

95 W. Mongomery Watt, 'Suffering in Sunnite Islam', *Studia Islamica* (http://www.jstor.org/stable/1595556, 50: Maisonneuve & Larose, 1979), pp.12-13.

96 Ormsby, *Theodicy in Islamic Thought: Dispute over Al-Ghazali's "Best of All Possible Worlds"*, p. 54.

97 See section 5.4.1 Ghazālī on God and Creation-in-time.

98 Freiherr Von Gottfried Leibniz, *Thodicy: Essays on the Goodness of God, the Freedom of Man and the Origin of Evil*, trans. E.M. Huggard (Charleston, SC: Bibliobazaar, 2007), pp. 130-31.

99 Ibid., p. 75.

100 Navid Kermani, *The Terror of God (Original Work in German)*, trans. Wieland Hoban (Cambridge, UK: Polity Press, 2011), p. 85.

101 Aslan, 'The Fall, Evil, and Suffering in Islam ', pp. 38-39.

102 Ibid.

103 Abū Ḥāmid Al-Ghazālī, *Kitāb Al-ṣabr Wa' L-Shukr', Patience and Thankfulness, Book Xxxii of Iḥyā' 'ulūm Al-Dīn*, trans. H.T. Littlejohn (Cambridge, UK: Islamic Text Society, 2011), p. 33.

104 Ibid., pp. 33-34.

105 Ibid., p. 40.

106 Ibid., p. 190.

107 Ibid., pp. 190-91.

108 See Margaretha T. Heemskerk, *Suffering in the Mu'tazilite Theology: 'Abd Al-Jabbar's Teachings on Pain and Divine Justice* (London: Brill, 2000), pp. 112-27.

109 See Zarrinkub, *Farar Az Madrasah - Life and Teachings of Al-Ghazali*, pp. 172-73.

110 For various aspects of Nursi's teachings, see Ibrahim M. Abu-Rabi' (ed.), *Spiritual Dimensins of Bediuzzaman Said Nursi's Risale-I Nur* (New York: State University of New York Press, 2008).

111 Bediuzzaman Said Nursi, 'Risale-I Nur, the Words: The Eighteenth Word', <http://www.erisale.com/index.jsp?locale=en#content.en.201.240>, accessed May 29, 2013.

112 Al-Ghazālī, *Kitāb Al-ṣabr Wa' L-Shukr', Patience and Thankfulness, Book Xxxii of Iḥyā' 'ulūm Al-Dīn* pp. 44; 194-96.

113 Zarrinkub, *Farar Az Madrasah - Life and Teachings of Al-Ghazali*, pp. 206-07.

114 Al-Ghazālī, *Kitāb Al-ṣabr Wa' L-Shukr', Patience and Thankfulness, Book Xxxii of Iḥyā' 'ulūm Al-Dīn* p. 55.

115 Ibid., p. 197.

116 Abū Ḥāmid Al-Ghazālī, *Kimyā' Al-Sa'āda, the Alchemy of Happiness* (2; Tehran, IR: Shirkat Intisharat Elmi va Farhangi, 1354), pp. 61-73.

117 Maha Elkaisy-Friemuth, *God and Humans in Islamic Thought, 'Abd Al-Jabbar, Ibn Sina and Al-Ghazali* (New York, NY: Routledge, 2006), p. 136.

118 Al-Ghazālī, *Kimyā' Al-Sa'āda, the Alchemy of Happiness*, pp. 78-80.

119 Hick, *Evil and the God of Love*, p. 255.

120 Ibid., pp. 61 & 257.

121 See Volume 4 in the Iḥyā', and Ormsby, *Theodicy in Islamic Thought: Dispute over Al-Ghazali's "Best of All Possible Worlds"*, pp. 61-63.

122 See Hick, *Evil and the God of Love*, pp. 253-364. Douglas Geivett has challenged some aspects of Hick's theodicy; see R. Douglas Geivett, *Evil and the Evidence for God: The Challenge of John Hick's Theodicy; Afterword by John Hick* (Philadelphia, PA: Temple University Press, 1993).

123 Barbara Freyer Stowasser, 'Theodicy and the Many Meanings of Adam and Eve', in Ibrahim M. Abu-Rabi' (ed.), *Theodicy and Justice in Modern Islamic Thought: The Case of Said Nursi* (Burlington, VT: Ashgate, 2010), pp. 15-16.

124 Sir Muhammad Iqbal, *The Reconstruction of Religious Thought in Islam* (Dubai, UAE: Kitab -al-Islamiyyah, 1934), pp. 12; 138-46.

125 Keith Ward, *Religion & Creation* (New York: Oxford University press, 1996), p. 65.

126 Iqbal, *The Reconstruction of Religious Thought in Islam*, p. 9.

127 For a possibility of developing a rational theodicy based on the Qur'an, see Muhammad Al-Ghazali, 'The Problem of Evil from Islamic Perspective', *Dialogue & Alliance* 8/2 (1994), 65-74.

Bibliography

(Averroes), Ibn Rushd (1921), *The Philosophy and Theology of Averroes*, trans. Mohammad Jamil Rehman (Lexington, KY: ForgottenBooks).

`Ulum, Bahrol (1367), *Resaleh Sir wa Soluk*, ed. Hassan Mostafawi (Tehran, IR: Amir Kabir).

Abdel Haleem, M.A.S. (2004), *The Qur'an, English Translation* (Oxford University Press, US).

Abdul Hakim, Khalifa (1959), *The Metaphysics of Rumi: A Critical and Historical Sketch* (New Delhi: Adam).

Abu-Dawūd 'Sunan Abu- Dawud', <http://www.searchtruth.com/>, accessed May 30, 2010.

Abu-Rabi', Ibrahim M. (ed.), (2008), *Spiritual Dimensins of Bediuzzaman Said Nursi's Risale-i Nur* (New York: State University of New York Press).

Aflaki, Shams al-Din Ahmad (1983), *Manageb al-Arefin* (Tehran, IR: Donya-ye Ketab).

al-Bukhārī, Muhammad Isma`il 'Hadith Collections of al-Bukhari', <http://www.hadithcollection.com/sahihbukhari.html>, accessed May 25, 2010.

Al-Ghazālī, Abū Ḥāmid (1354), *Kimyāʾ al-Saʿāda, The Alchemy of Happiness* (2; Tehran, IR: Shirkat Intisharat Elmi va Farhangi).

--- (1377), *Iḥyāʾ ʿulūm al-dīn*, trans. Mohammad Khajawii (4; Tehran, IR: Shirkat Intisharat Elmi va Farhangi).

--- (1962), *al-Iqtiṣād fiʾl-iʿtiqād* (Ankara).

--- (1992), *The Ninety-Nine Beautiful Names of God, al-Maqsad al-asnā fī sharḥ maʿānī asmāʾ Allāh al-ḥusnā* trans. David B. Burrell (Cambridge, UK: The Islamic Text Society).

--- (2001), *Kitāb al-tawḥīd waʾl-tawakkul, Faith in Divine Unity & Trust in Divine Providence*, trans. David Burrell (Louisville, KY: Fons Vitae).

--- (2006), *al-Munqidh min al-Dalal, Deliverance from Error*, trans. R.J. Mccarthy (Louisville, KY: Fons Vitae).

--- (2011), *Kitāb al-ṣabr waʾl-shukr', Patience and Thankfulness, Book XXXII of Iḥyāʾ ʿulūm al-dīn*, trans. H.T. Littlejohn (Cambridge, UK: Islamic Text Society).

--- (2012), *Kitāb al-arbaʿīn fī uṣūl al-dīn'*, trans. Aaron Spevack (Ghazālī on the Principles of Islamic Spirituality - Selections from The Forty Foundations of Religion Woodstock, VT: Sky Light Paths).

Al-Ghazali, Muhammad (1994), 'The Problem of Evil from Islamic Perspective', *Dialogue & Alliance* 8(2), 65-74.

Al-Hajjaj, Muslim 'Sahih Muslim', <http://www.hadithcollection.com/sahihmuslim.html>, accessed May 30, 2010.

al-Tabari, Abu Jafar Muhammad b. Jarir (1412), *Jami al-bayan an tawil ay al-Quran* (Beirut: Dar al-Marefa).

Ansari, Zafar Ishag (1988), *Towards Understanding the Qur'an: English version of Tafhim al-Qur'an* (London, UK: The Islamic Foundation).

Armstrong, Karen (1992), *Muhammad: A Biography of the Prophet* (New York, NY: HarperCollins).

Ashraf, Syed Ali (1987), 'The Inner Meaning of the Islamic Rites: Prayer, Pilgrimage, Fasting, Jihad', in Seyyed Hossein Nasr (ed.), *Islamic Spirituality - Foundations* (1; New York: Crossroad).

Aslan, Adnan (2001), 'The Fall, Evil, And Suffering in Islam ', in Peter Koslowski (ed.), *The Origin And The Overcoming of Evil And Suffering in The World Religions* (Netherlands: Kluwer Academic Publishers).

Augustine, ST. (2011), 'A Good Creation's Capacity for Evil (from City of God)', in Michael L. Peterson (ed.), *The Problem of Evil: Selected Readings* (Indiana, US: Univ. of Notre Dame), 191-96.

Ayoub, Mahmoud (1984), *The Qur'an and its Interpreters* (Albany: State University of New York Press).

--- (1988), 'The Speaking Qur'an and the Silent Qur'an: A Study of the Principles and Development of Imami Shi'i *tafsir*', in Andrew Rippin (ed.), *Approaches to the History of the Interpretation of the Qur'an* (Oxford, UK: Clarendon Press).

--- (2004), *Islam, Faith and History* (Oxford: Oneworld).

Ayoub, Mahmoud (2005), 'Qur'an: Its Role in Muslim Practice and Life', in Lindsay Jones (ed.), *Encyclopedia of Religion* (Detroit: McMillian Reference USA).

Azad, Maulana Abul Kalam (1978), *Tarjuman al- Qur'an*, trans. Syed Abdul Latif (3; New Delhi: Kitab Bhavan).

Balaghi, Sadreddin (1387 Solar), *Qisa al-anbiya (Stories of the Prophets)* (Tehran: Amir kabir Publishing).

Bar-Asher, Meir M. (1999), *Scripture and Exegesis in Early Imami Shiism* (London, UK: Brill).

Basinger, David (2011), 'Evil as Evidence against God's Existence', in Michael L. Peterson (ed.), *The Problem of Evil: Selected Readings* (Indiana, US: Univ. of Notre Dame), 141-52.

Bazargan, Abdol Ali (1381), *Nazm-e Qur'an* (Tehran, IR: Ghalam).

--- 'Man's Tests and Trials', <http://bazargan.com/abdolali/>, accessed 12/10/2010.

Becker, Ernest (1975), *Escape From Evil* (New York, USA: The Free Press).

Bowker, John (1970), *Problems of Suffering in Religions of the World* (Cambridge Univ. Press).

--- (1978), *The Religious Imagination and the Sense of God* (Oxford, ENG: Oxford University Press).

Brinner, William M. (2001), 'Noah', in Jane Dammen McAuliffe (ed.), *Encyclopedia of the Qur'an* (3; Washington, DC: Brill), pp. 544-47.

Brown, Jonathan A.C. (2009), *Hadith, Muhammad's Legacy in the Medieval and Modern World* (One World, UK).

Burckhardt, Titus (2006), 'Sufi Doctrine and Method', in Jean-Louis Michon and Roger Gaetani (ed.), *Sufism: Love & Wisdom* (Indiana: World Wisdom), 1-20.

Burrell, David (1990), 'Creation or Emanation', in David Burrell and Bernard Mcginn (ed.), *God and Creation: An Ecumenical Symposium* (Notre Dame, IN: University of Notre Dame Press).

Busse, Heribert (2001), 'Lot', in Jane Dammen McAuliffe (ed.), *Encyclopedia of the Qur'an* (3; Washington, D.C: Brill), pp, 231-32.

--- (2003), 'Jonah', in Jane Dammen McAuliffe (ed.), *Encyclopedia of the Qur'an* (3; Washington, D.C.: Brill), pp. 52-55.

Chittick, William C. (1983), *The Sufi Path of Love: The Spiritual Teachings of Rumi* (Albany, NY: State University of New York Press).

Danner, Victor (1987), *The Early Development of Sufism*, ed. Seyyed Hossein Nasr (Islamic Spirituality: Foundations; New York: Crossroad).

Denny, Frederick Mathewson (2011), *An Introdudion to Islam* (USA: Prentice Hall).

Dupre, Louis (1987), 'Mysticism ', *Encylopedia of Religion*.

Elkaisy-Friemuth, Maha (2006), *God and Humans in Islamic Thought, `Abd al-Jabbar, Ibn Sina and al-Ghazali* (New York, NY: Routledge).

Ernst, Carl W. (2003), *Folowing Muhammad, Rethinking Islam in the Contemporary World* (North Carolina, USA: The University of North Carolina Press).

Esack, Farid (2005), *The Qur'an: A user's Guide* (Oxford, England: Oneworld).

Este`alami, Muhammad (1371), *The Mathnawi of Jalaloddin Rumi* (Tehran, IR: Zavvar).

Firestone, Reuven (2001), 'Abraham', in Jane Dammen McAuliffe (ed.), *Encyclopedia of the Qur'an* (1; Washington, D.C.: Brill), pp. 5-10.

Furuzanfar, Badi`ozzaman (1333), *Risalah dar tahqiq-i ahwal wa zendegi-ye Mowlana Jalaloddin* (Tehran, IR: Taban).

--- (1361 Solar), *Ahadith-e Mathnavi* (Tehran, IR: Tehran Univ. Press).

--- (1367 Solar), *Sharh Mathnavi Sharif* (Tehran, IR: Zawwar).

Gaetani, Roger (2006), in Jean-Louis Michon and Roger Gaetani (ed.), *Sufism: Love & Wisdom* (Indiana: World Wisdom).

Gardet, L. 'Fitna', in P. Bearman, Bianquis (ed.), *Encyclopedia of Islam* (Second edn., II: Brill), p. 930.

Gatje, Helmut (1996), *The Qur'an and Its Exegesis: Selected Texts with Classical and Modern Muslim Interpretations*, trans. Alford T. Welch (Translated from German edn.; Oxford, England: Oneworld).

Geivett, R. Douglas (1993), *Evil and the Evidence for God: The Challenge of John Hick's Theodicy; Afterword by John Hick* (Philadelphia, PA: Temple University Press).

Geoffroy, Eric (2010), *Introduction to Sufism: The Inner Path of Islam*, trans. Roger Gaetani (Indiana: World Wisdom).

Ghayyem, Abbolnabi (1381 H.S.), 'Farhang-Moaser Arabic - Persian', (Tehran, Iran: Farhang Moaser).

Ghazali, Shaikh Muhammad Al (1999), *A Thematic Commentary on the Qur'an*, trans. `Ashur A. Shamis (Issues in Contemporary Islamic Thought, 14; Virginia, USA: International Institute of Islamic Thought).

Gimaret, D. (1993), 'Mu`tazila', in E. Van Donzel C.E. Bosworth and W.P. Heinrichs and CH. Pellat (eds.), *The Encyclopedia of Islam* (New edn., VII; Leiden: Brill).

Goldman, S. (2003), 'Joseph', in Jane Dammen McAuliffe (ed.), *Encyclopedia of the Qur'an* (3; Washington, D.C.: Brill), pp. 55-57.

Goodman, L. E. (2007), 'Time in Islam', in Ian Richard Netton (ed.), *Islamic Philosophy and Theology* (3; London, ENG: Routledge).

Green, Ronald M. (2005), 'Theodicy', in Lindsay Jones (ed.), *Encyclopedia of Religion* (2 edn., 13; Detroit, USA: Macmillan Reference).

Griffel, Frank (2009), *al-Ghazālī's Philosophical Theology* (New York, NY: Oxford University Press).

Grunebaum, G. E. Von (1970), 'Observations on the Muslim Concept of Evil', *Studia Islamica*, (31). accessed 12/25/2012.

Halabi, Ali Asghar (1385), *The Essentials of Mysticism and the Lives of the Muslim Mystics* (Tehran, IR: Asatir).

Hasker, William (2011), 'On Regretting the Evils of This World', in Michael L. Peterson (ed.), *The Problem of Evil, Selected Readings* (Indiana, USA: University of Notre Dame).

Hasson, Isaac (2001), 'David', in Jane Dammen McAuliffe (ed.), *Encyclopedia of the Qur'an* (1; Washington D.C.: Brill), pp. 495-97.

Heemskerk, Margaretha T. (2000), *Suffering in The Mu`tazilite Theology: `Abd al-Jabbar's Teachings on Pain and Divine Justice* (London: Brill).

--- (2006), 'Suffering', in Jane Dammen McAuliffe (ed.), *Encyclopedia of the Qur'an* (Leiden-Boston: Brill).

Helminski, Kabir (2004), *The Vision Of The Qur'an* (California: The Book Foundation).

Heschel, Abraham J. (2001), *The Prophets* (Perennial classics edn.; New York, USA: HarperCollins).

Hick, John (2004), *An Interpretation of Religion* (New Haven and London: Yale University Press).

--- (2007), *Evil and the God of Love* (New York, NY: Palgrave Macmillan).

Horten, Max (1974), 'Moral Philosophers in Islam', *Islamic Studies*, 13 (1). accessed 12/25/2012.

Huma`i, Jalal al-Din (1358), *Mulawi Nameh: What is Rumi Saying?* (Tehran, IR: Nashr-e Huma).

--- (1368), *Ghazālī-nāmah, Sharh-i hāl va āsār va `aqā'id* (Tehran, IR: Huma).

Huston, Smith (1991), *The World Religions* (New York: HarperCollins).

Huxley, Aldous (2009), *The Perennial Philosophy* (Harper Perennial Modern Classics edn.; New York: HarperCollins).

Ibn Ishag, Muhammad (1955 edition), *Ibn Hisham's Life of Prophet Muhammad*, trans. Seyed Hashim Rasouli Mahallati, 2 vols. (Tehran, IR: Ketabkhane Islamieh).

Ibn Khaldūn, Abdol Rahman (1375), *Muqaddimah of Ibn Khaldūn*, trans. Mohammad P. Ghonabadi, 2 vols. (Tehran, IR: Sherkat Elmi Farhangi).

Imam Amir al-Muminin, Ali bn Abi-Taalib (1999), *Nahjol-Balagha: Peak Of Eloquence, English Translation by Sayyid Ali Reza* (Ansariyan, Qum-Iran).

Inati, Shams C. (2000), *The Problem of Evil: Ibn Sina's Theodicy* (Albany, NY: State Univ. of New York Press).

Inwagen, Peter Van (2006), *The Problem of Evil* (New York, USA: Oxford University Press).

Iqbal, Afzal (1999), *The Life and Work of Jalaluddin Rumi* (London: Oxford University Press).

Iqbal, Sir Muhammad (1934), *The Reconstruction of Religious Thought In Islam* (Dubai, UAE: Kitab -al-Islamiyyah).

Izutsu, Toshibiko (2002), *Ethico - Religious Concepts In The Qur'an* (Montreal, CA: McGill-Queen's University Press).

Jahanbaksh, Jouya (1991a), 'Tafisr Mulla Fath Allah Kashani', in B. Khorramshahi (ed.), *The Encyclopedia of the Holy Qur'an* (Tehran, Iran: Dustan & Nahid Publishers), p. 766.

--- (1991b), '*Tafsir* Abul Futuh Razi', in B. Khorramshahi (ed.), *The Encyclopedia of the Holy Qur'an* (Tehran, IRan: Doustan & Nahid Publishers), pp. 661-62.

James, William (2002), *The Varieties of Religious Experience* (Centenary edn.; London, England: Routeldge).

Johns, A.H. (1999), 'Narrative, Intertext an Allusion in the Qur'anic Presentation of Job', *Journal of Qur'anic Studies*, 1 (1), pp. 1-25.

--- (2003), 'Job', in Jane Dammen McAuliffe (ed.), *Encyclopedia of the Qur'an* (3; Washington, D.C.: Brill), pp. 50-51.

Kashani, Mulla Fath Allah (1347 {solar} / 1969), *Minhaj al-sadigin fi ilzam al-mukhalifin* (Tehran, IR: Kitabfurushi-yi Islamiyah).

Kermani, Navid (2011), *The Terror of God (Original work in German)*, trans. Wieland Hoban (Cambridge, UK: Polity Press).

Khorramshahi, Baha-aldin (1386), *Qur'an and Mathnawi: The Influence of Qur'anic Narratives in Mathnawi* (Tehran, IR: Nashr Ghatreh).

Kramers, J.H (1960), 'Abd Allah Al-Abbas', *Encyclopedia of Islam* (UK: Brill).

Kulini, Abu Jafar *Usul al-Kafi, English translation by Muhammad Sarwar*, trans. Muhammad Sarwar (Islamic Seminary, New York, 2005).

Lane, Edward William (1968) *Arabic - English Lexicon* [online text], Williams and Norgate <http://www.studyquran.co.uk/LLhome.htm>.

Lawson, Todd (2009), *The Crucifixion and the Qur'an; A Study in the History of Muslim Thought* (Oxford, England: Oneworld).

Leibniz, Freiherr Von Gottfried (2007), *Thodicy: Essays on the Goodness of God, the Freedom of man and the Origin of Evil*, trans. E.M. Huggard (Charleston, SC: Bibliobazaar).

Lewis, Franklin D. (2008), *Rumi: Past and Present, East and West; The Life, Teachings and Poetry of Jalal al-Din Rumi* (Oxford, ENG: Oneworld).

Lings, Martin (1983), *Muhammad: His life based on the earliest sources* (Rochester, NY: Inner Traditions International).

Mackie, J. L. (1994), 'Evil and Omnipotence', in Marilyn McCord and Adams Adams, Robert Merrihew (ed.), *The Problem of Evil* (New York, USA: Oxford Univ. Press), 25-37.

Maleki Tabrizi, Javad (1385), *leqa'llah* (Qum: `Al Ali).

Marmura, Michael E. (2005a), *Avicenna: The Metaphysics of the Healing* (Provo, Utah: Brigham Young University Press).

--- (2005b), 'Al-Ghazālī', in Peter Adamson and Richard Taylor (ed.), *The Cambridge Companion to Arabic Philosophy* (Cambridge, UK: Cambridge University Press).

Marshall, David (2006), 'Zechariah', in Jane Dammen McAuliffe (ed.), *Encyclopedia of the Qur'an* (6; Washington, D.C.: Brill), pp. 574-5.

Martin, Michael (2011), 'Is Evil Evidence against the Existence of God?', in Michael L. Peterson (ed.), *The Problem of Evil: Selected Readings* (Indiana, US: University of Notre Dame), 135-39.

Martin, Richard C. and Woodward, Mark R. (1997), *Defenders of Reason in Islam: Mu`tazilism from Medieval School to Modern Symbol* (Oxford, ENG: Oneworld).

Mawdudi, Sayyid Abul A`la (2011), 'Tafhim al-Qur'an', <http://www.searchtruth.com/tafsir/tafsir.php?chapter=37>, accessed 16 April 2015.

Maybudi, Abolfazl Rashid al-din (1371 solar), *Kashf al-asrar (Unveiling of Mysteries)* (Tehran, IR: Amir Kabir).

McAuliffe, Jane Dammen (1991), *Qur'anic Christians, An Analysis of Classical and Modern Exegesis* (New York, USA: Cambridge University Press).

Michel, Thomas (2008), 'For You, Illness is Good Health: Said Nursi's Spirituality in His Approach to Physical Illness', in Ibrahim M. Abu-Rabi' (ed.), *Spiritual Dimensions of Bediuzzaman Said Nursi's Risale-i Nur* (State University of New York Press).

Michon, Jean-Louis (1987), 'The Spiritual Practices of Sufism', in Seyyed Hossein Nasr (ed.), *Islamic Spirituality* (1; New York, US: Crossroad).

Mulla Sadra Shirazi, Sadr al-Din (1387), *Mafatih al-Ghayb*, trans. Mohammad Khajawii (Tehran, IR: Mola).

Musafa, Muhammad Jafar (1380), *Ba Pir-e Balkh: Application of Masnavi in Self-Knowlege* (Tehran, IR: Parishan).

Mutahhari, Morteza (1385), `*Adl-e elahi* (Tehran, IR: Sadra).

Nagel, Tilman (2006), *The History of Islamic Theology From Muhammad to the Present*, trans. Thomas Thornton (Princeton, NJ: Markus Wiener).

Naji, Hamed (1999), 'Ibtila', in B. Khorramshahi (ed.), *The Encyclopedia of the Holy Qur'an* (1; Tehran, IR: Dustan & Nahid).

Nasr, Seyyed Hossein (1995), *Muhammad Man of God* (Chicago, IL: Kazi).

--- (1999), *Sufi Essays* (Chicago, IL: ABC International).

--- (2000), *The Ideals and Realities of Islam* (Chicago, IL: ABC International).

--- (2004), *The Heart Of Islam: Enduring Values for Humanity* (New York: HarperCollins).

--- (2006), *Islamic Philosophy from its Origin to the Present* (Albany, NY: State University of New York Press).

Nawas, John (2006), 'Trial', in Jane Dammen McAuliffe (ed.), *Encyclopedia of the Qur'an* (Leiden-Boston: Brill).

Nicholson, Reynold A. (1989), *The Mystics of Islam* (London, England: Penguin).

Nursi, Bediuzzaman Said 'Risale-i Nur, The Words: The Eighteenth Word', <http://www.erisale.com/index.jsp?locale=en#content.en.201.240>, accessed May 29, 2013.

Ormsby, Eric L. (1984), *Theodicy in Islamic Thought: Dispute Over Al-Ghazali's "Best of All Possible Worlds"* (Princeton, NJ: Princeton Univ. Press).

--- (1990), 'Creation in Time in Islamic Thought with Special Reference to al-Ghazali', in David Burrell and Bernard Mcginn (ed.), *God and Creation: An Ecumenical Symposium* (Notre Dame, IN: University of Notre Dame Press).

Otto, Rudolph (1957), *Mysticism East and West: A comparative Analysis of the Nature of Mysticism* (New York: Meridian Books).

Peterson, Michael L. (2011), *The Problem of Evil, Selected Readings* (Indiana, USA: Univ. of Notre Dame).

Picken, Gavin (2005), 'Tazkiat al-nafs: The Qur'anic Paradigm', *Journal of Qur'anic Studies*, 7 (2).

Plantinga, Alvin (1974), *God, Freedom, and Evil* (Cambridge, UK: WM. B. Berdmans).

Radfard, Aboulghasem (1999), 'Tafhim al-Qur'an', in B. Khorramshahi (ed.), *The Encyclopedia of the Holy Qur'an* (Tehran, Iran: Dustan & Nahid Publishers).

Rahman, Fazlur (1975), *The Philosophy of Mulla Sadra* (Albany, NY: State Univ. of NY Press).

--- (1990), 'Ibn Sina's Theory of the God-World Relationship', in David Burrell and Bernard Mcginn (ed.), *God and Creation: An Ecumenical Symposium* (Notre Dame, IN: University of Notre Dame Press).

--- (1994), *Major Themes of the Qur'an* (Second edn.; Minneapolis, USA: Bibliotheca Islamica).

Rasouli Mahallati, Seyed Hashim (1374 Solar), *Tales of the Prophets; From Adam to Muhamamd* (Tehran: Daftar Nashr Farhang Islami).

Razi, Abu Al-Futuh *Rawh al-jinan wa-ruh al-janan* (Tehran: Kitabfurush-yi Islamiyah 1384/1964).

Renard, John (1994), *All the King's Falcons, Rumi on Prophets and Revelation* (State University of New York Press, Albany).

--- (2004), *Knowledge of God in Classical Sufism* (Mahwah, NJ: Paulist Press).

Rippin, Andrew (2003), 'John the Baptist', in Jane Dammen McAuliffe (ed.), *Encyclopedia of the Qur'an* (3; Washington, D.C.: Brill), pp. 51-52.

Rizvi, Sajjad (2009), 'Mulla Sadra', *Stanford Encyclopedia of Philosophy*. accessed January 13, 2013.

Robinson, Neal (2003a), *Discovering The Qur'an: A Contemporary Approach to a Veiled Text* (Washington D.C: Georgetown University Press).

--- (2003b), 'Jesus', in Jane Dammen McAuliffe (ed.), *Encyclopedia of the Qur'an* (3; Washington, D.C.: Brill), pp. 11-24.

Rubin, Uri (2001), 'Prophets and Prophethood', in jane Dammen McAuliffe (ed.), *Encyclopaedia of the Qur'an* (4; Washington D.C.: Brill), pp. 289-306.

--- (2003), 'Muhammad', in Jane Dammen McAuliffe (ed.), *Encyclopedia of the Qur'an* (3; Washington, D.C.: Brill), pp. 440-57.

--- (2009), 'Prophets And Prophethood', in Andrew Rippin (ed.), *The Blackwell Companiion to The Qur'an* (West Sussex, UK: John Wiley & Sons Ltd.).

Rumi, Jalal al-Din *Masnawi-ye ma`navi* (Tehran, Iran: Amir Kabir,1957).

--- (1379), *Diwan Shams Tabrizi* (Tehran, IR: Peyman).

--- (1926), *The Mathnawi of Jalaluddin Rumi*, trans. Reynold A. Nicholson (Cambridge, ENG: E.J.W. Gibb Memorial, 2001).

--- (2004), *Fihi ma fihi (Discourses of Rumi)*, trans. Arthur John Arberry (London & New York: Routledge).

--- (2011/1390), *Majalis-i Sab'ah (The Seven Sessions)*, ed. Tofigh Sobhani (Tehran, IR: Keyhan).

Saeedimehr, Mohammad (2010), 'Islamic Philosophy and the Problem of Evil: a Philosophical Theodicy', *Intl. J. Humanities*, 17, 127-48.

Schimmel, Annemarie (1975), *Mystical Dimentions of Islam* (Chapel Hill, NC: The University of North Carolina Press).

--- (1993), *The Triumphal Sun: A Study of the Works of Jalalodin Rumi* (Albany, NY: State University of New York Press).

Schock, Cornelia (2001), 'Moses', in Jane Dammen McAuliffe (ed.), *Encyclopedia of the Qur'an* (3; Washington D.C.: Brill), pp. 419-26.

Schuon, Frithjof (1987), 'The Spiritual Significance of the Substance of the Prophet', in Seyyed Hossein Nasr (ed.), *Islamic Spirituality: Foundations* (New York: Crossroad).

--- (1998), *Understanding Islam* (Bloomington, Indiana: World Wisdon).

--- (2005), *The Transcendent Unity of Religions* (Wheaton, IL: Quest Books).

Sh'rani, Abu al-Hassan (1962), *Muhaddimah, Abu al-Futuh Razi's Rawh al-Jinan wa ruh al-Janan* (Tehran, Iran: Ketabfurushi-yi Islamiyah).

Shafiei Kadkani, Muhammad Reza (1388), *Mowlana Rumi's Ghazaliat Shams Tabrizi* (Tehran, IR: Sokhan).

Shah-Kazemi, Reza (2011), *Spiritual Quest: Reflections on Qur'anic Prayer According to the Teachings of Imam Ali* (London: I.B. Tauris).

Shoja`i, Muhammad (1375), *Maqalat dar Tazkie Nafs* (3; Tehran, IR: Sorush).

Smith, Wilfred Cantwell (1993), *What is Scripture?* (Minneapolis, USA: Fortress Press).

Sonn, Tamara (2009), 'Introducing', in Andrew Rippin (ed.), *The Blackwell Companion to The Qur'an* (West Sussex, UK: John Wiley & Sons).

Soroush, Abdolkarim (1373), *Hekmat wa Ma`ishat* (Tehran, IR: Serat).

--- (1379), *Ghomar-e `Asheghaneh: Rumi and Shams* (Tehran, IR: Serat).

Soucek, Priscilla (2006), 'Solomon', in Jane Dammen McAuliffe (ed.), *Encyclopedia of the Qur'an* (5; Washinton D.C.: Brill), pp. 76-78.

Stace, Walter T. (1960), *Mysticism and Philosophy* (Los Angeles, CA: Jeremy P. Tarcher, Inc.).

Stoddart, William (2006), 'Aspects of Islamic Esoterism', in Jean-Louis Michon and Roger Gaetani (ed.), *Sufism: Love & Wisdom* (Indiana: World Wisdom).

Stowasser, Barbara Freyer (2003), 'Mary', in Jane Dammen McAuliffe (ed.), *Encyclopedia of the Qur'an* (3; Washington, D.C.: Brill), pp. 288-95.

--- (2010), 'Theodicy and the Many Meanings of Adam and Eve', in Ibrahim M. Abu-Rabi' (ed.), *Theodicy And Justice In Modern Islamic Thought: The Case of Said Nursi* (Burlington, VT: Ashgate).

Surabadi, Abubakr `tigh Neishabur (1381 Solar), *Tafsir Surabadi*, ed. Sa`idi Sirjani (3; Tehran: Farhamg Nashr-Nu).

Tabarsi, Abu 'Ali al-Fadl ibn al-Hassan (1350 Solar), *Majma' al-Bayan fi Tafsir al-Qur'an*, trans. Ahmad Beheshti (Tehran, IR: Farahani).

Tabatabai, Muhammad Hussain (1367 Solar), *Al-Mizan*, trans. Seyed M. Bagher Musavi-Hamedani (Qum, Iran: Daftar Intisharat Islami).

--- (1387/2008), *Nihayah al-Hikmah (the Utmost of Philosophy)*, ed. Hadi Khosroshahi, trans. Mahdi Tadayyon (Ghom, IR: Bustan-e Ketab).

--- (1987), *The Qur'an in Islam*, trans. Seyyed Hossein Nasr (London, UK: Zahra).

Taleghani, Seyed Mahmoud (1347), *Partuvi az Qur'an (A Ray of the Qur'an)* (Tehran, IR: Sherkat Sahami Enteshar).

Tayob, Abdulkader (2002), 'An analytical survey of al-Tabari's exegesis of the cultural symbolic contstruct of fitna', in G.R. Hawting and Abdul-Kader A. Shareef (eds.), *Approaches to the Qur'an* (New York: Routledge).

Tirmidhi 'Sunan Tirmidhi', <http://www.hadithcollection.com/shama-iltirmidhi.html>, accessed May 30, 2010.

Turner, Colin (ed.), (2008), *The Six-Sided Vision of Said Nursi: Toward a Spiritual Architecture of the Risale-i Nur*, ed. Ibrahim M. Abu-Rabi' (Spiritual Dimensins of Bediuzzaman Said Nursi's Risale-i Nur, Albany, NY: State University of New York Press).

Tūsī, Nasīr al-Dīn (1370), *Kashf al-Morād, sharh Tajrid al-i`tiqad*, ed. `Allameh Helli, trans. Abol Hassan Sha`rani (Tehran, IR: Islami).

Underhill, Evelyn (1993), *Mysticism The Nature and Development of Spiritual Consciousness* (Oxford, England: Oneworld).

Ward, Keith (1996), *Religion & Creation* (New York: Oxford University press).

Watt, W. Mongomery (1979), 'Suffering in Sunnite Islam', *Studia Islamica*, 50. accessed 12/25/2012.

--- (1986), 'Ash`ariyya', in H.A.R. Gibb, Kramers, J.H. (ed.), *Encyclopedia of Islam* (I; Leiden: Brill).

--- (2004), 'Ghazali, Abu Hamid', in Lindsay Jones (ed.), *Encyclopedia of Religion* (Second edn., 5; USA: Macmillan Reference), 3469-72.

--- (2007), *The Faith and Practice of al-Ghazali* (Oxford: Oneworld).

Watt, W. Montgomery and Bell, Richard (1970), *Introduction to the Qur'an* (Edinburgh, UK: Edinburgh University Press).

Wheeler, Brannon M. (2002), *Prophets in the Qur'an, An Introduction to the Qur'an and Muslim Exegesis* (New York: Continuum).

--- (2009), 'Moses', in Andrew Rippin (ed.), *The Blackwell Companion to the Qur'an* (West Sussex, UK: John Wiley & Sons Ltd), pp. 248-65.

Wolfson, Harry Austryn (1976), *The Philosopy of Kalam* (Cambridge, MA: Harvard University Press).

Yasrebi, Seyed Yahya (1386/2007), *Erfan-e Nazari: Theoretical Mysticism, A Research into the Evolutionary Trend and the Principles and Issues of Tasawwuf* (Tehran, IR: Bustan-e Ketab).

--- (1389/2010), *Practical Mysticism* (Tehran, IR: Bustan-e Ketab).

Yusuf Ali, Abdullah *The Meaning of The Holy Qur'an* (11 edn.: Amana).

Zamakhshari, Abul Qasim Mahmud (1389 Solar), *al-Kashaf an haga`ig ghawamid al-tanzil wa-uyun al-aqawil fi wujuh al-tawi*, trans. Masud Ansari (Tehran, IR: Dar al-Kitab al- Arabi, Beirut / Qoqnoos, Tehran).

Zamani, Karim (1381 Solar), *Sharh Jame` Mathnavi Ma`navi (A Comprehensive Commentary of Mathnavi)* (Tehran, IR: Etela`at).

--- (1384 solar), *Minagar-e eshgh: A Thematical Commentary of the Mathnawi Ma`nawi* (Tehran, IR: Nashr-e Nay).

--- (1390), *Comprehensive Commentary of Rumi's Fihi ma Fihi* (Tehran, IR: Moin).

Zarrinkob, Abdolhusin (1373), *Step by Step Towards Meting God: Life and Spiritual Practices of Rumi* (Tehran, IR: Elmi).

Zarrinkub, Abd al-Husayn (1388), *Sirr Nay: A Critical Analysis and Commentary of Masnavi* (Tehran, IR: Ettellat).

Zarrinkub, Abdolhusin (1387), *Farar az madrasah - life and teachings of al-Ghazali* (Tehran, IR: Amir Kabir).